Traveler's Reading Guides:

Background Books, Novels, Travel Literature and Articles

Maggy Simony, ed.

Editorial Assistants:
Christine Donovan & Maria Simony

Freelance Publications Ltd
Bayport, New York 11705

Published by Freelance.Publications Ltd .
Box 8, Bayport, NY 11705

Copyright©1981 by Freelance Publications Ltd

Printed and bound in the United States of America

Library of Congress Cataloging in Publication Data

Simony, Maggy, date
  Traveler's reading guides.

  Includes index.
  Contents: v. 1. Europe.
  1. Travel–Bibliography. 2. Travel in literature–
Bibliography. I. Donovan, Christine, date   .
II. Simony, Maria, date   . III. Title.
Z6016.T7S54   [G151]   016.9104   80-65324
ISBN 0-9602050-1-2 (v. 1)   AACR2

*For Bill
and for Seth*

TABLE OF CONTENTS

TABLE OF CONTENTS

ACKNOWLEDGMENTS

I am grateful for permission to use the apt and persuasive quotations in the introductory pages to this series:

The Georg Schneider quotation was reprinted by permission from *Theory and History of Bibliography* by Georg Schneider, translated by Ralph Shaw (Metuchen, N.J.: Scarecrow Press, 1962). Copyright 1962 by Ralph Shaw.

The Frances Koltun quotation was reprinted by permission from *Complete Book for the Intelligent Woman Traveler* by Frances L. Koltun (New York: Simon & Schuster, 1967). Copyright 1967. by Frances L. Koltun.

The Neil Morgan quotation was reprinted by permission from Neil Morgan, syndicated travel columnist.

The book *World Travel Planner* (Los Angeles, CA: Nash Publishing, 1970) was the catalyst for this series, and I would like to thank its authors, Bob and Joan Watkins, and to acknowledge the role that their fine "how-to-travel" book played in the concept and idea for this series of *Traveler's Reading Guides.*

Preface

Armchair travel—described by Longfellow as "travels by the fireside ... while journeying with another's feet"—is a delightful form of reading as well as invaluable preparation for a real trip.

My interest in "armchair" travel, construed in its wider sense, goes back so many years I can't remember when it started. I do know it grew out of my father's reading habits and interest in far-away places. After one adventurous spurt when he emigrated at 17 from Stockholm to Brooklyn, Seth never was able to afford to travel more than a few hundred miles from home. But he was an armchair traveler—a trip to Maine meant reading Kenneth Roberts novels; his parting advice to me (leaving by car for Californiain 1948) was, characteristically, to "be sure to stop at a library *before* reaching Reno to read about the Donner party." And he was right! Crossing the mountains into California, for the first time, having just read that story, was a far more memorable experience with the history and heartbreak of those earlier travelers vividly in mind.

For me, then, in planning a trip to Europe, or anywhere else, making use of the local library is as important as finding a good travel agent.

The idea for compiling this series of Reading Guides stems directly from a great "how-to-travel" book, *World Travel Planner,* by Joan and Bob Watkins, which I came across back in 1971. They make a persuasive case for wide pre-travel reading as part of the travel planning process, and then go on to give a mini-course in *how* to prepare a travel reading list using your local library. While I didn't need convincing, having done precisely this all my adult life, it immediately occurred to me that there ought to be a reference book that provided ready-made reading lists for travelers, and that one day (if no one beat me to it) I would like to take on such a project myself.

This series is the end result, many years later and with many false starts along the way.

I am hoping for a few converts—that is, to entice those library users who never get beyond the latest Fodor or Frommer guide (essential as they certainly are) to begin using their local library for the marvelous travel-reading resource it is. Even one of the three-week "if it's Tuesday, this must be Belgium" tours can be greatly enhanced by reading beforehand about the places whizzing by.

Comments, both negative and positive, and suggestions for additions, deletions, changes in format, etc., will be gratefully received.

—*Maggy Simony, ed.*

Bibliography is for books what Ariadne's thread was for Theseus in the labyrinths, and what the compass is to sea travel.   —*Georg Schneider*

Introduction

In travel, as in most other things, what we understand best we enjoy the most. When you visit a country, you should know at least those facts about its religion, history, arts, and politics that are dearest to its people. (From *Complete Book for the Intelligent Woman Traveler*, by Frances Koltun.)

By now I am inured to the dreary truth that some of our best and brightest don't read. But I remain stunned that so many spend considerable money to travel with no sense of what they may find, and no insight to recognize it when they do. (From a travel column by Neil Morgan, syndicated travel writer.)

[Literature] ... shows us the world again so that we recognize it ... by bestowing on it insight, shape and concentration—with a glory not its own.   —Wordsworth

The quotations express perfectly the underlying philosophy, and reason for, *Traveler's Reading Guides*.

This is a series of informal bibliographies—"friendly bibliography"—meant for browsing, much as one browses in a library. They were compiled with the reasonably literate traveler in mind and they provide ready-made reading lists that include: background reading, classic travel writing, lighthearted travel memoirs, fiction (mysteries, family sagas, serious novels) set in the particular country, history (both "popular" and standard), perceptive commentary by knowledgeable observers, special interest books. Both for timeliness, and because they contain some of the best contemporary travel writing, the reading lists end with magazine articles of interest to travelers, from general and travel publications, as well as from the *New York Times Sunday Travel Section*.

In short, *Traveler's Reading Guides* represent a single-source, easy to use, time-saving research tool for library reference and/or travel collections and for the traveling public.

There are three volumes in this series: Volume 1 (Europe); Volume 2 (Western Hemisphere) to be published in December 1981; Volume 3 (Asia, Africa, Pacific) to be published in March 1982. Each volume is arranged alphabetically, by country, and reading lists are divided into Background Reading, Novels and Travel Articles.

Following are additional details regarding editorial decisions and reference sources used in compiling the *Guides*.

General approach and appearance of the series. In keeping with the informal approach of this series, the aim was to produce a very readable bibliography in a typography and format that could be easily scanned for items of interest without reading an entire entry. The text of the annotations also is deliberately informal.

When I began the project I hoped to end up with a comparable reading list for each country that included some cheerful fiction, some serious novels, a few histories, a few general background books, etc., etc. This proved to be a poor goal, and I ended up preparing reading lists that roughly represent both the quantity and type of bibliographic material available. Therefore, entries for the countries will vary widely. In many instances a country could do with some new books and articles, intended for the general traveler, to fill in the gaps. It occurs to me also, that the tourist offices of many countries would do well to commission or encourage American and English authors to write new novels and mysteries set in their most tourist-worthy cities and countryside.

In contrast to the countries for which a reading list had to be eked out, for some countries (favored with a deluge of books, articles and novels) the approach had to be selective, for reasons of space, and readers wishing to do so can find many alternative selections to those listed herein.

A word on the matter of spelling. Several geographical names, as well as "traveler" have alternative acceptable spellings. For book titles, or wherever quoted material is part of an annotation, the author's spelling of these words are used. In purely editorial text, I have used what I felt to be the most widely used American spelling for the word.

Background Reading. The standard reference sources used to select entries for this section were *Book Review Digest* and *Books in Print.* Many titles were culled from recommendations in travel books and articles collected over the years, and some were selected simply by browsing in the several small and medium-sized libraries used for research.

The lists are selective, and obviously, for some countries, many more books could have been included.

Most of the books listed here are annotated briefly. Often this is simply a few words from the jacket copy, or from reviewer comments, sufficient to "peg" a book. In some cases the title and sub-title were deemed sufficient to identify the contents of a book. Publisher and year of publication are noted.

Sub-heads have been used frequently to break up lengthy lists of background books into manageable segments. The sub-heads vary both as to title and content, depending on the total bibliographic material listed for the country. Thus, it might well be that a popular history is listed under the general heading of "Background Reading" for one country, under the sub-head "History" for a second, and under a still more specific sub-head (World War II, etc.) for a third.

Readers should at least scan all entries under Background Reading because of this flexible approach to categorizing the books.

Novels. The primary reference source used was the 9th Edition of *Fiction Catalog* and supplements to it for 1976-79. Occasionally listings were obtained from the 8th Edition. A second source for the entries in this section was the *Book Review Digest* under the Fiction (Location) category for the years 1976-80 with occasional reference to earlier editions of the *Digest*. Again, some books listed were in notes collected over the years.

Most of the novels are annotated briefly, but few have comments indicating relative literary merit. The annotations are meant merely to tag a book so that the reader can quickly determine if it is of interest or not. Geographical sub-heads are used where the list of titles is lengthy. Publisher, year of publication, and a review source are noted, with few exceptions.

Travel Articles. The basic reference source used was *The Magazine Index*. Information on articles for *Gourmet, Travel/Holiday, Travel & Leisure* and the *N.Y. Times Sunday Travel Section*, were taken directly from these publications. (*Travel & Leisure* is not indexed by either *The Magazine Index* or the *Reader's Guide*, but it was felt this publication had to be included as one of the few remaining purely travel magazines as well as for the quality of its articles.)

Entries cover a time frame of two years and are arranged alphabetically by media name.

Travel Article Supplements to update this section of the *Guides* will be available semi-annually (see order forms on pages 287 and 289).

Notes and Appendices. *Notes* at the beginning of each country section contain a key to the abbreviations used, a list of standard guides available for the country and any other special information pertinent to that country: cross-indexing, errata, etc.

Appendix 1 is a bibliography of the reference sources used in compiling the series, and of the standard guidebooks referred to in the *Notes*. Additional appendices may be added to individual volumes of the series as deemed necessary.

Introduction
(Volume 1—Europe)

Europe epitomizes travel for many Americans. Its combination of cultural treasures, fascinating history, the many nationalities within a relatively small geographic area, its travel history as the continent of the "Grand Tour" were all part of the decision to begin *Traveler's Reading Guides* with Europe as Volume 1.

The reading lists reflect the profound differences in the political and social histories of each country. Books for the several communist countries are largely gloomy, tragic, political, and I freely admit combining Albania with Yugoslavia to avoid beginning Volume 1 with a country that is probably last on the list of preferred tourist destinations. Austria, on the other hand, seemed the perfect "most European" country, with which to begin both the volume and the series.

England presented a problem, in compiling this *Reading Guide,* because of the sheer volume of books about England, and the number of novels by English authors. For reasons of space, therefore, novels listed herein are limited to those categorized by *Fiction Catalog* and *Book Review Digest* as being set in a specific county or city. And those listed for London have been further limited to fifty or so, mostly twentieth-century, novels.

Fortunately, there are several marvelous, comprehensive literary guides to England for travelers and these are listed on page 45 and 277. Also, in Appendix 2, is an alphabetical list of authors to use as a starting point in your library for locating the hundreds of additional novels and mysteries with English settings.

There is some emphasis on histories of all types in Volume 1 because a knowledge of at least the basic historical facts about a country seems essential to me for any European trip. Another way of absorbing history is by reading one of the many family chronicles listed under Novels.

As to the illustrations used for the inevitable few blank right hand pages, the choice of Victorian lady travelers was in part self-indulgence. Nevertheless, they are relevant, suggesting the "Grand Tour" and a kind of European travel now vanished, but which present-day tourists may vicariously recreate through several of the books listed herein.

Notes - Austria

1. Abbreviations of reference sources for novels:
   fc - Fiction Catalog, 9th Edition
   fc/s76 (77, etc.) - Supplement to 9th Edition
   fc/8ed - Fiction Catalog, 8th Edition
   brd/78 (79, etc.) - Book Review Digest for the year

2. Standard Series Guidebooks for Austria:
   Fodor
   Michelin Green Guide
   Nagel
   Foreign Area Study

3. See Appendix 1 for more complete data on the above.

4. See Europe, at end of country sections, for additional possible sources of reading and information for Austria.

Austria

Background Reading

Barea, I.   VIENNA
  "The legend and reality of an urban civilization, from its beginning
  as a frontier fortress to the dissolution of the Habsburg Empire."
  Knopf, 1966.

Barker, E.   AUSTRIA 1918-1972
  A "popular" history that describes an Austria, grim in the 1930's
  through the period of Hitler and WWII, and finally independent of
  its "lost empire" mentality.
  Univ. of Miami Press, 1973.

Brody, E.   MUSIC GUIDE TO AUSTRIA & GERMANY
  One of a series of guides for individual European countries—a handbook providing information for the widest range of travelers "from
  the music dilettante to the highly motivated specialist." Contains information on concert halls, opera houses, festivals, etc. as well as the
  country's musical history.
  Dodd, 1975.

Clark, R.   THE ALPS
  Knopf, 1973.

Cole, R. & James, T.   EUROPE: A SECOND TIME AROUND
  "An informal guide to selected places you may have missed on your
  first trip." Off-the-beaten track places to visit in Austria.
  Funk & Wagnall, 1971.

Comini, Alessandra   THE FANTASTIC ART OF VIENNA
    Knopf, 1978.
Crankshaw, E.   THE FALL OF THE HOUSE OF HABSBURG
    One of several histories listed here which tell of the nineteenth-
    century Austro-Hungarian Empire and its demise in the twentieth
    century.
    Viking, 1963.
Day, I.   GHOST WALTZ: A MEMOIR
    A daughter (now a New Yorker) uncovering, and coming to terms
    with the activities of her father as an Austrian-Nazi in WWII.
    Viking, 1980.
Deardorff, R.H.   A DAY OUTSIDE THE CITY
    Just what the title indicates—pleasant and interesting day-trips out-
    side major European cities, in this case Vienna.
    Holt, 1968.
Feldkamp, F.   NOT EVERYBODY'S EUROPE
    A grand tour of nine unique cities, including Salzburg, Austria.
    Harper's Magazine Press, 1976.
Gainham, S.   HABSBURG TWILIGHT
    Eight essays by a novelist who knows Vienna well, describing life in
    late nineteenth-century Vienna (see listing of her novels below).
    Atheneum, 1979.
Gunther, J.   TWELVE CITIES
    The author wrote a highly successful series of "Inside" books, and
    here "applies his unique zest and talent to cities" describing mood,
    temper, problems, politics, government in Vienna.
    Harper, 1969.
Handler, H.   THE SPANISH RIDING SCHOOL
    "Four centuries of classic horsemanship"—the Spanish Riding School
    is located in Vienna, despite its name.
    McGraw-Hill, 1972.
Hubmann, F.   THE HABSBURG EMPIRE
    Original photographs of the world of the Austro-Hungarian monarchy
    from 1840-1916.
    Library Press, 1972.
Kann, R.A.   HISTORY OF THE HAPSBURG EMPIRE 1526-1918
    Univ. of Calif. Press, 1974.
Kraus, K. ed.   MODERN AUSTRIAN LITERATURE
    M.S. Rosenberg, 1977.
Maass, W.B.   COUNTRY WITHOUT A NAME
    U.S. occupation in Europe after WWII. Written basically for Ameri-
    cans—a description of "the events in Austria before and during WWII."
    Ungar, 1979.

Marboe, E.   AUSTRIA
"Intended for Austrians . . . as well as for foreigners"—included because it was selected for one of this book's editors by an Austrian as
an ideal introduction to the country. Divided into three parts: history with many illustrations; land, people and national costume of
each of the provinces; transition from Empire to present-day Austria
"working out its approach to the year 2000 AD." English.
Osterreichesche Staatsdruckerei, 1969.

Marek, G.   THE EAGLES DIE
"Franz Joseph, Elisabeth, and their Austria." the drama of the Habsburg Empire presented "in terms of two individuals." Vienna is
brought vividly to life as are the cultural and intellectual life and the
personalities of the Emperor and his Empress.
Harper, 1974.

May, A.J.   THE HAPSBURG MONARCHY 1867-1914
Originally published by Harvard University Press in 1951.
Norton, 1968 (paper edition).

Morton, F.   A NERVOUS SPLENDOR: VIENNA 1888-1889
Built around the suicide at Mayerling, but the author describes all
levels of society within the time frame. Anecdotal portraits, gossip
and daily life.
Little Brown, 1979

Musulin, S.   AUSTRIA AND THE AUSTRIANS
Praeger, 1972.

Paumgartner, B.   SALZBURG: A WALK THROUGH A CITY
IPS, 1972.

Perl, L.   FOODS AND FESTIVALS OF THE DANUBE LANDS
World, 1969.

Pick, R.   THE LAST DAYS OF IMPERIAL VIENNA
Dial, 1976.

Schorske, C.E.   FIN-DE-SIECLE VIENNA: POLITICS & CULTURE
Knopf, 1979.

Taylor, A.J.P.   THE HABSBURG MONARCHY 1809-1918
"A history of the Austrian Empire and Austro-Hungary."
Univ. of Chicago Press, 1976.

Valiani, L.   THE END OF AUSTRIA-HUNGARY
Knopf, 1973.

Vergo, P.   ART IN VIENNA 1898-1918
Praeger, 1975.

Wechsberg, J.   THE VIENNA I KNEW
"Memories of a European childhood." Written by a noted food and
travel writer; reminiscences that make his family members come alive.
Doubleday, 1979.

Wolfson, V.   THE MAYERLING MURDER
    Questions the traditional acceptance of the deaths of Crown Prince
    Rudolf and Marie Vetsera as a suicide pact and makes the case that
    the Prince was murdered for being politically dangerous.
    Prentice-Hall, 1969.

Novels

Albrand, M.   A CALL FROM AUSTRIA
    Story of espionage set in a resort in the Austrian Alps.
    Random House, 1963. fc
Behrman, S.N.   THE BURNING GLASS
    Salzburg setting (and N.Y. and Hollywood), 1937-40.
    Little, Brown, 1968. fc
Brunngraber, R.   KARL AND THE TWENTIETH CENTURY
    Karl is victim of effects of WWI and the social and political forces of
    post-WWI Austria.
    Morrow, 1933.
Doderer, H. Von   THE DEMONS
    Portrait of Viennese society in the 1920's.
    Knopf, 1961. fc
Edgar, J.   COUNTESS
    Love and tragedy in WWI Vienna.
    St. Martin's, 1978. fc/s78
Fagyas, M.   THE DEVIL'S LIEUTENANT
    Pre-WWI Vienna and decline of the Austro-Hungarian Empire.
    Putnam, 1970. fc
Feuchtwanger, L.   THE UGLY DUCHESS
    A fictional account of the life of a fourteenth-century duchess.
    Viking, 1928.
Gainham, S.   NIGHT FALLS ON THE CITY
    This is the first of a trilogy that recounts the life of a prominent ac-
    tress in Vienna, beginning with the war years, 1938-45.
    Holt, 1967. fc
Gainham, S.   A PLACE IN THE COUNTRY
    Second volume of above trilogy, post-WWII.
    Holt, 1969. fc
Gainham, S.   PRIVATE WORLDS
    Final volume of the trilogy, the 1950's.
    Holt, 1971. fc

Gainham, S.   TO THE OPERA BALL
  An Austrian solider elopes with an heiress.
  Doubleday, 1977. fc/s77
Greene, G.   THE THIRD MAN
  The story *A Sense of Reality* from this book, was the basis for the
  popular movie of black marketeers and life in the period when Amer-
  can, Russian, French and British troops jointly occupied Vienna.
  Viking, 1950. fc
Haas, B.   THE HOUSE OF CHRISTINA
  Pre-WWII Vienna and an Austrian girl with three suitors—Nazi, Jew
  and American.
  Simon & Schuster, 1977. brd/78
Handke, P.   THE GOALIE'S ANXIETY AT THE PENALTY KICK
  Vienna; tale of a psychopath.
  Farrar, Straus, 1972. fc
Heaven, C.   CASTLE OF EAGLES
  Mid-nineteenth-century romance.
  Coward, McCann, 1974. fc
Irving, J.   SETTING FREE THE BEARS
  Picaresque novel of two young men.
  Random House, 1969. fc/8ed
MacInnes, H.   PRELUDE TO TERROR
  An American sent to Vienna to purchase a painting becomes involved
  in intrigue.
  Harcourt, 1978. brd/79
MacInnes, H.   THE SALZBURG CONNECTION
  A novel of intrigue that has its roots in WWII.
  Harcourt, 1968. fc
MacInnes, H.   THE SNARE OF THE HUNTER
  Flight of a refugee from Czechoslovakia to Austria.
  Harcourt, 1974. fc/8ed
Meyer, N.   THE SEVEN-PER-CENT SOLUTION
  "Pastiche" is the term used to describe this detective story of "Sher-
  lock Holmes" and Sigmund Freud joining forces to solve a mystery
  of criminal conspiracy set in Vienna.
  Dutton, 1974. brd/75
Musil, R.   THE MAN WITHOUT QUALITIES
  Two-volume novel by a leading standard writer of pre- and post-WWI.
  Coward, McCann, 1953-54.fc
Roth, J.   RADETSKY MARCH
  One man's story told in terms of the ending of the Austro-Hungarian
  Empire.
  Viking, 1932.

Schnitzler, A.   VIENNA 1900: GAMES WITH LOVE AND DEATH
   These stories were the basis of a haunting series shown on public tel-
   evision.
   Penguin, 1974. fc/s78
Solmssen, A.R.G.   ALEXANDER'S FEAST
   A colorful portrait of Salzburg, 1961.
   Little, Brown, 1971. fc
Stern, G.B.   MOSAIC
   One of four volumes in *The Matriarch Chronicles.*
   Knopf, 1930. fc
Stewart, M.   AIRS ABOVE THE GROUND
   A mystery set in rural Austria involving the Lipizzaner horses.
   Morrow, 1965. fc
Stone, I.   THE PASSIONS OF THE MIND
   A novel based on the life of Sigmund Freud.
   Doubleday, 1971. fc
Thompson, M.   THE CRY AND THE COVENANT
   Based on the life of Dr. Ignaz Semmelweis.
   Doubleday, 1949. fc
Werfel, F.   EMBEZZLED HEAVEN
   Vienna; an old woman is deceived by her nephew.
   Viking, 1940. fc
Wiseman, T.   THE QUICK AND THE DEAD
   A Viennese half-Jew survives the Nazi era.
   Viking, 1969. fc
Zweig, S.   BEWARE OF PITY
   The War of 1914.
   Viking, 1939. fc

Travel Articles

BICYCLING
   1980   Mar   Cycling in Eastern Europe, H.T. Lyon - p. 60

COSMOPOLITAN
   1979   Jul   Marvelous middle Europe, R. Ashley - p. 58

GLAMOUR
   1979   Jan   Austria: the most romantic, most old-world country
                   in Europe - p. 70

HARPER'S BAZAAR
1980   Dec   Travel highlights - p. 14

HI-FI
1979   Sep   Karajan's Easter Festival: the best and the most ex-
                pensive, J.H. Sutcliffe - p. 38

HORIZON
1980   Mar   The splendor of Vienna; the Hapsburg court sponsored
                sartorial magic, M. Holterhoff - p. 22
1979   Jun   An era remembered (Austrian festival) - p. 12
       Jul   Marvelous miscellany - p. 10

HOUSE & GARDEN
1980   May   Delicious Austria, P. Linck - p. 54

MADEMOISELLE
1980   Oct   Grab your bag and go—that's the beauty of Eurailing
                through Europe, R. Masello - p. 158

NEW YORKER
1979   Sep 17   Salzburg - p. 33

N.Y. TIMES SUNDAY TRAVEL SECTION (10)
1980   Jan 13   The coffeehouses of Old Vienna, P. Hofmann - p. 1
       May 25   A cheaper, friendlier, homier tour of the Alps,
                P. Hofmann, p. 1
       Aug 17   Schlossing your way through Austria,
                D. A. Andelman - p. 1
1979   Jan 7   Austria's zigeunerwagon, A. Levy - p. 14
       Feb 25   Marionettes: an alternative to grand opera in Salz-
                burg, I. Molotsky - p. 1
       May 20   How the landlady captured us, D. Pritchard - p. 37
       Jul 22   The Wolfgangsee: exploring a lake in Austria,
                A. Levy - p. 3
       Sep 30   Vienna's museum for everything, R. Blumenthal - p. 3
       Nov 4   Graz, an old imperial town in the green heart of
                Austria, A. Levy - p. 9

OPERA NEWS
1979   Oct   Tales from the Vienna shops (behind scenes at Staats-
                oper) - p. 22

POPULAR PHOTOGRAPHY
1979   Jul   Poland (yes!) surprises photographers; Vienna, unsur-
                prisingly, great too, K. Poli - p. 9

SATURDAY REVIEW
1979 Oct 13   For opera lovers only - p. 54

SKIING
1980 Spring Mountains mit schlag, J. Skow - p. 71
      Dec   A smuggler in Ischgl, J. Skow - p. 92
1979 Jan   A schladming sampler (skiing in Austria),
                 J. Skow - p. 86
      Sep   Ski the Alps, P. Gordon - p. 163
      Oct   Traveler in the Montafon, J. Skow - p. 142

SMITHSONIAN
1979 Oct   In the baroque world of Vienna all are on stage,
                 J. Wechsberg, p. 78

SPORTS AFIELD
1980 Nov   McClane's notebook: once you've seen its opening act
                 this high-finned trouper will entertain you with en-
                 core after encore (fishing in Austria) - A.J. McLane

TOWN & COUNTRY
1979 Dec   Gemutlichkeit in Lech, L. Ashland - p. 164
      Apr   Sound of music, D. Galloway - p. 11

TRAVEL & LEISURE
1980 Aug   The world around Vienna, H. Koenig - p. 57

TRAVEL/ HOLIDAY
1980 Jun   Beer garden picnic: Salzburg, L. Szathmary - p. 16
      Jul   Danube River cruise, B. Schemel - p. 39
1979 Mar   Salzburg Festival, C.E. Adeben - p. 44
      Mar   Vienna for the first time, H. and G. Koenig - p. 44

VOGUE
1979 Dec   Winter in Vienna . . . the season of splendor,
                 M.R. Henry - p. 172

WORKING WOMAN
1979 Mar   Traveling easy, E. Elliott - p. 95

WORLD PRESS REVIEW (formerly Atlas)
1979 May   Vienna's English theatre: pluck, luck, and artistic free-
                 dom far from Broadway, L. Ruff - p. 26

A ciel-blue satin Worth evening gown, bordered in fur and with a bead-embroidered iris design.

Notes - *Belgium and Luxembourg*

1. Abbreviations of reference sources for novels:
   fc - Fiction Catalog, 9th Edition
   fc/s76 (77, etc.) - Supplement to 9th Edition
   fc/8ed - Fiction Catalog, 8th Edition
   brd/78 (79, etc.) - Book Review Digest for the year

2. Standard Series Guidebooks for Belgium and Luxembourg:
   Blue Guide (Belgium and Luxembourg)
   Fodor (Belgium and Luxembourg)
   Michelin Red Guide (Benelux)
   Foreign Area Study

3. See Appendix 1 for more complete data on the above.

4. See Europe, at end of country sections, for additional possible sources of reading and information for Belgium and Luxembourg.

5. Errata: Add the Deardorff book (Brussels) to Background Reading for Belgium (see listing, page 2).

Belgium

INCLUDING: LUXEMBOURG

Background Reading

Aronson, T.   DEFIANT DYNASTY; THE COBURGS OF BELGIUM
Kings of the House of Saxe-Coburg-Gotha—"colorful, gossipy, scandalous chapters . . . imbedded in a solid historical matrix."
Bobbs-Merrill, 1968.

Bailey, A.HORIZON CONCISE HISTORY OF THE LOW COUNTRIES
American Heritage, 1974.

Brody, E.   THE MUSIC GUIDE TO BELGIUM, LUXEMBOURG, HOLLAND, AND SWITZERLAND
One of a series of guides for individual European countries—a handbook providing information for the widest range of travelers "from the music dilettante to the highly motivated specialist." Contains information on concert halls, opera houses, festivals, etc., as well as the country's musical history.
Dodd, 1977.

Cowie, D.   BELGIUM: THE LAND AND THE PEOPLE
Review of history, art, politics—somewhere between a history and a travel book.
Barnes, 1977.

Gunther, J.   TWELVE CITIES
See full entry under Austria on page 2. Brussels is one of the twelve.
Harper, 1969.

Hillaby, J.   A WALK THROUGH EUROPE
Account of a 1,300 mile walk from the North Sea to Nice—includes

Holland, Belgium, Germany, Swiss Alps, Italy and France. The book
reflects the zoologist author's enthusiasm for nature and people.
Houghton, 1972.

Hulst, R.A. d'   THE ROYAL MUSEUM
Great Galleries series.
Meredith, 1967.

Kossmann, E.H.   THE LOW COUNTRIES, 1780-1940
Oxford Univ. Press, 1978.

Lottman, H.   DETOURS FROM THE GRAND TOUR
"Off-beat, overlooked, and unexpected Europe" —travel writing that
includes material on Belgium.
Prentice-Hall, 1970.

Mallinson, V.   BELGIUM
Praeger, 1970.

McKenna, R.   FAR, FAR FROM HOME
Humorous account of an American family living in Brussels.
Harper, 1954.

Meeäs, A. de   HISTORY OF THE BELGIANS
Praeger, 1962.

Moulton, J.L. '   BATTLE FOR ANTWERP
Ex-army officer's story, 1944.
Hippocrene Books, 1978.

Nelson, N.   BELGIUM & LUXEMBOURG
Description and travel, one of the Batsford series.
Batsford, 1975.

Samson, P.M. & Dillon, J.   ANNE FRANK BRUSSELS WALK GUIDE
Malvaux, 1974.

Novels

Albrand, M.   MEET ME TONIGHT
Hungarians caught in Post-WWII intrigue in Brussels.
Random House, 1960. fc/8ed

Bronte, C.   THE PROFESSOR
School life in Brussels, first published 1857.
Oxford. fc

Bronte, C.   VILLETTE
School life in Brussels, first published 1853.
Oxford. fc

Darcy, C.   ALLEGRA
  Romance, nineteenth century.
  Walker, 1975. fc/s76
Fish, R.L.   WHIRLIGIG
  Brussels; mystery about smuggling.
  World, 1970. fc
Hulme, K.   THE NUN'S STORY
  A Catholic hospital is used as sanctuary for the underground in WWII.
  Little, Brown, 1956. fc
Hutchinson, R.C.   THE INHERITOR
  Returnee from WWII German labor camp discovers he is heir to a
  British fortune.
  Harper, 1961. fc
Johnson, P.H.   THE HOLIDAY FRIEND
  Belgian seacoast background; a student falls in love with her art his-
  tory teacher and follows the family on holiday. Grim ending.
  Scribner, 1972. fc
Johnson, P.H.   TOO DEAR FOR MY POSSESSING
  Love story of a man who spent his early years in Bruges, and returns
  to Belgium after his divorce.
  Scribner, 1973. fc
Johnson, P.H.   THE UNSPEAKABLE SKIPTON
  Bruges is the setting for this comedy of an English novelist who con-
  nives to profit from British tourists.
  Harcourt, 1959. fc
Johnston, J.   HOW MANY MILES TO BABYLON?
  Flanders; WWI and English soldiers.
  Doubleday, 1974. fc
Lambert, D.   TOUCH THE LION'S PAW
  Antwerp; jewelry heist.
  Sat. Review Press/Dutton, 1975. fc/s76
McGivern, W.P.   SOLDIERS OF '44
  Trapped American unit in WWII.
  Arbor House, 1979. brd/79
Sarton, M.   THE BRIDGE OF YEARS
  Farmlife, 1919-40
  Norton, 1971. fc
Stone, I.   LUST FOR LIFE
  Novel based on life of Van Gogh, nineteenth century.
  Doubleday, 1954. fc
Yates, R.A.   A SPECIAL PROVIDENCE
  An eighteen-year-old soldier in closing days of WWII.
  Knopf, 1969. fc/8ed

Travel Articles

BLACK ENTERPRISE
1979   Jul   Belgium, Z. Merchant - p. 51

DANCE MAGAZINE
1979   May   Koninklyk Ballet van Vlaanderen: phenomenon in
                          Flanders, R. Philip - p. 73

GOURMET
1980   Nov   A Belgian birthday, C.P. Reynolds - p. 62
1979   Jun   Shopping in Brussels, R. Deal - p. 22

HORIZON
1979   May   Brussels's grand place - p. 22
          Jul   Spectacular tradition (Brussels) - p. 10
          Aug   Music in great places - p. 11

NATIONAL GEOGRAPHIC
1979   Mar   Belgium: one nation divisible, J. Cerruti - p. 314

N.Y. TIMES SUNDAY TRAVEL SECTION (10)
1980   Apr 13   Where the wine of the country is beer, P. Lewis - p. 1
1979   Oct 14   What's doing in Bruges, V. Lewis - p. 7

SATURDAY REVIEW
1980   Feb 16   Bruges: gallery without a roof, H. Sutton - p. 18
          Sep   Brussel's Europalia, H. Sutton - p. 60

SOUTHERN LIVING
1979   Apr   Belgium offers a sampling of Europe - p. 90

TOWN & COUNTRY
1980   Apr   The chateaux heritage of Belgium, S. Roosevelt - p. 97
1979   Apr   One woman's Brussels (do the town with Countess de
                          Gouay), S. Wright - p. 133

TRAVEL & LEISURE
1980   May   Diminutive domains (Luxembourg), H. Koenig - p. 95
1979   Jan   Worth a stopover: Luxembourg, H. Koenig - p. 16
          Mar   Scenes from Flanders, M. Lee - p. 132

TRAVEL/HOLIDAY
1980   Sep   Walking through Luxembourg,
                          G. and H. Koenig - p. 50

WEIGHTWATCHERS MAGAZINE

A yachting costume from Worth is elaborate, in the French manner. British women wore more tailored and serviceable costumes for yachting made of serge or linen and with a sailor hat or yachting cap like those worn by the men.

Notes - Bulgaria

1. Abbreviations of reference sources for novels:
   fc - Fiction Catalog, 9th Edition
   fc/s76 (77, etc.) - Supplement to 9th Edition
   fc/8ed - Fiction Catalog, 8th Edition
   brd/78 (79, etc.) - Book Review Digest for the year

2. Standard Series Guidebooks for Bulgaria:
   Nagel
   Foreign Area Study

3. See Appendix 1 for more complete data on the above.

4. See Europe, at end of country sections, for additional possible sources of reading and information for Bulgaria.

Bulgaria

Background Reading

Brown, J.F.   BULGARIA UNDER COMMUNIST RULE
   Praeger, 1970.
Cary, W.H., Jr.   BULGARIA TODAY:
THE LAND AND THE PEOPLE
   Exposition, 1965.
Chase, I.   FRESH FROM THE LAUNDRY
A travel memoir, written with humor and perception, of this writer's
travels in some of the Communist bloc countries and Greece.
   Doubleday, 1967.
Dornberg, J.   EASTERN EUROPE:
A COMMUNIST KALEIDOSCOPE
The varieties of nationalities, ethnic groups, languages, religions, and
quality of life of an area that has "less in common than much of
Western Europe" except that they are communist in politics and eco-
nomics.
   Dial, 1980.
Haskell, A.L.   HEROES & ROSES
(A VIEW OF BULGARIA)
This is a book written by an Englishman who went to Bulgaria to act
as a judge in a ballet contest. He stayed on and learned to know and
love the people and shares this enthusiasm with his readers.
   Transatlantic, 1967.

Hoddinott, R.F.   BULGARIA IN ANTIQUITY
Particularly for the tourist interested in archaeology.
St. Martin's, 1975.
Johnson, S.   GAY BULGARIA
Apolitical, highly readable guide, based on two years of traveling by
car and staying at off-beat places rather than hotels frequented by
tourists.
Robert Hale, 1964.
Perl, L.   FOODS & FESTIVALS OF THE DANUBE LANDS
Bulgaria, along with other countries on the Danube.
World, 1969.
Perl, L.   YUGOSLAVIA, ROMANIA, BULGARIA;
                               NEW ERA IN THE BALKANS
History, government, culture and people.
Nelson, 1970.
Ristelhueber, R.   A HISTORY OF THE BALKAN PEOPLES
Twayne, 1971.
Stillman, E.   THE BALKANS
Time, Inc., 1964.
Todorov, N.   BULGARIA:
                    HISTORICAL & GEOGRAPHICAL OUTLINE
Vanous, 1969.

Novels

Gilman, D.   THE ELUSIVE MRS. POLLIFAX
Light mystery in Sofia with Mrs. Pollifax solving it.
Doubleday, 1971. fc
Littell, R.   THE OCTOBER CIRCLE
Group of Bulgarian performers resist the invasion of Czechoslovakia.
Houghton, 1976. fc/s76
Pelin, E.   SHORT STORIES
Stories about Sofia and peasants (Pelin is pseudonym for Ivanov).
Twayne.
Pinto, V. de S.   BULGARIAN PROSE & VERSE:
                    A SELECTION WITH AN INTRODUCTORY ESSAY
Univ. of London Press, 1957.
Talev, D.   THE IRON CANDLESTICK
First of a trilogy that is all about struggle against the Turks and one

family's experiences, from early nineteenth to early twentieth century. (Second and third volumes are *St. Elijah's Day* and *The Bells of Prespa.*)
Twayne.

Talev, D.   THE MONK OF HELENDAR
Eighteenth century Bulgaria.
Twayne, 1962.

Vazov, I.   UNDER THE YOKE
1876 uprising against the Turks.
Twayne.

Yovkov, Y.   SHORT STORIES
Tales of Bulgarian peasant life.
Twayne.

Travel Articles

HISTORY TODAY
  1980   Aug   Dependent independence? Eastern Europe 1918-1956,
                      L.P. Morris, p. 38

NATIONAL GEOGRAPHIC
  1980   Jul   Ancient Bulgaria's golden treasures,
                      C. Renfrew - p. 112
          Jul   The Bulgarians, B. Gibbons - p. 158

NATIONAL REVIEW
  1980   Aug 22 Bottled in Bulgaria, N. Hazelton - p. 1034
          Sep 19 Bulgaria the beautiful, N. Hazelton - p. 1153

WORLD PRESS REVIEW (formerly Atlas)
  1980   Jun   Exploring Bulgaria: the Balkan's rich heritage beckons,
                      M. Picchi - p. 62

Notes - Czechoslovakia

1. Abbreviations of reference sources for novels:
   fc - Fiction Catalog, 9th Edition
   fc/s76 (77, etc.) - Supplement to 9th Edition
   fc/8ed - Fiction Catalog, 8th Edition
   brd/78 (79, etc.) - Book Review Digest for the year

2. Standard Series Guidebooks for Czechoslovakia:
   Fodor
   Nagel
   Foreign Area Study

3. See Appendix 1 for more complete data on the above.

4. See Europe, at end of country sections, for additional possible sources of reading and information for Czechoslovakia.

Czechoslovakia

Background Reading

Burke, J.F.   CZECHOSLOVAKIA
One of the Batsford series.
Batsford, 1976.
Blunden, G.   ·   EASTERN EUROPE
CZECHOSLOVAKIA, HUNGARY, POLAND
Description and travel.
Time, Inc. 1965.
Bradley, J.F.N.   CZECHOSLOVAKIA: A SHORT HISTORY
Edinburgh Univ. Press, 1971.
Chapman, C.   AUGUST 21ST: THE RAPE OF CZECHOSLOVAKIA
1968 invasion by the Russians—on-the-spot accounts.
Lippincott, 1968.
Chase, I.   FRESH FROM THE LAUNDRY
One of the series of light, humorous, perceptive travel books written
by Miss Chase and based on her travels with her photographer-doctor
husband. This book describes a tour of the Communist satellite coun-
tries, including Czechoslovakia.
Doubleday, 1967.
Dornberg, J.   EASTERN EUROPE: A COMMUNIST KALEIDOSCOPE
See description under Bulgaria on page 17.
Dial, 1980.
Hermann, A.H.   A HISTORY OF THE CZECHS
Rowman & Littlefield, 1976.

Jelinkova, L.   CASTLES IN CZECHOSLOVAKIA
    Artia, 1962.
Korbel, J.   TWENTIETH-CENTURY CZECHOSLOVAKIA
    Columbia Univ. Press, 1977.
Kovaly, H. & Kohak, E.   THE VICTOR AND THE VANQUISHED
    This book is written from a unique perspective. Ms. Kovaly emerged
    from a German concentration camp at the end of WWII, and was the
    "victor" being a dedicated Communist and married to a top official
    in the party; Mr. Kohak was the "vanquished" as an anti-communist.
    Ms. Kovaly's husband was executed later on and this book tells of
    her disillusionment and the experiences of both authors from "oppo-
    site sides of the barricades."
    Horizon, 1973.
Levy, A.   ROWBOAT TO PRAGUE
    A personal account of the spring of 1968 by an American freelance
    writer living in Prague in the spring of 1968 when Czechoslovakia
    seemed to have regained its freedom only to be invaded by Russia.
    Orion, 1972.
Mlymar, Z.   NIGHTFROST IN PRAGUE
    The disillusionment of a former Communist party official.
    Karz, 1980.
Muacho, L.   THE SEVENTH NIGHT
    Moving account of week's events leading to invasion by the Soviets
    and exile of the author.
    Dutton, 1969.
Neustupný, E.   CZECHOSLOVAKIA BEFORE THE SLAVS
    Praeger, 1961.
Pachman, L.   CHECKMATE IN PRAGUE
    Pachman (chess grandmaster) comments on '68 occupation by the
    Soviets—"a footnote to history."
    Macmillan, 1975.
Parrott, C.   THE SERPENT AND THE NIGHTINGALE
    Autobiography of a diplomat who served for many years in Czecho-
    slovakia, and of his last visit in 1967-68 after retirement—ambience.
    Faber, 1978.
Perl, L.   FOODS AND FESTIVALS OF THE DANUBE LANDS
    World, 1969.
Szulc, T.   CZECHOSLOVAKIA SINCE WW II.
    Written by leading expert on the Communist world.
    Viking, 1971.
Sterling, C.   THE MASARYK CASE
    Biography of Jan Masaryk.
    Harper, 1969.

Volavkova, H.   A STORY OF THE JEWISH MUSEUM IN PRAGUE
   Artia, 1968.
Wallce, W.V.   CZECHOSLOVAKIA
   Westview Press, 1977.
Wechsberg, J.   PRAGUE: THE MYSTICAL CITY
   The riches of the thousand-year old city described beautifully by
   a leading travel writer and one with special empathy for the country
   —"like an unplanned stroll through the ancient quarters of the city
   letting imagination and impression have full play . . . depth and
   panorama."
   Macmillan, 1971.
Wechsberg, J.   THE VOICES
   The author's objective was "to preserve for posterity an act of enormous contribution made by the communications media, especially
   the radio, to the civilian opposition. . ." Wechsberg records the voices
   in his hotel room in Vienna as the network of clandestine radio sta-
   tions operate for many days after the Soviet invasion.
   Doubleday, 1969.
Zeman, Z.   THE MASARYKS:
                     THE MAKING OF CZECHOSLOVAKIA
   Personal biography and "popular" and readable history of Masaryk's
   life and the period.
   Harper, 1976.

Novels

Benes, J.   SECOND BREATH
   Labor camp in the 1950's
   Orion, 1969. fc/8ed
Bieler, M.   THE THREE DAUGHTERS
   Prague in the 1930's and story of one family.
   St. Martin's, 1978. fc/s78
Fuks, L.   MR. THEODORE MANDSTOCK
   A Jew in Prague prepares himself to face the concentration camp.
   Orion, 1968. fc
Harkins, W.   ANTHOLOGY OF CZECH LITERATURE
   King's Crown Press, 1953.
Jacot, M.   THE LAST BUTTERFLY
   WWII concentration camp near Prague (Terezin).
   Bobbs, 1974. fc

Kohout, P. WHITE BOOK...
Full title is (really!)—Adam Juracek, professor of drawing and physical education at the Pedagogical Institute in K, vs Sir Isaac Newton, professor of physics at the University of Cambridge, reconstructed from contemporary records and supplemented by most interesting documents. A satire; professor defies law of gravity in "K" which is a fictitious resort town.
Braziller, 1977. brd/78

Kundera, M. THE FAREWELL PARTY
Outrageous plot and an entertaining account of life in a communist country.
Knopf, 1976. fc/s76

Kundera, M. THE JOKE
A college student, and prankster, plays a joke on Stalin, and fifteen years later seeks vengeance from the man who had turned him in to the authorities.
Coward, McCann, 1969. fc

Kundera, M. LAUGHABLE LOVES
Short stories first published in 1969.
Knopf, 1974. fc

Kundera, M. LIFE IS ELSEWHERE
Communism and the 1948 takeover.
Knopf, 1974. fc

Littell, R. THE OCTOBER CIRCLE
1968 intervention by the Soviet Union and the reaction of a group of traveling Bulgarian performers.
Doubleday, 1975. fc/s76

Peters, E. THE PIPER ON THE MOUNTAIN
Adventure and mystery in Slovakia.
Morrow, 1966. fc

Pynsent, R., ed. CZECH PROSE AND VERSE;
A SELECTION WITH INTRODUCTORY ESSAY
Athlone, 1979.

Selver, P.   AN ANTHOLOGY OF CZECHOSLOVAK LITERATURE
First published in 1929.
Kraus, 1969.

Škvoreckỹ, J. THE BASS SAXOPHONE
This is two novellas. In the one a teenaged Czech, and an ardent jazz lover, plays for the Nazis against his true feelings for them. The second novella is a love story.
Knopf, 1979. brd/79

Škvoreckỹ, J. MISS SILVER'S PAST
A satire on the publishing scene under communism.
Grove, 1975. brd/76

Travel Articles

BICYCLING
1980   Mar   Cycling in eastern Europe, H.T. Lyon - p. 60

HI-FI
1979   Mar   Czechs: all out for Janacek, R.T. Jones - p. 35

HISTORY TODAY
1980   Aug   Dependent independence? Eastern Europe 1918-1956,
                  L.P. Morris, p. 38

HOUSE & GARDEN
1979   Apr   Castles in Bohemia, D. Guimaraes - p. 111
       Nov   Old Bohemia and new Czech glass, H. Harris - p. 266

HOUSE BEAUTIFUL
1980   Sep   Great spas: where the water works, M. Gough - p. 30

NATIONAL GEOGRAPHIC
1979   Apr   Old Prague in winter, P.T. White - p. 546

NEW YORKER
1979   Jul 23   Letter from Prague (Life in Czechoslovakia),
                  A. Bailey - p. 55

OPERA NEWS
1979   May   Czechs at my table, F. Tobey - p. 8

Notes - Denmark

1. Abbreviations of reference sources for novels:
   fc - Fiction Catalog, 9th Edition
   fc/s76 (77, etc.) - Supplement to 9th Edition
   fc/8ed - Fiction Catalog, 8th Edition
   brd/78 (79, etc.) - Book Review Digest for the year

2. Standard Series Guidebooks for Denmark:
   Blue Guide
   Nagel (Denmark and Greenland)
   Fodor (Scandinavia)
   Frommer $ Guide

3. See Appendix 1 for more complete data on the above.

4. See Europe, at end of country sections, for additional possible sources of reading and information for Denmark.

5. The asterisks indicate books on Scandinavia as a whole, but entered only in Denmark; the Notes for the rest of the Scandinavian countries include appropriate cross-reference.

Denmark

Background Reading

*Blankner, F., ed.   THE HISTORY OF THE
                                              SCANDINAVIAN LITERATURES
  " . . . a survey of the literatures of Norway, Sweden, Denmark, Iceland and Finland from their origins to the present day including
  Scandinavian-American authors and selected bibliographies . . ."
  Kennikat, 1966.

Brochman, O.   COPENHAGEN: A HISTORY
                                              TOLD THROUGH ITS BUILDINGS
  Vanous, 1970.

*Butler, E.   THE HORIZON CONCISE HISTORY OF SCANDINAVIA
  American Heritage, 1973.

*Connery, D.S.   THE SCANDINAVIANS
  Background information and the clear differences between the Scan-
  dinavian countries and their inhabitants; " . . . rich in detail . . ."
  Simon & Schuster, 1966.

Deardorff, R.H.   A DAY OUTSIDE THE CITY
  Pleasant and interesting day trips using the city of Copenhagen as
  a base.
  Holt, 1968.

*Derry, J.K.   A HISTORY OF SCANDINAVIA; NORWAY, SWEDEN
                                DENMARK, FINLAND AND ICELAND
  Univ. of Minnesota Press, 1979.

Flender, H.   RESCUE IN DENMARK
Rescue of the Jews of Denmark during WWII.
Manor, 1974.
Foote, P.G. and Wilson, D.M.   THE VIKING ACHIEVEMENT
"A comprehensive survey of the society and culture of early medieval Scandinavia."
Praeger, 1970.
Harvey, W.J. and Reppien, C.   DENMARK AND THE DANES
"A survey of Danish life, institutions and culture."
Kennikat Press, 1970.
Lauring, P.   A HISTORY OF THE KINGDOM OF DENMARK
Host, 1973.
Lottman, H.   DETOURS FROM THE GRAND TOUR
"Off-beat, overlooked, and unexpected Europe"—travel writing that includes material on the Scandinavian capital cities.
Prentice-Hall, 1970.
MacHaffie, I. and Nielsen, M.   OF DANISH WAYS
Dillon Press, 1976.
Magnusson, M.   VIKINGS!
Based on ten-part public television series; Viking culture, religion, mythology, literature and a reconstruction of origins.
Dutton, 1980.
Michelsen, P.   FRILANDS MUSEET: THE DANISH
                          MUSEUM VILLAGE AT SORGENFRI
A history of an open air museum and its buildings.
Humanities, 1973.
Munksgaardd, E.   DENMARK: AN ARCHAEOLOGICAL GUIDE
Faber, 1974.
Nelson, N.   DENMARK
Part of the Batsford series.
Hastings, 1974.
Oakley, S.   A SHORT HISTORY OF DENMARK
Praeger, 1972.
Petrow, R.   THE BITTER YEARS: THE INVASION AND
                        OCCUPATION OF DENMARK AND NORWAY
April/40 - May/45.
Morrow, 1979.
Sansom, William   THE ICICLE AND THE SUN
Author's memoir and guide based on visit to Scandinavia.
Greenwood, 1976. (First published in 1959)
*Shirer, W.L.   THE CHALLENGE OF SCANDINAVIA
Economic and social achievements of Scandinavian countries as a model for the world.
Little, Brown, 1955.

Simpson, C.   THE VIKING WORLD
" . . . an authentic and vivid picture of life in Viking times."
St. Martin's, 1980.

Streeter, Ed.   SKOAL SCANDINAVIA
Perceptive and pleasant account of author's trip by car through Scandinavia with his wife and another couple.
Harper, 1952.

Strode, H.   DENMARK IS A LOVELY LAND
Beautifully written and descriptive travelog—almost like being there.
Harcourt, 1951.

Thomas, J.O.   THE GIANT KILLERS
The story of the Danish resistance movement, 1940-45, recounting " . . . Dane's communal and individual acts of resistance against their Nazi occupiers" including the rescue of nearly all Danish Jews and on to liberation in 1945.
Tapllinger, 1976.

Novels

Albrand, M.   NIGHTMARE IN COPENHAGEN
American scientist involved in cold war mystery.
Random House, 1954. fc/8ed

Arnold, E.   A NIGHT OF WATCHING
Fourth year of German occupation (1943) and Danish Jews are being smuggled out of the country.
Scribner, 1967. fc

Bjarnhof, K.   THE GOOD LIGHT
Boy's acceptance of his blindnesss, pre-WWII (sequel to book below).
Knopf, 1960. fc

Bjarnhof, K.   THE STARS GROW PALE
Boy who is going blind must go to special school in Copenhagen.
Knopf, 1958. fc

Bodelsea, A.   THINK OF A NUMBER
Suspenseful police investigation novel.
Harper, 1968. fc

Dinesen, I.   WINTER'S TALES
Short stories—"seven gothic tales."
Random House, 1942. fc

Eden, D.   THE SHADOW WIFE
Contemporary gothic.
Coward, McCann, 1968. fc

Freuchen, P.   WHITE MAN
   Eighteenth-century attempt to colonize Greenland with imprisoned
   army deserters.
   Rinehart, 1946. fc
Kelly, M.   ASSAULT
   Copenhagen; WWII episode involving British and the Danish under-
   ground.
   Harcourt, 1969. fc/8ed
Lofts, N.   THE LOST QUEEN
   Sister of George III is married off to the crown prince of Denmark;
   eighteenth century.
   Doubleday, 1969. fc
Nielsen, T.   UNSUCCESSFUL MAN
   Suspense novel of a suspicious suicide that leads to murder.
   Harper, 1976. brd/77.
Nexo, M.A.   PELLE THE CONQUEROR
   Four-volume work originally published 1906-10. It deals with dairy
   farm life and a boy leaving for Copenhagen to become a political ac-
   tivist.
   P. Smith. fc
Ørum, P.   NOTHING BUT THE TRUTH
   Murder mystery with psychological insights solved by an introspective
   detective and his brash assistant.
   Pantheon, 1976. brd/77
Ørum, P.   SCAPEGOAT
   West Jutland setting for a murder mystery.
   Pantheon, 1975. fc/s76
Sorensen, V.   KINGDOM COME
   Rural Danish life in 1850's; families oppose a love affair.
   Harcourt, 1960. fc
Stegner, W.   THE SPECTATOR BIRD
   Aging man in twentieth-century California reflects on past and a
   Danish adventure.
   Doubleday, 1976. fc/s76

Travel Articles

CRUISING WORLD
   1980   Oct   Exploring Scandinavia's heartland,
                     J. McKelvey - p. 134

FORTUNE
1980   Dec 29   A holiday harvest of Danish pheasant (pheasant hunt-
                ing in Denmark), M. Wellemeyer - p. 21

GOURMET
1980   Jun   Bornholm: a Danish idyll, J. Jones - p. 34

HORIZON
1980   Aug   Tivoli frivolity - p. 18

INTERNATIONAL WILDLIFE
1980   Sep-Oct A Danish delight called Dyrehaven (wildlife preserve),
                D. Hinrichsen - p. 29

MOTHER EARTH NEWS
1980   Nov-Dec Journeys we know you'll enjoy - p. 86

NATIONAL GEOGRAPHIC
1979   Dec   Magic world of Hans Christian Andersen,
                H. Arden - p. 824

N.Y. TIMES SUNDAY TRAVEL SECTION (10)
1980   Jul 20   Aero, a Danish island that holds off change,
                R. W. Apple, Jr. - p. 1

SATURDAY REVIEW
1980   Feb 16   Something dazzling in the state of Denmark (ballet),
                W. Terry - p. 40

SOUTHERN LIVING
1980   Aug   Holidays in Denmark - p. 22

TRAVEL & LEISURE
1979   Feb   Funen: the place to go if you believe in fairytales,
                M. Spring - p. 107
       Jul   Eating in Copenhagen, E. Jones - p. 72

TRAVEL/HOLIDAY
1980   Apr   Copenhagen—after dark, J.H. Silverman - p. 30
       Aug   Denmark's Jutland, T.B. Lesure - p. 42

Notes - England

1. Abbreviations of reference sources for novels:
   fc - Fiction Catalog, 9th Edition
   fc/s76 (77, etc.) - Supplement to 9th Edition
   fc/8ed - Fiction Catalog, 8th Edition
   brd/78 (79, etc.) - Book Review Digest for the year

2. Standard Series Guidebooks for England and Great Britain:
   Blue Guides (England, London)
   Fodor (London, Great Britain)
   Fodor Budget (Great Britain)
   Frommer $ Guide
   Frommer Dollarwise (England and Scotland)
   Michelin Green Guide (London)
   Michelin Red Guides (Greater London, Great Britain and Ireland)
   Nagel (Great Britain and Ireland)

3. See Appendix 1 for more complete data on the above.

4. See Europe, at end of country sections, for additional possible sources of reading and information for England.

5. The asterisks indicate books on Great Britain as a whole, but entered only under England; the Notes for Scotland, Ireland, Wales include appropriate cross-reference.

6. See special Appendix 2 for England as explained in Introduction (Europe).

England

Background Reading

Beadle, M.   THESE RUINS ARE INHABITED
    Anecdotal account of the wife of an American professor at Oxford
telling of their year-long stay in England, with a teen-age son, and
their travels and holidays.
    Doubleday, 1961.

Burton, E.   HERE IS ENGLAND
    "An informal introduction to a great country, written especially
for American readers" is the lengthy sub-title.
    Farrar, 1965.

Dobie, J. Frank   A TEXAN IN ENGLAND
    Originally published in 1945; a year at Cambridge as professor of
American history in 1943 is basis for this chronicle—"charming,
moving, eloquent chapters" combined with political commentary.
    Univ. of Texas Press, 1980.

Fellows, A.   ENGLAND AND WALES,
                           A TRAVELLER'S COMPANION
    Readability combined with scholarship and careful research; history
in terms of architecture—house, castle, cathedral, parish church. Originally published in 1937.
    Oxford, Clarendon, 1964.

*Glyn, A.   THE BRITISH, PORTRAIT OF A PEOPLE
    Social commentary by an "insider who is also an outsider" and able

"to describe with detachment and humor . . . British sexual habits, eating and drinking customs . . . class distinctions . . . other matters that go to make up a distinct culture and way of life."
Putnam, 1970.

* Irving, C.   POX BRITANNICA
Critical analysis of Britain today—"antidote to the many tomes written by Anglophiles."
Sat. Review Press, 1974.

McKenney, R. and Bransten, R.   HERE'S ENGLAND
First published in 1955; useful and entertaining in helping to get a focus, especially for a first trip to England. Authors feel you must have some understanding of English history and church architecture if the country is not to "slide out from under you." Contains suggested two-week stay in London and seven brief trips out of the city, as well as "A Sightseer's Handy Key to History and Architecture."
Harper, 1971.

* Morton, H.V.   MORTON'S BRITAIN
The "In Search of" series of travel guides by this leading travel writer written in the 20's and 30's have been culled for the excerpts in this newer book with comments to bring the reader up to date. Includes material on England, Ireland, Scotland, Wales.
Dodd, 1970.

Priestley, J.B.   THE ENGLISH
". . . highly personal choice of subjects" to illustrate what the author considers essentially English characteristics—biographical essays plus chapters on arts, future, etc. of England. Lavishly illustrated.
Viking, 1973.

Roberts, C.   AND SO TO BATH
Entertaining, informative, anecdotal and historical—"a different kind of travel book"—account of author's three-month long trip from London to Bath (three hours by car) visiting every historic building and re-telling stories of those in history who traveled this bit of highway.
Macmillan, 1940.

* Sampson, A.   ANATOMY OF BRITAIN TODAY
A journalist's critical analysis of "the workings of Britain—who runs it and how they got there."
Harper, 1965

Simon, K.   ENGLAND'S GREEN AND PLEASANT LAND
A leading travel writer is the author; "contains topographically arranged description of the aesthetic, historic, and legendary interest of numerous English towns and villages."
Knopf, 1974.

*Winks, R.W.   AN AMERICAN'S GUIDE TO BRITAIN
Advice for Americans by a literate and "frankly opinionated" American who has traveled extensively in Britain.
Scribner, 1977.

London

Bell, W.G.   UNKNOWN LONDON
Eighteen essays on antiquities in London about which everyone has heard but most really know very little. An ". . . admirable guide to old London . . . unfailingly entertaining."
Spring Books, 1966.

Bermant, C.   LONDON'S EAST END; POINT OF ARRIVAL
London's immigrants—" . . . colorful, anecdotal and well researched."
Macmillan, 1976.

Borer, M.C.   THE CITY OF LONDON; A HISTORY
Social and institutional history for the general reader-traveler.
McKay, 1978.

Borer, M.C.   TWO VILLAGES: THE STORY OF CHELSEA
                                        AND KENSINGTON
" . . . traces fascinating and enchanting story of two villages which . . . retain an atmosphere and beauty all their own."
W.H. Allen, 1973.

Collier, R.   THE CITY THAT WOULD NOT DIE,
                    THE BOMBING OF LONDON, MAY 10-11, 1941
Dutton, 1960.

Edel, L.   BLOOMSBURY; A HOUSE OF LIONS
Biographies and critique of writers and artists of the "Bloomsbury" group; turn of the century.
Lippincott, 1979.

Ehrlich, B.   LONDON ON THE THAMES
"Rambles through London neighborhoods" of real people and literary figures.
Little, Brown, 1966.

Flanner, J.   LONDON WAS YESTERDAY
Reports from London, 1934-39, to the New Yorker magazine, giving contemporary view of pre-WWII London, including Windsor story.
Viking, 1975.

Gadd, D.   THE LOVING FRIENDS
Bloomsbury group of intellectuals—"sorts out the legends about this famous intellectual circle—who they were, what they believed in, what influence they had . . . what became of them."
Harcourt, 1974.

Gray, R.   A HISTORY OF LONDON
Architectural and social history intended for the layman.
Taplinger, 1979.
Green, M.R.   A TAXI DRIVER'S LONDON
Arco, 1969.
Hanff, H.   84 CHARING CROSS ROAD
Letters between a New York woman and a London book store. Has
become a kind of minor classic for Anglophiles.
Grossman, 1971.
Hanff, H.   DUCHESS OF BLOOMSBURY STREET
A "sequel" to the book above; the author of the letters and the re-
sulting book, becomes something of a celebrity and is invited to visit
the London she has been so enthralled with over the years, but has
never seen.
Lippincott, 1973.
Harrison, M.   THE LONDON OF SHERLOCK HOLMES
Drake, 1972.
Hibbert, C.   THE COURT OF ST. JAMES; THE MONARCH
                   AT WORK FROM VICTORIA TO ELIZABETH II
" . . . court traditions and working habits of five monarchs."
Morrow, 1980.
Hibbert, C.   LONDON: THE BIOGRAPHY OF A CITY
2000 years of London history concisely presented—". . . instructive
. . . exuberant . . . witty text."
Morrow, 1970.
Howard, P.   LONDON'S RIVER
Anecdotes and history of that section of the Thames that flows
through Greater London.
St. Martin's, 1977.
Laurie, P.   SCOTLAND YARD; A STUDY
                       OF THE METROPOLITAN POLICE
Holt, 1970.
Lawson, A.   DISCOVER UNEXPECTED LONDON
Recommended highly by J. Bainbridge, in *Gourmet's* London Jour-
nal, as "providing an off-beat armchair stroll through the city (that
will) . . . prompt many readers to embark on their own tours of dis-
covery."
Elsevier-Phaidon, 1977.
Lillywhite, B.   LONDON COFFEE HOUSES; A REFERENCE BOOK
                   OF THE 17TH, 18TH AND 19TH CENTURIES
G. Allen, 1963.
Meiland, J.   FIRST TIME IN LONDON
For the independent traveler; gives suggestions and advice on sched-

uling a 1, 2 or 3 week visit including "less frequented places of exceptional interest." Twenty original walks.
Scribner, 1979.

Miller, E.   THAT NOBLE CABINET: A HISTORY
OF THE BRITISH MUSEUM
Ohio Univ. Press, 1974.

Minney, R.J.   NO. 10 DOWNING STREET, A HOUSE IN HISTORY
Little, Brown, 1963.

Nelson, W.H.   THE LONDONERS; LIFE IN A CIVILIZED CITY
". . . a delight to read . . . real insight into the personality of one of the world's great cities" by an American who chooses to live there.
Random House, 1974.

Plimmer, C. and D.   LONDON: A VISITOR'S COMPANION
A companion-guide by American journalist-authors; narrative style, good preparation for a trip to London. Includes lesser known sites.
Norton, 1977.

Pritchett, V.S. and Hofer, E.   LONDON PERCEIVED
A "picture book" but one with a superior text by a British critic and travel writer.
Harcourt, 1963.

Rasmussen, S.E.   LONDON: THE UNIQUE CITY
Written by a Danish architect and town planner—"London has developed organically out of the life of the people."
MIT Press, 1934. (Paper ed. 1967)

Rickards, M.   WHERE THEY LIVED IN LONDON:
A GUIDE TO FAMOUS DOORSTEPS
Taplinger, 1972.

Roose-Evans, J.   LONDON THEATRE;
FROM THE GLOBE TO THE NATIONAL
Dutton, 1977.

Rowse, A.L.   THE TOWER OF LONDON
IN THE HISTORY OF ENGLAND
The Tower as "a mirror in which much of English history may be seen"—executions, coronations, processions, comic episodes.
Putnam, 1973.

Simon, K.   LONDON PLACES AND PLEASURES
An "uncommon guidebook" written by a leading travel writer. Some of the practical information on hotels, prices, etc., may be outdated, but the book is highly descriptive and one of the classic guides.
Putnam, 1970.

Trease, G.   LONDON: A CONCISE HISTORY
The sweep of London history in readable style.
Scribner, 1975.

Vevers, G.   LONDON'S ZOO
    Chatto Bodley, 1979.
Weintraub, S.   THE LONDON YANKEES; PORTRAITS OF
    AMERICAN WRITERS AND ARTISTS IN ENGLAND, 1894-1914
    Harcourt, 1979.
Weiss, D.   THE GREAT FIRE OF LONDON
    Crown, 1968.

Oxford

Morris, J., ed.   THE OXFORD BOOK OF OXFORD
    "Traces the history of the University from its foundation in the Middle
    Ages through to 1945, combining extracts from contemporary ob-
    servers with Jan Morris's own linking commentary."
    Oxford, 1978.
Morris, James   OXFORD
    Comprehensive guide that is a "mixture of rhapsody and anecdote."
    A perfect preparatory book for the visitor to Oxford.
    Harcourt, 1965.
Piper, D.   THE TREASURES OF OXFORD
    Oxford's art.
    Paddington, 1977.
Rowse, A.L.   OXFORD IN THE HISTORY OF ENGLAND
    Its "contributions to the politics and culture of England."
    Putnam, 1975.

Stonehenge

Balfour, M.   STONEHENGE AND ITS MYSTERIES
    Scribner, 1980.
Fowles, J. and Bruhoff, B.   THE ENIGMA OF STONEHENGE
    Summit, 1980.

Village Life

Blythe, R.   AKENFIELD—PORTRAIT OF AN ENGLISH VILLAGE
    In-depth portrait of village in E. Anglia 90 miles from London.
    Pantheon, 1969.
Colls, R.   THE COLLIER'S RANT;
             SONG AND CULTURE IN THE INDUSTRIAL VILLAGE
    Life in mining villages.
    Rowman & Littlefield, 1977.
Crookston, P.   VILLAGE ENGLAND
    Villages that have meaning in the context of English history but are

not necessarily well-known to tourists: includes information also on where to stay, etc.
Methuen, 1980.
Deindorfer, R.G.   LIFE IN LOWER SLAUGHTER
N.Y.C. writer's two-year experiment living in an English village.
Dutton, 1971.
Rowse, A.L.   CORNISH CHILDHOOD
Pre-WWI account of historian's childhood and education in the village school—"how an extraordinary little boy escaped his working class environment and became an Elizabethan scholar." Originally published in 1942.
Crown, 1979.

Countryside and Country Life

Bradley, H.   MISS CARTER CAME WITH US
Text and paintings; Yorkshire social life and customs from author's childhood.
Little, Brown, 1974.
Collis, J.S.   THE WORM FORGIVES THE PLOUGH
"Character and psychology of the English farm labourer."
Braziller, 1975.
Creaton, D.   BEASTS AND BABIES
Life on the farm..
St. Martin's, 1978.
DuMaurier, D.   VANISHING CORNWALL
People, places, landscape, history—synthesized by author who has made Cornwall the setting for many of her novels.
Doubleday, 1967.
Hartley, D.   LOST COUNTRY LIFE
"Captures country living in England . . . " twelfth to eighteenth centuries. Details of crafts, folklore, etc.
Pantheon, 1980.
Herriot, J.   JAMES HERRIOT'S YORKSHIRE
The veterinarian-writer around whose practice in Yorkshire the TV public broadcasting station series revolves.
St. Martin's, 1979.
Hillaby, J.   JOURNEY THROUGH LOVE
Walks along the coast of England, South Downs and Hampshire by the British naturalist.
Houghton, 1977.
Hillaby, J.   WALK THROUGH BRITAIN
"Journey from Land's End to John o' Groat's during spring-summer

1966 . . . detailed and highly readable account of that adventure
. . . " by a zoologist and nature lover.
Houghton, 1969.

Mingay, G.E.   RURAL LIFE IN VICTORIAN ENGLAND
"Daily life of the several classes of people who lived in the English
countryside in the nineteenth century."
Heinemann, 1977.

Wyatt, J.   SHINING LEVELS
"The story of a man who went back to nature" in the Lake District.
Lippincott, 1974.

Waterways and Seaside

*Darwin, A.   CANALS AND RIVERS OF BRITAIN
Hastings House, 1976.

Hern, A.   THE SEASIDE HOLIDAY
"The history of the English seaside resort."
Cresset, 1967.

Rolt, Lionel T.C.   THE THAMES FROM MOUTH TO SOURCE
Batsford, 1951.

Walton, J.K.   THE BLACKPOOL LANDLADY; A SOCIAL HISTORY
"Study of the rise of the seaside holiday industry from the late nine-
teenth century to the present."
Manchester Univ. Press, 1979.

Wheeler, A.   THE TIDAL THAMES;
                    THE HISTORY OF A RIVER AND ITS FISHES
England reverses a polluted river.
Routledge & Paul, 1979.

History

* Beloff, Max   IMPERIAL SUNSET
"Britain's liberal empire 1897-1921."
Knopf, 1969.

* Childs, D.   BRITAIN SINCE 1945; A POLITICAL HISTORY
St. Martin's, 1980.

* Churchill, Sir W.L.S.   HISTORY OF THE
                              ENGLISH-SPEAKING PEOPLES
Abridged edition.
Dodd, 1965.

Costigan, G.   MAKERS OF MODERN ENGLAND
"The force of individual genius in history"—leading figures in British
history.
Macmillan, 1967.

* Derry, T.K., et al   GREAT BRITAIN: ITS HISTORY FROM
                               EARLIEST TIMES TO THE PRESENT DAY
    A standard, scholarly history.
    Oxford Univ. Press, 1962.

Feiling, K.   A HISTORY OF ENGLAND
    One-volume, readable history by an Oxford professor; pre-Roman
    times to WWII.
    McGraw-Hill, 1951.

* Hamilton, R.   THE VISITOR'S HISTORY OF BRITAIN
    Intended for orientation of the tourist before going to England.
    Houghton, 1964.

Johnson, P.   THE OFFSHORE ISLANDERS
    "England's people from Roman occupation to present."
    Holt, 1972.

* Morris, J.   HEAVEN'S COMMAND, AN IMPERIAL PROGRESS
    First in a three-part "popular" history written by the renowned tra-
    vel writer. The "material is marshalled with immense narrative skill
    and the sweep of the whole achievement carries the reader along. . .
    a nostalgic tour de force . . ." The first volume begins with Queen
    Victoria's accession to the throne in 1837 and ends with her Jubi-
    lee in 1897.
    Harcourt, 1974.

* Morris, J.   PAX BRITANNICA, THE CLIMAX OF AN EMPIRE
    The British empire at its zenith (1897) " . . . anyone who is half in
    love with the late Victorian Age will be still further captivated."
    Harcourt, 1969.

* Morris, J.   FAREWELL THE TRUMPETS: AN IMPERIAL RETREAT
    Final volume of the trilogy.
    Harcourt, 1978.

Uttley, J.   A SHORT HISTORY OF THE CHANNEL ISLANDS
    Praeger, 1966.

White, R.J.   THE HORIZON CONCISE HISTORY OF ENGLAND
    American Heritage, 1971.

Social and Folk History

Booker, C.   THE NEOPHILIACS
    "A study of the revolution in English life in Swinging England of
    the fifties and sixties."
    Gambit, 1970.

Bragg, M.   SPEAK FOR ENGLAND
    "An oral history of England; 1900-1975, based on interviews with
    inhabitants of Wigton, Cumberland."
    Knopf, 1977.

Grossman, L.   A SOCIAL HISTORY OF ROCK MUSIC,
                        FROM THE GREASERS TO GLITTER ROCK
    McKay, 1976.
Hibbert, C.   HORIZON BOOK OF DAILY LIFE
                              IN VICTORIAN ENGLAND
    McGraw-Hill, 1975.
* Hole, C.   BRITISH FOLK CUSTOMS
    "Particularly useful for the potential visitor . . ."
    Hutchinson Pub. Group, 1977.
Longmate, N.   THE WORK HOUSE
    Victorian social history.
    St. Martin's, 1974.
Perry, G.   VICTORIANS: A WORLD BUILT TO LAST
    Viking, 1974.
* Seaman, L.C.B.   LIFE IN BRITAIN BETWEEN THE WARS
    Putnam, 1970.
Sutcliffe, A.   BIRMINGHAM, 1939-1970
    An industrial city from pre-WWII, through the Blitz and post-War
    period.
    Oxford Univ. Press, 1974.
Watson, F.   YEAR OF THE WOMBAT; ENGLAND 1857
    Unique angle—"using as a symbol the first Australian wombat to be
    shown in the London Zoo, the author has written a social history of
    the events of the year."
    Harper, 1974.
Winter, G.   THE GOLDEN YEARS, 1903-1913
    A pictorial survey in contemporary photographs of the decade.
    David & Charles, 1975.

Kings and Queens

Brook, S.G.   UNCLE OF EUROPE
    "The social and diplomatic life of Edward VII."
    Harcourt, 1975.
Burke, J.   LIFE IN THE CASTLE IN MEDIEVAL ENGLAND
    Rowman & Littlefield, 1978.
Fraser, A.   LIVES OF THE KINGS AND QUEENS OF ENGLAND
    "Readable" biogrpahical sketches.
    Knopf, 1975.
Hibbert, C.   THE COURT OF ST. JAMES
    "The monarch at work from Victoria to Elizabeth II."
    Morrow, 1980.
Lofts, N.R.   QUEENS OF ENGLAND
    By a leading contemporary British novelist; history "through the

lives of the women who have . . . reigned as queen or consort."
Doubleday, 1977.

Morris, J.   THE MONARCHS OF ENGLAND
" . . . as readable and full of antic eccentricity as a novel . . ."
Charter House, 1975.

Murphy, C.J.V.   THE WINDSOR STORY
An account of the pre-WWII romance of Wallis Simpson and the King
of England which resulted in his renouncing the throne.
Morrow, 1979.

Murray, J.   THE KINGS AND QUEENS OF ENGLAND;
A TOURIST GUIDE
Short history of each one, bibliography and index to historically
interesting buildings.
Scribner, 1974.

* Seymour, W.   SOVEREIGN LEGACY
"An historical guide to the British monarchy" as well as castles and
other buildings still open to tourists which are connected with the
various monarchs.
Doubleday, 1980.

Thomas, G.Z.   RICHER THAN SPICES
Charles II and Catherine, 1662—"how a royal bride's dowry . . . revo-
lutionized taste, manners, craftsmanship and history."
Knopf, 1965.

"Upstairs/Downstairs"

Buckle, K. ed.   U AND NON-U REVISITED
"Updating Nancy Mitford's *noblesse oblige* which maintained that a
person's social place . . . is made manifest by the language he or she
uses . . . the changes that have occurred in England and America since
the fifties."
Viking, 1978.

Brander, M.   VICTORIAN GENTLEMAN
Description of Victorian gentleman from "personal diaries and then
current books."
Atheneum, 1975.

Cook, O.   ENGLISH COUNTRY HOUSE:
AN ART AND A WAY OF LIFE
Existing houses and "the kinds of people for whom the houses were
built" with photos.
Putnam, 1974.

Fisher, J.   THE WORLD OF THE FORSYTES
Universe, 1976.

Girouard, M.   LIFE IN THE ENGLISH COUNTRY HOUSE:
                                A SOCIAL AND ARCHITECTURAL HISTORY
    Views English houses as "archeological digs."
    Yale Univ. Press, 1978.
Girouard, M.   THE VICTORIAN COUNTRY HOUSE
    All about: from architecture to domestic organization.
    Yale Univ. Press, 1979.
Harrison, R.   ROSE: MY LIFE IN SERVICE
    "Recollections of life in one of England's grandest households, by
    the personal maid to Nancy Lady Astor."
    Viking, 1975.
Huggett, F.E.   LIFE BELOW STAIRS; DOMESTIC SERVANTS
                                IN ENGLAND FROM VICTORIAN TIMES
    Scribner, 1977.
Leslie, A.   THE MARLBOROUGH HOUSE SET
    The "beautiful people" of 1860-1910.
    Doubleday, 1972.
Sutherland, D.   THE ENGLISH GENTLEMAN
    First in a series describing the "system" of upper class life in England
    by an insider with wit. Following books on the wife and child of
    the English gentleman round out the series, but this first one is re-
    viewed as best and funniest.
    Penguin, 1980.
Sutherland, D.   THE ENGLISH GENTLEMAN'S WIFE
    Viking, 1979.
Sutherland, D.   THE ENGLISH GENTLEMAN'S CHILD
    Viking, 1980.
Sykes, C.S.   THE GOLDEN AGE OF THE COUNTRY HOUSE
    Photographs from private albums, 1850-WWII.
    Mayflower, 1980.

Cathedrals and Churches

Betjeman, J.   AN AMERICAN'S GUIDE TO ENGLISH PARISH
                                CHURCHES INCLUDING THE ISLE OF MAN
    A selective guide to parish churches deemed most worth seeing for
    architecture and/or setting.
    McDonald, 1959.
Morris, R.   CATHEDRALS AND ABBEYS OF
                                ENGLAND AND WALES
    Cathedrals "were built with sweat, skill and cash, not by miracles,"
    is the point made by this book written by an archaeologist with an
    emphasis on the social, economic and technical setting.
    Norton, 1979.

Literary Guides for Travelers

Altick, R.D.   TO BE IN ENGLAND
  A literary guide to homes of English authors and poets.
  Norton, 1969.

*Daiches, D. and Flower, J.   LITERARY LANDSCAPES OF THE
                                     BRITISH ISLES: A NARRATIVE ATLAS
  Literary London (Chaucer, Shakespeare, Dr. Johnson, Dickens,
  V. Woolf including a walking tour with Mrs. Dalloway); Bath (Austen,
  Dickens, Smollett); the Lake District poets; Yorkshire (Bronte coun-
  try); Midlands and Wessex (Hardy); Dublin; Scotland.
  Paddington, 1979.

*Drabble, M.   A WRITER'S BRITAIN; LANDSCAPES IN LITERATURE
  By a leading novelist who combines English literary quotations with
  relevant photographs—Shakespeare to Tolkien, "good balance of
  . . . unfamiliar writers and well-knowns."
  Knopf, 1979.

Harting, E.C. LITERARY TOUR GUIDE TO ENGLAND & SCOTLAND
  "Homes and haunts" of leading English authors and settings for
  some of their major works"—includes London walking tours. Useful
  paperback and introduction to combining reading with literary tours.
  Morrow, 1976.

*Morley, F.   LITERARY BRITAIN; A READER'S GUIDE
                                TO ITS WRITERS AND LANDMARKS
  Delightfully written, leisurely "journey through the literary highways
  and byways of England, Scotland and Wales in company with a remarkable and enthusiastic bibliophile." Unique format in that the
  journeys take the reader along the six ancient roads out of London
  (now main A roads) and back again to London.
  Harper, 1980.

Parker, E.   POETS AND THE ENGLISH SCENE
  "Poems arranged by location."
  Scribner, 1976.

Music and Art

Brody, E.   MUSIC GUIDE TO GREAT BRITAIN;
                                 ENGLAND, SCOTLAND, WALES, IRELAND
  See full annotation for this series under Austria (Brody), page 1.
  Dodd, 1975.

*Harris, J.   THE ARTIST AND THE COUNTRY HOUSE
  "A history of country house and garden view painting in Britain
  1540-1870."
  Sotheby Parke Bernet Publications, 1979.

Plumb, J.H.   ROYAL HERITAGE:
                                 THE TREASURES OF THE BRITISH CROWN
    A TV program, repeated periodically, has been made based on this
    book.
    Harcourt, 1977.

The Pub

Jackson, M.   THE ENGLISH PUB
    Harper, 1976.
Monckton, H.A.   A HISTORY OF THE ENGLISH PUBLIC HOUSE
    The Bodley Head Ltd., 1969.

World War II

*Deighton, L.   BATTLE OF BRITAIN
    Illustrated review of a pivotal battle of WWII—a day by day account
    of the summer of 1940 through September 15.
    Coward, McCann, 1980.
*Deighton, L.   FIGHTER: THE TRUE STORY
                                      OF THE BATTLE OF BRITAIN
    Knopf, 1978.
*Longmate, N.   IF BRITAIN HAD FALLEN
    Stein & Day, 1972.
*Longmate, N.   THE GI'S: THE AMERICAN IN BRITAIN, 1942-1945
    Scribner, 1975.

Intriguing Miscellany

*Burl, A.   RINGS OF STONE: THE PREHISTORIC STONE CIRCLES
                                   OF BRITAIN & IRELAND
    Stonhenge is the most visited; this book goes beyond to other such
    antiquities.
    Ticknor & Fields, 1980.
Brander, M.   THE LIFE AND SPORT OF THE INN
    List of inns based on "author's personal experience over many years
    . . . the devotee of nineteenth-century literature will take one look at
    this volume and be trapped."
    St. Martin's, 1975.
Cherry, M.S.   WOULD YOU LIKE TO LIVE IN ENGLAND?
    Times Books, 1974.
*Cheshire, D.F.   MUSIC HALL IN BRITAIN
    Entertaining account of music halls at their height, 1843-1923.
    Fairleigh Dickinson Univ. Press, 1974.

*Deal, W.   A GUIDE TO FOREST HOLIDAYS
                                        IN GREAT BRITAIN AND IRELAND
"Pleasures and pastimes of several hundred forest parks . . . giving
detailed information on how to get there and what you will find in
the way of plant and animal life . . ."; includes information on camp-
ing, sporting and cultural facilities, places of local interest, nearby
accommodations.
David & Charles, 1976.

Forbes, A.   TOWNS OF NEW ENGLAND AND OLD ENGLAND,
                                        IRELAND AND SCOTLAND
Commissioned by the State Street Trust Co., Boston, to commemo-
rate the tercentenary of the landing of the Pilgrims in Massachusetts;
describes towns in Great Britain which have same-name counter-
parts in the U.S.
Putnam, 1921.

Fowles, J.   ISLANDS
A "deeply personal work" by this outstanding novelist (*French Lieutenant's Woman*) about the Scilly Islands in particular and islands,
and the mystique of islands, in general.
Little, Brown, 1978.

*Hippisley-Coxe, A.D.   HAUNTED BRITAIN: A GUIDE TO
                                        SUPERNATURAL SITES
McGraw-Hill, 1973.

Holden, E.   THE COUNTRY DIARY OF AN EDWARDIAN LADY
A facsimile reproduction of a naturalist's diary. This is a lovely book
with a unique publishing history.
Holt, 1977.

Itkowitz, D.C.   PECULIAR PRIVILEGE; A SOCIAL HISTORY
                                  OF ENGLISH FOX HUNTING, 1753-1885
" . . . casts light on social relationships in the nineteenth-century
countryside."
Harvester, 1977.

Longrigg, R.   ENGLISH SQUIRE AND HIS SPORT
History of country squire to present vis-a-vis hunting, fishing, cro-
quet, etc.
St. Martin's, 1977.

McPhee, J.   WIMBLEDON: A CELEBRATION
"Vignettes for tennis buffs"—a series of articles in book form.
Viking, 1972.

* Wilson, C.A.   FOOD AND DRINK IN BRITAIN
A historical and social history of the subject, from the stone age to
the eighteenth century.
Harper, 1974.

Novels

London

Amis, K.   GIRL, 20
  Farce—a middled-aged musician and his affairs with young girls.
  Harcourt, 1972. fc
Atwater, J.D.   TIME BOMB
  Suspense novel of planned IRA bombings in Picadilly Circus, West-
  minster Abbey and St. Paul's.
  Viking, 1977. brd/78
Bawden, N.   FAMILIAR PASSIONS
  Marrage and divorce and a search for the truth about real parents.
  Morrow, 1979. fc/s79
Bryher   BEOWULF
  Wartime London through the experiences of two ladies who run a
  tea shop.
  Pantheon, 1956. fc
Buckley, W.F., Jr.   SAVING THE QUEEN
  American CIA agent in London, post-WWII, and secrets leaked to
  the USSR.
  Doubleday, 1976. fc/s76
Burnley, J.   THE WIFE
  Affair of the wife of a TV personality who has been neglected by her
  husband.
  Simon & Schuster, 1977. fc/s77
Cadell, E.   THE ROUND DOZEN
  London and environs; romantic suspense novel involving missing fam-
  ily treasure.
  Morrow, 1978. fc/s78
Cooke, J.   NEW ROAD
  Residents fight to save a Georgian terrace in South London.
  St. Martin's, 1976. brd/76
Danby, M.   A SINGLE GIRL
  British-American romance in the sixties era of drugs.
  McGraw-Hill, 1973. fc
Dane, C.   BROOME STAGES
  Chronicles two hundred years of one family in the English theatre,
  from Shakespeare to the last Broome who goes into the movies.
  Doubleday, 1931. fc
Davidson, L.   ·   MURDER GAMES
  Murder of art school students, models and film makers in Chelsea sec-
  tion of London, with quotations from writers who once lived in the

area (Wilde, Belloc, etc.) signalling the murders.
Coward, 1978. brd/78

Deighton, L.   SS-GB; NAZI-OCCUPIED BRITAIN 1941
Fantasy in which Germany has won the war in 1941 and King George
is held prisoner in London.
Knopf, 1979. brd/79

Delderfield, R.F.   THE AVENUE
Twenty people's lives, from 1919 to 1947, who live in a South Lon-
don suburb.
Simon & Schuster, 1969. fc

Dibdin, M.   THE LAST SHERLOCK HOLMES STORY
Jack the Ripper and London of 1888.
Pantheon, 1978. brd/78

Dickinson, P.   THE LIVELY DEAD
A rooming house in Kensington is the scene for this mystery with a
zany set of characters.
Pantheon, 1975. brd/76

Donleavy, J.P.   SCHULTZ
An American expatriate in London's West End musical comedy scene,
by the author of *The Ginger Man.*
Delacorte, 1979. brd/80

Drabble, M.   THE MIDDLE GROUND
Contemporary novel of a woman journalist involved in the women's
movement.
Knopf, 1980. brd/80

Duffy, M.   CAPITAL: A FICTION
A history professor, and an oddball student who audits his course,
give a composite picture of London from earliest days to the present
—"a celebration of London" told with irony and humor.
Braziller, 1976. brd/76

Frankau, P.   SING FOR YOUR SUPPER
First in a trilogy of an English theatrical family. This book is set in a
seaside town in the summer of 1926. The second and third volumes
(*Slaves of the Lamp* and *Over the Mountains*) are set in London and
take the family on through World War II.
Random House, 1964. fc

Freeman, C.   THE DAYS OF WINTER
Family saga, 1914-1940.
Arbor House, 1978. fc/s79

Gardner, J.   THE NOSTRADAMUS TRAITOR
A traveler on tour in London makes an unusual request; internation-
al intrigue and a complex plot inolving the Nazis.
Doubleday, 1979. fc/s79

Gilbert, H.   GWEN THE AMMUNITION
Suspense novel with a "Patty Hearst-like situation" that captures
contemporary mood and mores.
Harper, 1976. fc/s76

Godden, R.   AN EPISODE OF SPARROWS
First published in 1955; a little girl and ally are determined to have a
garden in a bombed-out section of London.
Viking, 1968. fc

Godden, R.   TAKE THREE TENSES
Chronicle of three generations of an English family.
Little, Brown, 1945. fc

Greene, G.   THE HUMAN FACTOR
British intelligence agent becomes a double-agent working on behalf
of South Africa; the moral dilemma of "doing wrong things for right
reasons."
Simon & Schuster, 1978. brd/78

Graham, W.   ANGELL, PEARL AND LITTLE GOD
Unusual triangle with much London background and detail of the
life of the affluent.
Doubleday, 1970. fc

Hardwick, M.   THE DUCHESS OF DUKE STREET
Adaptation of TV series about the woman who owned an exclusive
residential hotel where many prominent people visited, including the
Prince of Wales (Edward VII).
Holt, 1977. fc/s77

Heath, C.   LADY ON THE BURNING DECK
A contemporary widow coping with life and her impossible children;
"acute perception of social foibles . . . hard to believe they aren't actually living somewhere in North London. . . ."
Taplinger, 1979. brd/80

Hoban, R.   TURTLE DIARY
Funny book of two men with a bizarre plan to free all the sea-turtles
in the London Zoo.
Random House, 1976. fc/s76

Household, G.   HOSTAGE: LONDON;
                               THE DIARY OF JULIAN DESPARD
High suspense as the heart of London becomes hostage to anarchist
plot. A member of the group defects and the "chase" includes London and the Cotswolds.
Little, Brown, 1977. fc/s77

Jameson, S.   THE EARLY LIFE OF STEPHEN HIND
Social climber's ruthless journey to the top.
Harper, 1966. fc

Johnson, P.H.   A SUMMER TO DECIDE
First published in 1948; the story of two complicated marriages.
Scribner, 1975. fc/s76

Jones, M.   NOBODY'S FAULT
Heroine is unable to choose between two men; "meticulously observed facets of modern English life."
Mason/Charter, 1977. brd/76

Kennedy, L.   MAGGIE
Story of a "survivor" from the depression to post-WWII prosperity.
Paddington Press, 1979. fc/s79

Lessing, D.   THE SUMMER BEFORE THE DARK
Wife and mother goes off to find herself.
Knopf, 1973. fc

MacInnes, C.   THE LONDON NOVELS OF COLIN MACINNES
Deal with various aspects of modern London life.
Farrar, Straus, 1969. fc

MacKenzie, D.   RAVEN AND THE KAMIKAZE
A detective living on a Thames River houseboat is involved in international intrigue as a Polish emigre tries to assassinate a Soviet agent.
Houghton, 1977. brd/78

McCrum, R.   IN THE SECRET STATE
Computers and British espionage.
Simon & Schuster, 1980. brd/80

Palmer, L.   THE RED RAVEN
Pre-WWII love triangle written by the actress Lilli Palmer.
Macmillan, 1978. brd/79

Pearson, J.   THE BELLAMY SAGA
The public TV series is basis for this book version.
Praeger, 1976. fc/s76

Pym, B.   QUARTET IN AUTUMN
Four elderly, single retirees and the welfare state.
Dutton, 1978. fc/s78

Read, P.P.   A MARRIED MAN
Murder involving a London barrister; a portrait of bourgeois Britain.
Lippincott, 1979. brd/80

Rendell, R.   A DEMON IN MY VIEW
A seedy West London suburb is the setting for this novel of a psychopath and one who is writing a thesis on the psychopathic personality.
Doubleday, 1977. fc/s77

Scholefield, A.   VENOM
An Eaton Square boy is taken hostage but his captors must also deal with a pet snake.
Morrow, 1978. fc/s78

Sharp, M.   BRITANNIA MEWS
  Family saga, 1865-1940, set in the Mews as it changes from slum to
  fashionable residential area.
  Little, Brown, 1946. fc
Sharp, M.   THE FAITHFUL SERVANTS
  Beneficiaries of a family trust (good and faithful servants now too
  old to work) and the trustees and family descendents, in a series of
  vignettes.
  Little, Brown, 1975. brd/75
Snow, C.P.   A COAT OF VARNISH
  Snow's first mystery; set in 1976 in upper middle class London.
  Scribner, 1979. brd/80
Seymour, G.   THE GLORY BOYS
  Terrorists (Palestinian and IRA) plan to kill an Israeli nuclear scien-
  tist.
  Random House, 1976. fc/s76
Theroux, P.   THE FAMILY ARSENAL
  An American ex-State Department employee becomes involved with
  IRA.
  Houghton, 1976. fc/s76
Wells, D.   JANE
  Liberated American woman (a movie critic) living in Covent Garden
  area of London.
  Viking, 1974. fc
West, R.   THE FOUNTAIN OVERFLOWS
  Large London family in the Edwardian era.
  Viking, 1956. fc
Winslow, P.G.   COPPER GOLD
  Scotland Yard superintendent must solve a murder involving his as-
  sistant who has become involved with a Soho nightclub owner.
  St. Martin's, 1978. brd/78

Berkshire

Eden, D.   THE STORRINGTON PAPERS
  Sorting out of her employer's family papers leads to mystery and ro-
  mance for the heroine.
  Coward, McCann, 1978. fc/s79

Buckinghamshire

Milne, A.A.   MR. PIM
  A comedy; "dead" husband returns to his remarried wife.
  Dutton, 1930. fc

Cambridgeshire

Butterworth, M.   THE MAN IN THE SOP WITH CAMEL
> Bank clerk impersonates his dead boss in this thriller with a sense of the ridiculous.
> Doubleday, 1975. fc

James, P.D.   AN UNSUITABLE JOB FOR A WOMAN
> Woman detective and death of a microbiologist at Cambridge.
> Scribner, 1972. fc

Johnson, P.H.   THE GOOD LISTENER
> Three students in the 1950's and how their lives turn out.
> Scribner, 1975. fc/s76

Raphael, F.   THE GLITTERING PRIZES
> Twentieth-century Cambridge and its many societies.
> St. Martin's, 1977. fc/s78

Sharp, T.   PORTERHOUSE BLUE
> Satire; graduate of Porterhouse College becomes master and wreaks revenge for his own unhappy school days.
> Prentice-Hall, 1974. brd/75

Snow, C.P.   THE MASTERS
> Election of a college master.
> Scribner, 1975. fc

Channel Islands

Christopher, J.   THE RAGGED EDGE
> Earthquake on Guernsey and chilling aftermath.
> Simon & Schuster, 1966. fc

Goudge, E.   GREEN DOLPHIN STREET
> Begins on the Islands, but is also a story of the New Zealand frontier in the nineteenth century.
> Coward, McCann, 1944. fc

Marsh, N.   LAST DITCH
> University don vacationing on one of the Channel Islands becomes involved in drug smuggling and a fatal accident.
> Little, Brown, 1977. brd/77

Robinson, D.   KRAMER'S WAR
> American pilot bails out in German-occupied Isle of Jersey in June, 1944.
> Viking, 1977. fc/s77

Cornwall

Brent, M.   TREGARON'S DAUGHTER
> Turn of the century gothic.
> Doubleday, 1971. fc

Burley, W.J.   DEATH IN A SALUBRIOUS PLACE
  Detective thriller in the Scilly Isles (Cornwall).
  Walker, 1973. fc
DuMaurier, D.   THE KING'S GENERAL
  Historic novel of the period of the Parliamentary Wars.
  Doubleday, 1946. fc
  (Other books by Daphne DuMaurier, and set in Cornwall, include:
  *Frenchman's Creek, The House on the Strand, Jamaica Inn, Rebecca,
  My Cousin Rachel, Rule Britannia*.)
Ford, H.   A BRIDE FOR BEDIVERE
  Romance and suspense.
  Harper, 1977. fc/s77
Godden, R.   CHINA COURT
  Remembrances of life in a family house through five generations.
  Viking, 1961. fc
Graham, W.   THE ANGRY TIDE
  Adventure story set in Cornwall.
  Doubleday, 1978. fc/s78
Graham, W.   THE FOUR SWANS, A NOVEL OF CORNWALL
  Family saga.
  Doubleday, 1977. fc/s77
Heyer, G.   PENHALLOW
  Middle 1930's murder story, first published in 1942.
  Dutton, 1971. fc
Holt, V.   BRIDE OF PENDORRIC
  Typical gothic by one of the most prolific authors of the genre.
  Doubleday, 1963. fc
  (Other gothics set in Cornwall, by Victoria Holt, include: *Curse of
  the Kings, Legend of the Seventh Virgin, Manfreya in the Morning,
  Mistress of Mellyn, Lord of the Far Island*.)
Howatch, S.   THE DARK SHORE
  Return to Cornwall with his new wife, and mystery of hero's first
  wife's death.
  Stein & Day, 1965. fc
Innes, M.   THE AMPERSAND PAPERS
  Sir John Appleby, retired Scotland Yard inspector, gets back into
  harness in a murder mystery involving Ampersand ancestor's corres-
  pondence with Percy Bysshe Shelley.
  Dodd, 1979. fc/s79
Marsh, N.   DEAD WATER
  Island off the Cornwall coast is setting for mystery involving Scotland
  Yard and faith healing.
  Little, Brown, 1963. fc

Michaels, B.   WAIT FOR WHAT WILL COME
    American school teacher in Cornwall.
    Dodd, 1978. fc/s79
Quiller-Couch, A. and DuMaurier, D.   CASTLE DOR
    Modern day Tristan and Isuelt; started by Quiller-Couch and finished,
    at the request of his daughter, by DuMaurier.
    Doubleday, 1962. fc
Roberts, D.J.   THE ENCHANTED CUP
    Tristan and Isuelt legend based on *Morte d'Arthur* by Malory.
    Appleton, 1953. fc
Salisbury, C.   THE WINTER BRIDE
    Nineteenth-century gothic romance.
    Doubleday, 1978. fc/s78
Tattersall, J.   LYONESSE ABBEY
    Girl married off to pay a gambling debt; gothic, of course.
    Morrow, 1968. fc

Cumberland

Bragg, M.   THE HIRED MAN
    Turn of the century; a man's attempt to raise his family's social status.
    Knopf, 1970. fc
Gaskin, C.   THE PROPERTY OF A GENTLEMAN
    Romance and mystery when art expert visits an estate in the Lake
    District.
    Doubleday, 1974. fc
Raymond, E.   THE MOUNTAIN FARM
    Love story.
    Sat. Review Press, 1966. fc

Devonshire

Canning, V.   QUEEN'S PAWN
    Thief is blackmailed into stealing the queen's gold.
    Morrow, 1975. fc
Canning, V.   THE MASK OF MEMORY
    An intelligence thriller that is also a study of the relationship of the
    British agent with his wife.
    Morrow, 1975. fc
Canning, V.   THE KINGSFORD MARK
    Gothic murder mystery in a setting of lonely moors.
    Morrow, 1976. fc/s76
Crispin, E.   THE GLIMPSES OF THE MOON
    Oxford professor on sabbatical solves a messy triple murder.
    Walker, 1978.

Delderfield, R.F.   A HORSEMAN RIDING BY
First in a family saga, beginning in 1902.
Simon & Schuster, 1966. fc

Delderfield, R.F.   THE GREEN GAUNTLET
Continues above saga from WWII to sixties.
Simon & Schuster, 1968. fc

Delderfield, R.F.   TO SERVE THEM ALL MY DAYS
Schoolmaster's account of life at an English public school between
WWI and II.
Simon & Schuster, 1972. fc

Delderfield, R.F.   ALL OVER THE TOWN
Happenings in a seaside town when a girl takes over local newspaper
along with an ex-RAF assistant editor. First published in 1947.
Simon & Schuster, 1977. fc/s77

Eden, D.   DARKWATER
Romance and terror on an English estate.
Coward, McCann, 1963. fc

Eyre, K.W.   THE LUTE AND THE GLOVE
American goes to England and meets ancestral ghost.
Appleton, 1955. fc

Gilbert, M.   THE EMPTY HOUSE
Intrigue revolving around bio-warfare station.
Harper, 1979. brd/79

Goudge, E.   THE ROSEMARY TREE
Writer, who has been in jail, and his relationships in a Devon village
with ex-sweetheart and schoolmistress.
Coward, McCann, 1956. fc

Goudge, E.   GENTIAN HILL
The legend of St. Michael's chapel at Torquay sets pattern for story
set on the Devonshire coast at the time of Napoleonic invasions.
Coward, McCann, 1949. fc

Harris, M.   THIS OTHER EDEN
Late eighteenth century historical novel.
Putnam, 1977. fc

Household, G.   RED ANGER
Secret agents pursue young man unjustly accused of treason through
the countryside.
Little, Brown, 1975. brd/75

Macardle, D.   THE UNINVITED
Haunted house on the Devon cliffs.
Doubleday, 1942. fc

Sharp, M.   CLUNY BROWN
Amusing novel of a young girl, who simply will not remember her

social place as a plumber's niece, and who runs off with a Polish
emigre.
Little, Brown, 1944. fc

Stevenson, D.E.   THE HOUSE ON THE CLIFF
Actress leaves London when she inherits a Devonshire estate, and
also finds love.
Holt, 1966. fc

Dorset

Cook, L.   THE MANIPULATOR
"Spooky, shivery" tale of an old lady who preys on others.
Coward, McCann, 1978. fc/s78

Fowles, J.   THE FRENCH LIEUTENANT'S WOMAN
Lyme Regis is setting for a love story told in Victorian style but with
modern insights.
Little, Brown, 1969. fc

James, P.D.   THE BLACK TOWER
Scotland Yard Commander Dalgliesh involved in a mystery of deaths
in a home for the disabled.
Scribner, 1975. brd/76

Maybury, A.   THE MINERVA STONE
Gothic romance involving a TV personality, his wife, and the obliga-
tory "stately home" in Dorset.
Holt, 1968. fc

Murdoch, I.   THE NICE AND THE GOOD
A love story as well as a mystery and "sexual comedy."
Viking, 1968. fc

Wade, J.   THE SINGING WIND
Victorian gothic; London novelist is summoned to Dorset only to
find a murder.
Coward, McCann, 1977. fc/s78

East Anglia

James, P.D.   DEATH OF AN EXPERT WITNESS
A forensic science lab, in a small village, is the scene for the murder
of a senior biologist.
Scribner, 1977. fc/s78

Lofts, N.   THE HOUSE AT OLD VINE
History of a house and the people who inhabited it.
Doubleday, 1961. fc

Lofts, N.   THE HOMECOMING
Fifteenth-century knight and his family.
Doubleday, 1976. fc/s76

Lofts, N.   BLESS THIS HOUSE
    Chronicle of a house and its inhabitants over 350 years.
    Doubleday, 1954. fc
Rendell, R.   MAKE DEATH LOVE ME
    A bank manager (at heart a "romantic") and two teenaged bank
    robbers; a thriller with psychological insight.
    Doubleday, 1979. fc/s79
Seymour, G.   KINGFISHER
    Hijackers from Russia, en route to Israel, are forced to land in Stan-
    sted.
    Simon & Schuster, 1978. brd/78
Sharp, M.   THE INNOCENTS
    Poignant story of a retarded girl and the two women want to care
    for her.
    Little Brown, 1972. fc
Sharp, M.   SUMMER VISITS
    Saga of an estate in East Anglia from 1800-1940's.
    Little, Brown, 1978. fc/s78
Smith, D.   THE NEW MOON WITH THE OLD
    Secretary-housekeeper must deal with four precocious children when
    her employer leaves England.
    Little, Brown, 1963. fc
Stow, R.   THE GIRL GREEN AS ELDERFLOWER
    British colonial, and writer, returns to England; medieval myths in a
    modern novel.
    Viking, 1980. brd/80

Gloucestershire

Delving, M.   NO SIGN OF LIFE
    American book buyer becomes involved in solving a murder; much
    description of the countryside.
    Doubleday, 1979. brd/79

Hampshire

Goudge, E.   THE BIRD IN THE TREE
    First of a trilogy of the Eliot family, beginning in 1938. Second and
    third titles are *Pilgrim's Inn* and *The Heart of the Family*.
    Coward, McCann, 1940-53. fc

Hertfordshire

Amis, K.   THE GREEN MAN
    Ghost story with humour; *The Green Man* is a pub.
    Harcourt, 1970. fc

Isle of Man

Gash, J.   GOLD BY GEMINI
An antique dealer, a search for early Roman coins, and murder.
Harper, 1978. fc/s79

Kent

Holt, V.   THE SHIVERING SANDS
Gothic involving a piano teacher's search for her archaeologist sister.
Doubleday, 1969. fc
Mayhew, M.   THE CRY OF THE OWL
Suspense and romance—"owlers" are a band of smugglers.
Doubleday, 1977. fc/s77

Lancashire

Bainbridge, B.   QUIET LIFE
Setting is a village near Southport in Lancashire; story of acute family
strife told in flashback.
Braziller, 1977. brd/77
Bainbridge, B.   YOUNG ADOLF
Novel growing out of a diary entry that at 23, young Adolf Hitler
visited Liverpool.
Braziller, 1979. fc/s79
Hartog, Jan de   THE PEACEABLE KINGDOM
Quaker life in England, 1652-53, and Pennsylvania, 1754-55.
Atheneum, 1972. fc
Stubbs, J.   BY OUR BEGINNINGS
Lancashire family saga.
St. Martin's, 1979. fc/s79

Northumberland

Cookson, C.   THE CINDER PATH
Serious story of a man's boyhood in an unhappy home, WWI.
Morrow, 1978. fc/s79
Cookson, C.   A GRAND MAN
Daughter's love for her father and efforts to find a way out of their
tenement life for a farm job and cottage in the country.
Morrow, 1975. fc
Cookson, C.   THE MALLEN STREAK
A family saga with unusual and complicated relationships; mid-1800's
to WWI (followed by *The Mallen Girl* and *The Mallen Lot).*
Dutton, 1973. fc

Cookson, C.   PURE AS THE LILY
    1933-1973, working class family.
    Bobbs, 1973. fc
Cronin, A.J.   THE STARS LOOK DOWN
    Life in a mining community in the first half of the century.
    Little, Brown, 1935. fc
Marchant, C.   MISS MARTHA MARY CRAWFORD
    Motherless family kept together by the daughter; nineteenth century.
    Morrow, 1976. fc/s76
Melville, J.   DRAGON'S EYE
    Island off the north coast is setting for this romantic mystery.
    Simon & Schuster, 1976. fc/s76
Stewart, M.   THE IVY TREE
    Northumberland countryside is the setting for this mystery of a Can-
    adian girl posing as an heiress.
    Mill, 1962. fc

Nottingham

Sillitoe, A.   THE WIDOWER'S SON
    The son becomes a highly successful military officer, but does not
    manage his private life as well.
    Harper, 1977. fc/s77
Sillitoe, A.   SATURDAY NIGHT AND SUNDAY MORNING
    An angry young man, his love affairs and life, as part of the working
    class in industrial area of Britain.
    Knopf, 1959. fc

Oxfordshire

Amis, K.   JAKE'S THING
    Comedy of Oxford University life and one of its don's fears of sexual
    impotence.
    Viking, 1979. fc/s79
Ashe, R.   MOTHS
    Oxford don becomes involved with murder, a lustful ghost, a special
    house.
    Holt, 1976. fc/s77
Butler, G.   SARSEN PLACE
    Oxford in the 1880's; a governess-tutor involved in strange happen-
    ings in an old house.
    Coward, McCann, 1974. fc
Clarke, A.   THIS DOWNHILL PATH
    Suspense and murder involving death of a female poet.
    McKay, 1977.

Dexter, C.   LAST BUS TO WOODSTOCK
Inspector Morse and Sgt. Lewis are the murder-solving team of detectives in this and the following books by C. Dexter.
St. Martin's 1975. brd/76

Dexter, C.   LAST SEEN WEARING
St. Martin's, 1976. brd/76

Dexter, C.   THE SILENT WORLD OF NICHOLAS QUINN
St. Martin's, 1977. brd/78

Fowles, J.   DANIEL MARTIN
Two friends at Oxford marry sisters and realize years later they chose the wrong one.
Little, Brown, 1977. fc/s77

French, M.   THE BLEEDING HEART
Two Americans, working temporarily in England, fall in love.
Summit, 1980. brd/80

Goudge, E.   THE SCENT OF WATER
Woman at fifty inherits a house and journals of an earlier resident and finds spiritual regeneration and happiness.
Coward, McCann, 1963. fc

Larkin, P.   JILL
Student life at Oxford in 1940. Poignant story of a student from the working class, who conjures up a sister Jill to help cope with his loneliness. First published in 1946.
Overlook, 1976. fc/s76

Sayers, D.L.   GAUDY NIGHT
College gaudy (a gathering of alumni) precipitates blackmail and Lord Peter Wimsey's involvement.
Harper, 1960. brd/75

Smith, G.   CAVIARE
A love story that involves espionage and defection.
Coward, 1976. brd/s77

Stewart, J.I.M.   THE GAUDY
This begins a series of novels on Oxford—"... attuned to the finer nuances of Oxford life"—and having the collective title, *A Staircase in Surrey.* They were written by an Oxford don who also writes mysteries under the name of Michael Innes. *The Gaudy* is an alumni gathering of "old boys" of the 1940's. The second book, *Young Patullo,* reverts to an earlier period in the hero's life as he arrives to attend an Oxford memorial service. In the third, *A Memorial Service,* Patullo, now a playwright, returns to Surrey College as a fellow. The fourth, *The Madonna of the Astrolabe,* concerns a newly-discovered portrait intended to help finance repair of the bell tower only to disappear.
Norton, 1975-77. fc (and supplements for 76-78)

Shropshire

Webb, M.   PRECIOUS BANE
Farming life and country people; a disfigured woman finds a husband who appreciates her.
Dutton, 1926. fc

Wodehouse, P.G.   NO NUDES IS GOOD NUDES
The nude is a portrait who resembles various people, depending upon the eye of the beholder.
Simon & Schuster, 1970. fc

Somerset

Cadell, E.   GAME IN DIAMONDS
Light romance of grandmother's matchmaking efforts on behalf of her grandson.
Morrow, 1976. fc/s76

Canning, V.   THE RUNAWAYS
One is a fifteen-year old from reform school, the other a cheetah from Longleat Animal Park.
Morrow, 1972. fc

Heyer, G.   LADY OF QUALITY
This book (as well as *Bath Tangle*), written by a leading writer of historical novels, is set in the city of Bath.
Dutton, 1972. fc

Surrey

Braddon, R.   THE FINALISTS
Suspense at Wimbledon as Russian defector must thwart a plan to assassinate the queen during the singles finals.
Atheneum, 1977. fc/s77

Gardner, J.   THE WEREWOLF TRACE
A furniture importer living in Surrey is discovered to have been present in the bunker where Hitler died, and is his spiritual heir.
G.K. Hall, 1978. fc/s77

Haldeman, L.   THE LASTBORN OF ELVIN WOOD
Adult fantasy of villagers attempts to preserve a band of aging fairies.
Doubleday, 1978. fc/s79

Sussex

Gibbons, S.   COLD COMFORT FARM
A parody of the "earthy" novel, as an orphan intrudes upon her relatives' careless lives.
Dial Press, 1964. fc

Godden, R.   THE DIDDAKOI
   Poor little gypsy girl and her horse.
   Viking, 1972. fc
Heyer, G.   THE RELUCTANT WIDOW
   Regency period mystery of a governess who is married off to a dying
   man. First published in 1946.
   Putnam, 1971. fc
Household, G.   WATCHER IN THE SHADOWS
   A British agent believed to be a Nazi is hunted down by a former
   enemy.
   Little, Brown, 1960. fc
Howatch, S.   THE SHROUDED WALLS
   Turn of the century gothic.
   Stein & Day, 1968. fc
Tattersall, J.   THE WILD HUNT
   1810 gothic.
   Morrow, 1974. fc

Wiltshire

Golding, W.   THE PYRAMID
   Three separate incidents in a boy's life, growing up 1920-40.
   Harcourt, 1967. fc
Golding, W.   THE SPIRE
   Building of the highest spire ever becomes an obsession of the dean
   of a medieval cathedral.
   Harcourt, 1964. fc
Shelby, G.   THE CANNAWAYS
   First of a family trilogy beginning in 1697.
   Doubleday, 1978. fc/s78

Yorkshire

Braine, J.   THE QUEEN OF A DISTANT COUNTRY
   A successful novelist re-examines his life.
   Coward, McCann, 1973. fc
Braine, J.   LIFE AT THE TOP
   This is the sequel to *Room at the Top*. In this book, the hero has ar-
   rived "at the top" and thus made good his ambition to escape his
   background.
   Houghton, 1962. fc
Braine, J.   ROOM AT THE TOP
   Story of a man's ruthless ambition for escape from his mining town
   beginnings.
   Houghton, 1957. fc

Byatt, A.S.   THE VIRGIN IN THE GARDEN
     The time is 1953 just before, during and after the coronation of the
     present queen, Elizabeth II. The book concerns a pageant celebrating
     that event.
     Knopf, 1979. brd/79
Caine, J.   HEATHCLIFF
     This is a book to be read in connection with the classic *Wuthering
     Heights.* In that book the hero, Heathcliff, disappears for a period of
     time and returns with his fortunes considerably improved. This is the
     author's version of what happened to Heathcliff during his absence.
     Knopf, 1978. brd/78
Caldwell, T.   GRANDMOTHER AND THE PRIESTS
     Leeds; tales of priests told to a woman through her grandaugter's
     eyes and ears.
     Doubleday, 1963. fc
Holt, V.   KIRKLAND REVELS
     Gothic set on the Yorkshire moors.
     Doubleday, 1962. fc
Michaels, B.   GREYGALLOWS
     Gothic set in the 1840's as London girl is married off to the owner
     of Greygallows.
     Dodd, 1972. fc
Sharp, M.   ROSA
     A comedy of manners set in England of the 1890's. Rosa is a grooms-
     man's daughter who marries the estate owner; contrasts Yorkshire
     and London society.
     Little, Brown, 1970. fc
Storey, D.   SAVILLE
     A coal miner's education and breaking away from his working class
     family.
     Harper, 1977. fc/s77
Woods, S.   AND SHAME THE DEVIL.
     Corruption in a small city in Yorkshire involving the arrest of two
     Pakistanis and police.
     Holt, 1967. fc
Woods, S.   THEY LOVE NOT POISON
     Murder, black marketing in Yorkshire country in post-WWII (1947),
     a period of shortages and rationing in England.
     Holt, 1972. fc
Woods, S.   DONE TO DEATH
     Detective mystery with the same couple involved as in *They Love
     Not Poison.*
     Holt, 1974. fc/s76

Travel Articles

ANTIQUES
1980	Apr	Lindisfarne Castle - p. 818
	Jun	Callaly Castle, C. and J. Wainwright - p. 1260
	Oct	Horace Walpole & Strawberry Hill (Orleans House Gallery), C. and J. Wainwright - p. 694
1979	Apr	Bethnal Green Museum, C. and J. Wainwright - p. 720
	May	Rockingham Castle (Northamptonshire), C. Wainwright - p. 948
	Jul	Cragside opens to the public (Northumberland), C. and J. Wainwright - p. 102
	Sep	Wallington Hall, Northumberland, C. and J. Wainwright - p. 520
		Washington Old Hall, C. and J. Wainwright - p. 308

ANTIQUES JOURNAL
1979 Mar   Studying antiques in England, B. Levin - p. 18

APARTMENT LIFE
| 1980 | May | Ye old resorts: England's country house hotels offer old world pleasures to new world travelers, R. Nadelson - p. 22a |
| *1979 | Dec | The B and B way through Britain, R.L. Costas - p. 4 |

ATLANTIC
1979 Feb   The barge of Avon, R. Bendiner - p. 84

BETTER HOMES & GARDENS
1980 Jun   Norwich, one of England's best kept secrets - p. 224

BIKE WORLD
* 1979 May-Jun Riding the rails and trails of Great Britain, P. Wexler - p. 48

BLACK ENTERPRISE
* 1980 Aug   Her majesty's isles: pubs, bagpipes and regal—all yours in the culturally diverse British Isles, J. Whitlow - p. 115

COSMOPOLITAN
| 1979 | Oct | Brown's Hotel (London), K.T. MacLay - p. 100 |
| | Oct | Insider's Guide to London, K.T. MacLay - p. 86 |

| | Oct | The Savoy Lounge, the Dorchester lounge, K.T. MacLay - p. 100 |

CUISINE
1980   Jun   Ma Cuisine (London), W. Rice - p. 84

ESQUIRE
1979   Jan 30   Haut sport: English pheasant for the American squire, A. Horne - p. 50

ESSENCE
1980   Sep   London's black mosaic (blacks in London), J. Harris - p. 22

          May   Spring flings in Paris and London, J. Harris - p. 64

50 PLUS
1980   Apr   A vacation in England by foot, L. Sabin - p. 34

GOURMET
1980   Mar   London Journal (Tate Gallery), J. Bainbridge - p. 6

          May   Gourmet Holiday: Dorset, M. Costa - p. 28

          Jun   London Journal (*Debrett's Peerage,* Cambridge), C.P. Reynolds - p. 16

          Jul   An excursion from London—the American Museum and Hunstrete House (Bath), R. McDouall - p. 24

          Sep   London Journal (*Debrett's Peerage,* ancestry research in general), J. Bainbridge - p. 4

          Oct   Young chefs of London, E.L. Ortiz - p. 33

          Nov   Ludlow—a Shropshire sojourn, I.C. Kuhn - p. 26

          Dec   London Journal (a model train shop and the London Times on Valentine's Day), J. Bainbridge - p. 10

1979   Mar   London Journal (helicopter tour of London, caviar bar restaurant), J. Bainbridge - p. 10

          Apr   Ramblings from Chewton Glen, M. Elder - p. 24

          Jun   An Oxford gaudy, M. Kenyon - p. 44

          Jun   The great kitchen at Brighton, L. Langseth-Christensen - p. 40

          Jun   London Journal (garden party at Buckingham Palace, Andrew Lawson book—see Background Reading), J. Bainbridge - p. 4

          Jul   An excursion from London—Cliveden and Waterside, Inn, R. McDouall - p. 44

          Jul   In search of Victor Hugo (apartment in Paris and Hauteville House on Isle of Jersey), N. Barry - p. 32

          Sep   Hadrian's Wall revisited, M. Kenyon - p. 30

INTERNATIONAL WILDLIFE
*1980 Mar-Apr   Britain's primeval moors are not always what they
                seem: so stark, so lonely, so beguiling,
                T. Andrews - p. 12

LADIES' HOME JOURNAL
*1980   Aug   Country holiday in the British Isles, P. Funke - p. 56

MADEMOISELLE
1980   Mar   London (antique markets) - S.D. Wood - p. 54

MODERN BRIDE
1979 Dec-Jan   London, P. Brooks - p. 176

MONEY
1980   Apr   Up and about in Paris, London & Rome,
                R. Beardwood - p. 60

MOTHER EARTH NEWS
1980 Nov-Dec   Journeys we know you'll enjoy - p. 86

NATIONAL GEOGRAPHIC
1980   Nov   The grandeur of Windsor, J. David - p. 616
       Nov   Windsor Castle, A. Holden and J.L. Stanfield - p. 604
1979   Oct   Two Englands (traditional and modern),
                A.C. Fisher - p. 442

NATIONAL GEOGRAPHIC WORLD
1980   Apr   Victory at Skipton Castle - p. 22

NEW YORKER
1980   Jan 21   The enormous mind (British Museum),
                M. Panter-Downes - p. 42
       Mar 10   Letter from London, M. Panter-Downes - p. 138
       Dec 22   Covent Garden (new series of shops in old Covent
                Garden Market), C. Trillin - p. 82
       Dec 29   Letter from London, M. Panter-Downes - p. 56

N.Y. TIMES SUNDAY TRAVEL SECTION (10)
1980   Feb 17   Experiencing the iron age at England's Butser Farm
                reconstruction, D. Wickers - p. 5
       Mar 9   Visiting the guildhalls in London's financial district,
                R. Heskey - p. 3
       Mar 16   The Yorkshire of the Brontes, Sterne, Herriot,
                S. Salmans - 1

	Mar 30	In England's York, arts festival goes outdoors - p. 33
	Apr 20	A country home for monarchs, S. Carr - p. 1
*	May 11	Britain school courses for vacationers, S. Salmans - p. 7
*	May 18	The youth hostel route in Britain, F. Bailinson - p. 3
	Jun 1	A distinctively English way with opera, Glyndebourne, M. Sterne - p. 1
	Jun 22	Tracing the art of heraldry in London, B. Lovenheim - p. 13
	Jul 6	Sailing rented cruisers on England's Norfolk Broads, J.E. Mann - p. 3
	July 6	The Dolphin Yard at Sittingbourne, Kent, recalls the age of barges, D. Wickers - p. 3
	Aug 10	London's new Covent Garden Market, W. Borders - p. 3
	Aug 17	What's doing in Bristol, F. Bailinson - p. 5
	Oct 12	Thame's boats serve lunch and dinner with the sights, J.E. Mann - p. 3
	Nov 9	Some meditations on the enigma that is Stonehenge, J. Fowles - p. 1
*	Nov 16	Landmarks for rent in Britain, D. Guimaraes - p. 1
	Nov 30	What's doing in London, W. Borders - p. 7
	Dec 14	A careful planner turns footloose, J. Cook - p. 3
1979	Jan 21	A cozy cottage in England, V. Sampson - p. 1
	Jan 28	Europe revisited: a nostalgic tour with grandchildren (France, England), V. Royster - p. 1
	Feb 4	American Museum in Britain, I.H. Freeman - p. 14
	Feb 18	An unseasonable visit to Cornwall, S. Marker - p. 3
	Mar 18	How to win at Wimbledon by scoring as a spectator, G. Lichtenstein - p. 1
	Apr 1	Swapping yachts across the Atlantic, R.L. Chapman and A. Jackson - p. 1
	Apr 1	What's doing in York, J. Collins - p. 11
	Apr 22	Crowd problems at English cathedrals, S. Carr - p. 9
	Jun 3	What's doing around Brighton, I. Lyon - p. 9
	Jun 10	Miracle plays are staged in Glastonbury Abbey ruins, T. Cowan - p. 5
	Jun 24	The 'three choirs' festival—Hereford, A. Lewis - p. 5
	Jul 8	A literary pilgrimage to London's Bloomsbury, S. Marker - p. 1
	Jul 29	The English lakes: a diverse journey, I. Molotsky - p. 1
	Aug 19	Country houses near Picadilly, M. Sterne - p. 1
	Oct 21	A pilgrim's tour of old churches in East Anglia, G. M. Gibson - p. 1
	Dec 9	Those nostalgic English music halls, S. Salmans - p. 1

SATURDAY REVIEW
 *1980   Feb 2   Some of their favorite places (Great Britain),
                     H. Sutton - p. 40
  1979   Mar 17   Far out guide to places you never thought of (Isle of
                     Man), P. Brook - p. 46
          Mar 17   To the tables down at Guernsey, C.N. Parkinson - p. 57
          Jun 23   Touch of Russian abandon in London's Nikita's,
                     G. Feifer - p. 47

SMITHSONIAN
  1979   Jul   The British Museum honors flaming birth of industry
                     (Museum of Iron), W. and R. Vandivert - p. 58

SOUTHERN LIVING
  1980   Sep   The Tower has a new museum - p. 55
  *   Aug   Britain by car and train rail-drive packages - p. 20
           Sep   Paris via BritRail (prices, accommodations) - p. 54

SUNSET
  1980   Nov   South of London plant adventure (Jermyn's Arbore-
                     tum) - p. 252
           Dec   Shopping and shop browsing in the elegant heart of
                     London - p. 38
  1979   Jun   America's past in Plymouth, England - p. 28

TOWN & COUNTRY
  1980   Feb   Madame Tussaud's: after 177 years still waxing
                     famous, W. Petschek - p. 52
           Oct   The English countryside, L. Gwinn - p. 246
  1979   Apr   Cruisin' down the canal, S.H. Anderson - p. 18
           Apr   England's staying power (English country houses to-
                     day), D.M. Meenan and D. Moore - p. 85
           Apr   The gourmet shires of England, J. Villas - p. 116
           Apr   The Dorchester, L. Gwinn - p. 132

TRAVEL & LEISURE
  1980   Jan   A passenger's approach to Heathrow,
                     D. Wickers - p. 28
           Mar   Parliamentary performance, L. Probst - p. 24
           Mar   Latest from London, S. H. Anderson - p. 46
           Apr   Bookish London, R. Poe - p. 43
           May   Food worlds—Harrods, M. Leech - p. 68
           Jul   Knightsbridge—a walk through fashionable London,
                     K.H. Mackey - p. 53

	Sep	Into the English countryside on a Green Line bus, D. Wickers - p. 144
	Dec	St. Paul's Cathedral, E. Venant - p. 138
1979	Jan	London's small hotels, M. Leech - p. 13
	Feb	Briefcase: capital hotels for the executive (London), Argus - p. 10
	Mar	Driving around London—and putting, too—where to go if you want to golf, P. Arnold - p. 30
	Mar	The inimitable Mr. Carrier, G. Lang - p. 106
	Apr	Lunch in the City of London, Argus - p. 12
	May	The posh pads of London, J. Herbert Silverman - p. 28
	Jun	A shopping spree in London, P. Brooks - p. 27
	Jun	How to see London with kids, M. Spring - p. 34
	Dec	Fortnum & Mason, F. Ferretti - p. 77

TRAVEL/HOLIDAY

1980	Feb	London's wine bars, F. Green - p. 12
	Apr	York, P. Brooks - p. 54
1979	Feb	Britain's smallest royal palace (Queen Charlotte's cottage in Kew), A. Glaze - p. 16
	Mar	London's small hotels, E. Antrobus - p. 48
	Jun	Dollar-stretching for seniors on the Isle of Man, K. Simmon - p. 54

VOGUE

1979	Jun	On the magic Isle of Man—once-in-a-thousand-years-fun, J. Fritz - p. 147

WORLD PRESS REVIEW (formerly Atlas)

1980	Feb	Drinking like an Englishman: the high and low life of British pubs, R.W. Leonhardt - p. 59

YACHTING

1979	Jun	Cruising England's midland canals, M. Lostiom - p. 72

Notes - Finland

1. Abbreviations of reference sources for novels:
   fc - Fiction Catalog, 9th Edition
   fc/s76 (77, etc.) - Supplement to 9th Edition
   fc/8ed - Fiction Catalog, 8th Edition
   brd/78 (79, etc.) - Book Review Digest for the year

2. Standard Series Guidebooks for Finland:
   Fodor (Scandinavia)
   Frommer $ Guide (Scandinavia)
   Nagel
   Foreign Area Study

3. See Appendix 1 for more complete data on the above.

4. See Europe, at end of country sections, and items with an asterisk under Denmark, for additional possible sources of reading and information for Finland.

5. Errata: Add the Foote, Magnusson and Simpson books to Background Reading for Finland (see listings, pages 28, 29).

‛Finland

Background Reading

Bradley, D.   LION AMONG ROSES: A MEMOIR OF FINLAND
The author lived in Finland, with his wife and five children, and
worked as a teacher of English literature. The book is descriptive of
daily life, family adjustments, the celebration of Christmas, etc.
Holt, 1965.

Hall, W.   THE FINNS AND THEIR COUNTRY
History, politics and the nature of the land by an enthusiastic admirer
of the Finns.
Eriksson, 1968.

Ingold, T.   SKOLT LAPPS TODAY
Finnish reindeer herders in today's Finland.
Cambridge, 1977.

Irwin, J.   THE FINNS AND THE LAPPS
                                 HOW THEY LIVE AND WORK
Praeger, 1973.

Jutikkala, E. and Pirinen, K.   A HISTORY OF FINLAND
Praeger, 1974.

Kirby, D.G.   FINLAND IN THE 20TH CENTURY
Univ. of Minnesota Press, 1980.

Lister, R.P.   THE HARD WAY TO HAPARANDA
"A journey in Lapland"–Haparanda is the Swedish beginning of an
adventurous trip (1800 miles) through all of Lapland.
Harcourt, 1966.

Nickels, S.   THE TRAVELLER'S GUIDE TO FINLAND
Pre-travel background reading as well as practical travel information.
Chatto-Bodley, 1979.
Nicol, G.   FINLAND
Part of the Batsford series.
Hastings, 1975.
Sansom, W.   THE ICICLE AND THE SUN
Four essays on Scandinavia (including Finland), by a gifted travel
writer—" . . . offering truth and magic." First published in 1959.
Greenwood, 1976.
Sykes, J.   DIRECTION NORTH: A VIEW OF FINLAND
The author served in the ambulance corps during the 1940 war with
Russia and this book describes his return visit 25 years later and liv-
ing with the families of two old acquaintances.
Chilton, 1967.
Von Hertzen, H. and Spreiregen, P.D.   BUILDING A NEW TOWN:
"Finland's new garden city, Tapiola."
MIT Press.
Wuorinen, J.H.   A HISTORY OF FINLAND
Columbia Univ. Press, 1965.

Novels

Janssen, T.   THE SUMMER BOOK
Summer idyll is shared by a girl and her grandmother on a Finnish
island.
Pantheon, 1975. brd/75
Sariola, M.   THE HELSINKI AFFAIR
A good detective story; a lawyer is the hero and the courtroom scenes
and procedures "fascinatingly different" from those in the U.S.
Walker, 1971. fc
Schoolfield, G.C. (intro.)   SWEDO-FINNISH SHORT STORIES
Regional and modern psychological stories by Finns whose native
tongue is Swedish.
Twayne, 1975.
Sillanpää, F.E.   THE MAID SILJA
Well-to-do family is brought to ruin by father's ineptitude. Originally
published in 1931; this is a classic novel in Finland and won a Nobel
prize in 1939.
N.S. Berg, 1974. fc

Travel Articles

COSMOPOLITAN
1980   Feb   Cross country fun, R. Ashley - p. 68

HORIZON
1979   Aug   Music and more (Helsinki Festival) - p. 11

HOUSE & GARDEN
1979   Jul   Special weaving course in Finland - p. 48

MOTHER EARTH NEWS
1980 Nov-Dec   Journeys we know you'll enjoy - p. 86

N.Y. TIMES SUNDAY TRAVEL SECTION (10)
1979   May 27 A chain of islands in the midnight sun (Alands),
                     C. Wren, - p. 1

TRAVEL & LEISURE
1980   Jun   Helsinki, C.N. Bernard - p. 100

WORLD PRESS REVIEW (formerly Atlas)
1979   Jan   Wintering with the Lapps, G.J. van Laas - p. 57

Notes - France

1. Abbreviations of reference sources for novels:
   fc - Fiction Catalog, 9th Edition
   fc/s76 (77, etc.) - Supplement to 9th Edition
   fc/8ed - Fiction Catalog, 8th Edition
   brd/78 (79, etc.) - Book Review Digest for the year

2. Standard Series Guidebooks for France:
   Blue Guides (Northwestern France, South of
       France, Paris)
   Fodor (France, Paris)
   Fodor Budget
   Frommer Dollarwise
   Michelin Green Guides (Brittany, Chateaux of
       the Loire, Dordogne, Fr. Riviera, Normandy,
       Paris, Provence)
   Michelin Red Guides (France, Paris)
   Nagel (Chateaux of the Loire, Fr. and Italian
       Riviera)

3. See Appendix 1 for more complete data on the
   above.

4. See Europe, at end of country sections, for additional possible sources of reading and information
   for France.

5. Errata: Add the Chase book to Background Reading
   for France (see listing, page 115).

France

INCLUDING: MONACO

Background Reading

Ardagh, J.   A TALE OF FIVE CITIES; LIFE IN EUROPE TODAY
   An in-depth portrait of five provincial cities: Newcastle (England), Toulouse (France), Stuttgart (Germany), Bologna (Italy) and Ljubljana (Yugoslavia)—interesting and fascinating approach as the author compares cities that are not ordinarily first on a tourist's list.
   Harper, 1980.
Cole, R. and James, T.   EUROPE: A SECOND TIME AROUND
   "An informal guide to selected places you may have missed on your first trip." Off-the-beaten track places to visit in France.
   Funk & Wagnall, 1971.
Deardorff, R.H.   A DAY OUTSIDE THE CITY
   Pleasant and interesting day trips with Paris or Nice as a base.
   Holt, 1968.
Durrell, L.   SPIRIT OF PLACE
   An anthology of excerpts of Durrell's letters, essays and early novels; a combination of fact, fiction and travel reflections, that includes the Rhone River wine country and Southern France.
   Dutton, 1969.
Edwards, H.   FRANCE AND THE FRENCH
   Nelson, 1973.
Feldkamp, F.   NOT EVERYBODY'S EUROPE
   A grand tour of nine unique cities including Lyon, France.
   Harper's Magazine Press, 1976.

Fisher, M.F.K.   A CONSIDERABLE TOWN
   Marseilles—"its glory and wickedness, past and present; its life, its
   legends, its mystery."
   Knopf, 1978.
Fisher, M.F.K.   MAP OF ANOTHER TOWN
                                        A MEMOIR OF PROVENCE
   Two years lived in Aix-en-Provence described delightfully and with
   a "spirit of place"—daily adventures of living.
   Little, Brown, 1964.
Gramont, S. de   THE FRENCH; PORTRAIT OF A PEOPLE
   The author ". . . seeks to explain . . . why French are admired, de-
   tested, misunderstood, and unique."
   Putnam, 1969.
Hess, J.L.   VANISHING FRANCE
   French life and politics along with some history.
   Quadrangle, 1975.
Hillaby, J.   A WALK THROUGH EUROPE
   See entry under Belgium on page 11.
   Houghton, 1972.
Larfillon, L.   ONE HUNDRED HOURS TO VISIT
                                 THE CHATEAUX OF THE LOIRE
   Larousse, 1973.
Lottman, H.   DETOURS FROM THE GRAND TOUR
   "Off-beat, overlooked, and unexpected Europe"—travel writing that
   includes material on Paris and Normandy.
   Prentice-Hall, 1970.
Morris, J.   PLACES
   Literate essays by a leading travel genre writer—". . . entertainment
   and information fused in imaginative prose." Trouville is the "place."
   Harcourt, 1972.
Myhill, II.   THE LOIRE VALLEY
   Routes into the area from Paris and other major cities as well as
   touring the Valley itself. Personal observations and historical anec-
   dotes combined with practical tourist information.
   Faber, 1978.
Nourissier, F.   THE FRENCH
   "Today's 50 million Frenchmen looked at lovingly, critically, wittily,
   . . . and with hope, by a sparkling writer who is one of them."
   Knopf, 1968.
Oliver-Michel, F. and G.C.   GUIDE TO THE ART
                                        TREASURES OF FRANCE
   Companion guide for the traveler interested in art; what to see, ar-
   ranged geographically into fifteen areas.
   Dutton, 1966.

Pope-Hennessy, J.   ASPECTS OF PROVENCE
     The landscape and mood of Provence conveyed by a literary travel
     writer who is an artist as well.
     Little, Brown, 1967.

Stern, L. and P.V.D.   BEYOND PARIS
     A TOURING GUIDE TO THE FRENCH PROVINCES
     Norton, 1967.

Streeter, E.   ALONG THE RIDGE
     A travel memoir describing ". . . an unusually beautiful and diversi-
     fied automobile trip" from Paris, south to Andorra and Spain, back
     across southern France to the Dolomites, ending in Dubrovnik.
     Harper, 1964.

White, F.   WAYS OF AQUITAINE
     Also *Three Rivers of France* (Merrimack/1979) and *West of the
     Rhone* (Faber), by the same author; companion guides to take along
     covering central and southwestern France.
     Norton, 1968.

Wylie, L.W.   VILLAGE IN THE VAUCLUSE
     "Life in the French town where the author, his wife, and two small
     sons lived for a year."
     Harvard Univ. Press, 1957.

Paris

Barry, J.   THE PEOPLE OF PARIS
     An interpretation of Paris, through its people, by an American cor-
     respondent who arrived with Patton's 3rd Army and stayed on.
     Doubleday, 1966.

Brassai, G.H.   THE SECRET PARIS OF THE 30'S
     Pantheon, 1976.

Chiang, Y.   THE SILENT TRAVELLER IN PARIS
     A Chinese traveler ("silent" for lack of fluency in French) describes
     his encounter with the city and its inhabitants.
     Norton, 1962.

Cobb, R.   THE STREETS OF PARIS
     Unfashionable, unchanged, back streets of Paris, photographed (be-
     fore they do change) and accompanied by text.
     Pantheon, 1980.

Collins, L.   IS PARIS BURNING?
     Suspenseful and exciting retelling of the liberation of Paris in 1944
     and a German general's decision to save the city from burning.
     Simon & Schuster, 1965.

Dill, M.   PARIS IN TIME
     A historical guide to Paris in "chatty" style.
     Putnam, 1975.

Ehrlick, B.   PARIS ON THE SEINE
The city, the river, the romance of the centuries, told with pictures, but mostly text.
Atheneum, 1962.

Flanner, J. (Genêt)   PARIS WAS YESTERDAY, 1925-1939
Selections from letters to the New Yorker; the left bank literary colony of the period. *Paris Journal* (Atheneum, 1965) contains selections from the period 1944-1971.
Viking, 1972.

Frégnac, C.   THE GREAT HOUSES OF PARIS
History, social mores in an " . . . entertaining and gossipy text."
Vendome Press, 1979.

Gajudsek, R.E.   HEMINGWAY'S PARIS
With photographs; all about Paris and Hemingway.
Scribner, 1978.

Gault, H. and Millau, C.   A PARISIAN'S GUIDE TO PARIS
An ". . . amusing, irreverent view of eating, shopping, drinking, sitting and looking in Paris." An "inside" guide written with Americans particularly in mind.
Random House, 1969.

Gunther, J.   TWELVE CITIES
See full entry under Austria, Paris is one of the twelve.
Harper, 1969.

Harriss, J.   TALLEST TOWER; EIFFEL AND BELLE EPOQUE
Social history of the Eiffel Tower.
Houghton, 1975.

Hemingway, E.   A MOVEABLE FEAST
Sketches of 1921-26 years in Paris; published posthumously.
Scribner, 1964.

Jacobson, S. and E., eds.   THE DANCE HORIZONS TRAVEL GUIDE
TO SIX OF THE WORLD'S DANCE CAPITALS
Dance-related information for professional dancers or enthusiasts, that includes festivals, theatre seating charts, etc. etc.—invaluable for travelers in planning visits to the six cities covered in the book. Four of the cities are in Europe (Lond, Paris, Leningrad and Moscow).
Dance Horizons, 1978.

Knowles, J.   DOUBLE VISION: AMERICAN THOUGHTS ABROAD
For travelers (armchair or otherwise) as well as ". . . anyone who enjoys . . . polished and civilized writing." Included: London and Cambridge, Paris, Nice, Antibes, Rome, Venice.
Macmillan, 1969

Landes, A. and S.   PARIS WALKS: CLOSE-UPS OF THE LEFT BANK
Ready-made walking tours.
New Republic, 1978.

Longstreet, S.   WE ALL WENT TO PARIS:
AMERICANS IN THE CITY OF LIGHT 1776-1971.
    Macmillan, 1972.

Marx, S.   QUEEN OF THE RITZ
    Hotel Ritz during the war years.
    Bobbs, 1978.

Morrow, C.   BOHEMIAN PARIS OF TODAY
    Gordon, 1977.

Paul, E.H.   THE LAST TIME I SAW PARIS
    Sketches of life on the Rue de la Huchette, in pre-WWII Paris, until
the Germans came. (*Springtime in Paris* depicts the same street ten
years later.)
    Random House, 1942.

Shaw, I.   PARIS! PARIS!
    The experiences and impressions of a noted novelist.
    Harcourt, 1977.

Simon, K.   PARIS: PLACES AND PLEASURES;
AN UNCOMMON GUIDEBOOK
    Written by a leading travel writer; comments on Paris and its sights,
sounds, institutions and inhabitants. Intended for a ten-day visit
with various alternatives suggested.
    Putnam, 1970.

Skinner, C.O.   ELEGANT WITS AND GRAND HORIZONTALS
    Paris during the 1890's and a ". . . sparkling panorama of 'la belle
epoque,' its gilded society, irrepressible wits and splendid courtesans."
    Houghton, 1962.

Stein, G.   PARIS, FRANCE
    A "love letter" to the city by Ms. Stein who had known Paris since
1900; published as Paris fell to the Germans.
    Liveright, 1970.

Monaco

Fielding, X.   THE MONEY SPINNERS:
MONTE CARLO AND ITS FABLED CASINO
    Little, Brown, 1977.

Herald, G.W. and Radin, E.D.   THE BIG WHEEL;
MONTE CARLO'S OPULENT CENTURY
    Morrow, 1963.

Jackson, S.   INSIDE MONTE CARLO
    "A social history of Monaco's past one hundred years and of its resi-
dent and visiting celebrities and reigns of the Grimaldi princes, including the present Ranier III."
    Stein & Day, 1975.

Corsica

Carrington, D.   CORSICA: PORTRAIT OF A GRANITE ISLAND
    John Day, 1974.
Deane, S.   ·IN A CORSICAN VILLAGE
    Autobiographical account of social life and customs.
    Vanguard, 1965.

Rivers and Waterways

Glyn, A.   THE SEINE
    A portrait of the river, its history, geography, people and legends.
    Putnam, 1966.
Kimbrough, E.   FLOATING ISLAND
    Enjoyable memoir of a barge trip through France with a group of
    friends by this writer of travel books.
    Harper, 1968.
Liley, J.   FRANCE, THE QUIET WAY:
                                      A GUIDE TO ITS WATERWAYS
    Beekman, 1975.

History

Brogan, D.W.   THE FRENCH NATION
    1814-1940.
    Harper, 1957.
Codevilla, A.   MODERN FRANCE
    ". . . a valuable guide" for the American traveler.
    Open Ct., 1974.
Davidson, M.B.   HORIZON CONCISE HISTORY OF FRANCE
    American Heritage, 1971.
Hamilton, R.   THE HOLIDAY HISTORY OF FRANCE
    Chatto-Bodley, 1978.
Hampson, N.   THE FRENCH REVOLUTION: A CONCISE HISTORY
    "For the layman who enjoys reading history."
    Scribner, 1975.
Lofts, N. and Weiner, M.   ETERNAL FRANCE
    A history of France, 1789-1944, by a novelist-historian team.
    Doubleday, 1968.
Maurois, André   A HISTORY OF FRANCE
    History by the learned novelist and biographer.
    Farrar, 1957.
Tuchman, B.   A DISTANT MIRROR
    Life in the fourteenth century.
    Knopf, 1978.

Kings, Queens, Rulers

Backer, D.A.L.   PRECIOUS WOMEN
Seventeenth-century France through the eyes of the socially elite
women of the day.
Basic Books, 1974.

Barry, J.   PASSIONS AND POLITICS;
A BIOGRAPHY OF VERSAILLES
Doubleday, 1972.

Cronin, V.   LOUIS & ANTOINETTE
A favorable view of the royal couple who are seen as the innocent
victims of history; highly readable style.
Morrow, 1975.

Cronin, V.   NAPOLEON BONAPARTE, AN INTIMATE BIOGRAPHY
Seen as something of a "whitewash" by some reviewers, but "a pleas-
ure to read."
Morrow, 1972.

Denieul-Cormier, A.   A TIME OF GLORY;
THE RENAISSANCE IN FRANCE 1488-1559
Wise and foolish royalty.
Doubleday, 1968.

Law, J.   FLEUR DE LYS:
THE KINGS AND QUEENS OF FRANCE
An entertaining, anecdotal view of French monarchs from inside the
palace.
McGraw-Hill, 1976.

Lewis, W.H.   THE SPLENDID CENTURY
". . . not only a story of Louis XIV, his life, loves, the people and
events that made his reign memorable, but a story of seventeenth-
century France and its way of life."
Sloane, 1953.

Mitford, Nancy   THE SUN KING
Biography of Louis XIV beautifully illustrated and written by a nov-
elist known for her wit and style.
Harper, 1966.

Seward, D.   BOURBON KINGS OF FRANCE
"A series of light and heretofore scattered facts about the most color-
ful ruling family in European history."
Harper, 1976.

Cathedrals

Adams, H.   MONT ST. MICHEL AND CHARTRES
". . . eloquent and profound . . . expression concerning the glory of

medieval art and the elements that brought it into being."
Houghton, 1914.
Holbrook, S.   JOY IN STONE
The Cathedral of Reims.
Farrar, Straus, 1973.
Hurlimann, M.   FRENCH CATHEDRALS
Viking, 1967.
Temko, A.   NOTRE-DAME OF PARIS
A "biography" of the cathedral.
Viking, 1955.

Eating and Drinking

Aron, J.P.   ART OF EATING IN FRANCE;
MANNERS AND MENUS IN THE NINETEENTH CENTURY
Harper, 1976.
Blake, A.   GREAT CHEFS OF FRANCE; THE MASTERS OF
HAUTE CUISINE AND THEIR SECRETS
A history of French cuisine and description of the chef-owners of
three-star (Guide Michelin) restaurants outside of Paris.
Lichine, A.   ALEXIS LICHINE'S GUIDE TO WINES
AND VINEYARDS OF FRANCE
A "unique guide for touring the vineyards."
Knopf, 1979.
Price, P.V.   EATING AND DRINKING IN FRANCE TODAY
A book for the serious gourmet.
Scribner, 1974.
Wildman, F.S., Jr.   A WINE TOUR OF FRANCE: A CONVIVIAL
GUIDE TO FRENCH VINTAGES AND VINEYARDS
Random House, 1976.

Novels

Backer, D.   THE PARMA LEGACY
Seventeenth-century historical novel about two women—peasant and
princess.
Norton, 1978. fc/s78
Boissard, J.   A MATTER OF FEELING
Contemporary family life in France, and their teenager's affair with
an older man.
Little, Brown, 1980. brd/80

Chaix, M.   LAURELS OF LAKE CONSTANCE
Using her father's diaries, a daughter writes a memoir-novel of his life from WWII to the present and his ideological journey from anti-Bolshevism to Nazi collaborator.
Viking, 1977. brd/77

Freeling, N.   THE NIGHT LORDS
British justice becomes involved in a murder while vacationing in France.
Pantheon, 1978. brd/79

Mitford, N.   THE BLESSING
"Dull" English woman marries Parisian gay blade.
Random House, 1951. fc

Neumann, A.   THE DEVIL
Louis IX.
Knopf, 1928.

Neumann, A.   ANOTHER CAESAR
Napoleon.
Knopf, 1935.

Ormesson, J. d'   AT GOD'S PLEASURE
Decline of an aristocratic French family
Knopf, 1977. brd/78

Pinget, R.   THE LIBERA ME DOMINE
Picture of a small rural town through a series of grisly events.
Red Dust, 1978. fc/s79

Prou, S.   LA BELLE EDMEÉ
Story of a woman "survivor" 1940-45.
Harper, 1978. fc/s78

Rolland, R.   THE SOUL ENCHANTED
French woman's story, early 1900's (five novels).
Holt, 1925-34.

Romains, J.   MEN OF GOOD WILL
Life during pre-WWI decade.
Knopf, 1932.

Saul, J.R.   THE BIRDS OF PREY
Novel based on real-life 1968 plane crash.
McGraw-Hill, 1978. fc/s78

Simenon, G.   THE HATTER'S PHANTOMS
Study of a psychotic killer in French town.
Harcourt, 1976. fc/s76

Stevenson, A.   THE FRENCH INHERITANCE
Neo-Nazism in present-day France is subject of mystery set in small town outside of Paris.
Putnam, 1974. fc

Warner, S.T.   SUMMER WILL SHOW
    1848 revolution.
    Viking, 1936.
Wiser, W. THE WOLF IS NOT NATIVE TO THE SOUTH OF FRANCE
    American expatriate, divorced with son.
    Harcourt, 1978. fc/s78
Zola, Emile   THE DOWNFALL
    Franco-Prussian War.
    Published 1892.

Paris

Ajar, E.   MOMO
    Old woman takes in the children of prostitutes.
    Doubleday, 1978. brd/78
Anthony, C.   THE RETURN
    A thriller set in Paris.
    Coward, McCann, 1978. fc/s79
Beauvoir, S. de   LES BELLES IMAGES
    Putnam, 1968.
Beauvoir, S. de   THE MANDARINS
    World, 1956.
Cocteau, J.   THE HOLY TERRORS
    Brother and sister and their excessive dependence on each other; first
    published in 1929.
    New Directions, 1957. fc
Colette   BREAK OF DAY
    Semi-autobiographical; first published in 1928.
    Farrar, Straus, 1966. fc
    (Other novels with a Paris background by Colette include: *Claudine
    in Paris, Gigi, Julie De Carneilhan, Chance Acquaintances, The Inno-
    cent Libertine, The Vagabond.)*
Cortázar, J.   A MANUAL FOR MANUEL
    Latin-American exiles plot to kidnap VIP.
    Pantheon, 1978. brd/79
Deighton, L.   AN EXPENSIVE PLACE TO DIE
    A clinic and its illegal experiments, concoctions, creations.
    Putnam, 1967. fc
Dutourd, J.   THE HORRORS OF LOVE
    A good man goes (very) bad in middle age.
    Doubleday, 1967. fc
Freeling, N.   THE BUGLES BLOWING
    A government official is involved in a murder that reaches into the
    offices of the president of France.
    Harper, 1976. fc/s76

Freeman, C.   THE DAYS OF WINTER
    Twentieth-century family saga.
    Arbor House, 1978. fc/s79

Gallico, P.   MRS 'ARRIS GOES TO PARIS
    A charwoman and Christian Dior.
    Doubleday, 1958. fc

Gary, R.   YOUR TICKET IS NO LONGER VALID
    A man's declining business and sexual prowess seen as France's
    "emasculating" dependence on Arab oil.

    Braziller, 1977. brd/78

Geñet, J.   OUR LADY OF THE FLOWERS
    Grove, 1963. fc

Geñet, J.   FUNERAL RITES
    Grove, 1969. fc

Gide, A.   THE COUNTERFEITERS
    First published in 1925.
    Modern Library, 1962. fc

Giraudoux, J.   LYING WOMAN
    Woman involved in two parallel love affairs.
    Winter House, 1972. fc

Goldberg, M.   THE KARAMANOV EQUATIONS
    American doctor is asked to save a Russian scientist in Paris; CIA
    and KGB are involved.
    World, 1972. fc

Handke, P.   MOMENT OF TRUE FEELING
    Exisential novel of 48 hours in the life of a press attache—"magic
    creation of Paris places and moods . . . "
    Farrar, Straus, 1977. brd/77

Harris, R.   THE LAST ROMANTICS
    Paris between the wars.
    Simon & Schuster, 1980.

Hemingway, E.   THE SUN ALSO RISES
    Post-WWI "lost" generation; scene shifts between Paris and Spain.
    Scribner, 1926. fc

Johnston, V.   A ROOM WITH DARK MIRRORS
    Drug intrigue aboard N.Y.-Paris flight, and thereafter.
    Dodd, 1975. fc/s76

Jones, J.   THE MERRY MONTH OF MAY
    The 1968 student uprising in Paris.
    Delacorte, 1971. fc

Lyons, N. & I.   CHAMPAGNE BLUES
    Comedy; travel guide authors in the grandest hotel in Paris.
    Simon & Schuster, 1979.

Lyons, N. & I.   SOMEBODY'S KILLING
                                           THE GREAT CHEFS OF PARIS
  A mystery.
  BJ Pub. Group, 1978.
MacInnes, H.   THE VENETIAN AFFAIR
  A plot to assassinate De Gaulle.
  Harcourt, 1963. fc
Martin du Gard, R.   SUMMER 1914
  Pre-WWI narrative of a family.
  Viking, 1941. fc
Martin du Gard, R.   THE THIBAULTS
  Continuation of family saga begun in *Summer 1914.*
  Viking, 1939. fc
Miller, H.   TROPIC OF CANCER
  Autobiographical novel of an American in Paris in the early 30's.
  Grove, 1961. fc
Monteilhet, H.   MURDER AT THE FRANKFURT BOOK FAIR
  Plot begins in Paris with a professor's attempts at plagiarism.
  Doubleday, 1976. fc/s76
Moore, B.   THE DOCTOR'S WIFE
  Love affair in Paris of a London doctor's wife and an American.
  Farrar, Straus, 1976. fc/s76
Nin, A.   CITIES OF THE INTERIOR
  Three novels: *Ladders to Fire* tells of Americans in Paris.
  Swallow, 1974. fc
Oldenbourg, Z.   THE AWAKENED
  1930's and war years; love story.
  Pantheon, 1957. fc
Pilhes, R.   THE PROVOCATEUR
  Corporate life in French division of American corporation.
  Harper, 1977. brd/78
Queneau, R.   THE BARK TREE
  Mystery of hidden money, first published 1933.
  New Directions, 1971. fc
Read, P. P.   POLONAISE
  Saga of Polish family ending in Paris, 1925-58.
  Lippincott, 1976. fc/s76
Remarque, E.M.   ARCH OF TRIUMPH
  Paris just before WWII; another novel you can catch in movie form
  on late night TV occasionally.
  Appleton, 1945. fc
Rhys, J.   QUARTET
  An English girl, in Paris, is victim of a husband and wife.
  Harper, 1971. fc

Rhys, J.   GOOD MORNING, MIDNIGHT
"Has been" returns to Paris. Originally published 1939.
Harper, 1970. fc

Romains, J.   THE DEPTHS AND THE HEIGHTS
Political novel of Paris heading toward WWI.
Knopf, 1937. fc

Romains, J.   THE EARTH TREMBLES
1910-11 socio-political novel. ·
Knopf, 1936. fc

Sabatier, R.   THE SAFETY MATCHES
Paris orphan and high society, 1930's.
Dutton, 1972. fc

Sabatier, R.   THREE MINT LOLLIPOPS
Sequel to *The Safety Matches* (above).
Dutton, 1974. fc

Sagan, F.   A CERTAIN SMILE
Love affair of a young student and an older married man.
Dutton, 1956. fc

Sagan, F.   LA CHAMADE
Love affair of "hedonist" (she) and "romantic" (he).
Dutton, 1966. fc

Sagan, F.   THE UNMADE BED
Paris romance is rekindled five years later.
Delacorte, 1978. brd/79

Sartre, J.P.   THE AGE OF REASON
Existentialism in Paris of 1938.
Knopf, 1947. fc

Simenon, G.   MAIGRET AND THE HOTEL MAJESTIC
Murder of a woman in a luxury hotel.
Harcourt, 1978. brd/78
(Other Simenon books with a Paris setting include: *The Old Man Dies, The Prison, The Little Saint, The Glass Cage, The Girl with a Squint.*)

Stead, C.   HOUSE OF ALL NATIONS
Story of international finance in 1920-30; first published in 1938. A huge cast of characters with a banker the central figure along with his family, servants, employees, mistresses, victims, associates.
Holt, 1972. fc

Steinbeck, J.   THE SHORT REIGN OF PIPPIN IV
The monarchy is reinstated in the person of an amateur astronomer.
Viking, 1957. fc

Troyat, H.   STRANGERS ON EARTH
Darov family as exiles in Paris (a sequel to *The Red and the White* set in Russia of 1917).
Crowell, 1958. fc

Troyat, H.   AMELIE IN LOVE
First in a five-part family saga of a lower middle class family in Paris.
This volume covers the period 1912-1915 and beginning of WWI.
Simon & Schuster, 1956. fc

Troyat, H.   AMELIE AND PIERRE
Sequel to *Amelie In Love*. Continues family saga as Amelie manages
the family cafe in Paris while Pierre goes off to war in 1914.
Simon & Schuster, 1957. fc

Troyat, H.   ELIZABETH
                                       TENDER AND VIOLENT ELIZABETH
Continue Troyat's five-part chronicle of a family; daughter Elizabeth
at a convent school in the country and then her love affairs and marriage set in a ski resort.
Simon & Schuster, 1959 and 1960. fc

Troyat, H.   THE ENCOUNTER
The fifth and final book of this series is back in Paris as WWII begins
and Nazis occupy the city.
Simon & Schuster, 1962. fc

Uris, L.   TOPAZ: A NOVEL
Russian espionage penetrates the French government.
McGraw-Hill, 1967. fc

Waller, L.   TROCADERO
Terrorists are holding the Trocadero where art treasures are stored in
order to free a political prisoner, with American and French security
officers working to solve the situation.
Delacorte, 1978. fc/s78

Bourgogne (Burgundy)

Colette   MY MOTHER'S HOUSE, AND SIDO
Autobiographical novel of author's early years in the region. First
published in 1922.
Farrar, Straus, 1975. fc

Bordeaux (and Guienne Region)

Daley, R.   STRONG WINE RED AS BLOOD
Story of the region and wine-making as American businessman who
is sent to buy a wine chateau becomes enthralled with the life and
wine-making process.
Harper's Mag. Press, 1975. fc/s76

Mauriac, F.   A MAURIAC READER
Five novels set in Bordeaux and environs. First published in 1922;
the author won Nobel prize for literature in 1952.
Farrar, Straus, 1968. fc

Mauriac, F.   MALTAVERNE
Autobiographical novel (age 17-22) of conflict between a mother
and son over his life's direction. Maltavese is the family estate.
Farrar, Straus, 1970. fc

Mauriac, F.   QUESTIONS OF PRECEDENCE
"Explores the moral implications of using another human being for
an unworthy purpose"—in this case, to enter Bordeaux society.
Farrar, Straus, 1959. fc

Mauriac, F.   WOMAN OF THE PHARISEES
Woman interferes in others' lives out of religious conviction. First pub-
lished in 1942.
Holt, 1946. fc

Brittany

Balzac, H. de   BEATRIX
Love story set in Brittany of early nineteenth century. Originally
published in 1839.
Prentice-Hall, 1970. fc

Fowles, J.   THE EBONY TOWER
Four stories based on ancient Celtic tales, retold.
Little, Brown, 1974. fc

Genêt, J.   QUERELLE
"A sailor in the port of Brest, is central figure."
Random House, 1974. fc

Loti, P.   AN ICELAND FISHERMAN
Nineteenth-century writer's account of the dangerous, hard lives
of Breton fishermen.
Dutton, 1935. fc

MacInnes, H.   ASSIGNMENT IN BRITTANY
British officer is sent on mission to Brittany following the disaster
of Dunkirk in WWII.
Harcourt, 1971. fc

French Alps (Haute Savoie Region)

Habe, H.   THE MISSION
Story based on actual conference held in Evian-les-Bains in 1938
to plan the "purchase" of Jews from Germany as a method of
saving them.
Coward, McCann, 1966. fc

Stewart, M.   NINE COACHES WAITING
Contemporary gothic. English governess encounters murder and ro-
mance.
Morrow, 1959. fc

Normandy

Flaubert, G.   MADAME BOVARY
Flaubert's masterpiece of a woman's disintegration and French pro-
vincial life in the nineteenth century. Originally published 1857.
Dutton. fc

Keyes, F.P.   CAME A CAVALIER
American girl at Red Cross hospital in WWI, stays on through WWII.
Messner, 1947. fc

Maupassant, G. de   PIERRE AND JEAN
Bourgeois story of infidelity. Originally published in 1888.
fc

Provence

Boulle, P.   FACE OF A HERO
Murder complicated by an eye-witness account.
Vanguard, 1956. fc

Cooper, L.F.   BREAKAWAY
Avignon. Woman wanders through France and finds love.
Knopf, 1977. fc/s77.

Durrell, L.   LIVIA
Avignon, between wars.
Viking, 1979. fc/s79

Riviera

Bedford, S.   A COMPASS ERROR
A seventeen-year-old's summer on the Riviera just before WWII. (This
novel is a sequel to *A Favourite of the Gods;* see listings under Rome
and London.)
Knopf, 1969. fc

Fitzgerald, F.S.   TENDER IS THE NIGHT
Set on the Riviera of wealthy Americans and intellectuals, pre-WWII.
Psychiatrist marries an American heiress who is psychologically dis-
turbed.
Scribner, 1951. fc

Gallico, P.   THE ZOO GANG
Exploits of former resistance fighters in WWII who now use their skills
against the underworld.
Coward, McCann, 1971. fc

Knowles, J.   MORNING IN ANTIBES
Riviera vignettes.
Macmillan, 1962. fc

Sagan, F.   BONJOUR TRISTESSE
Attempts of young girl to keep her father from remarrying.
Dutton, 1955. fc

Shaw, I.   EVENING IN BYZANTIUM
   "Has-been" Hollywood producer at the Cannes film festival.
   Delacorte Press, 1973. fc
Simenon, G.   SUNDAY
   Murder of spouse involving arsenic.
   Harcourt, 1966. fc
Simenon, G.   THE CONFESSIONAL
   Young man's disillusion with parents.
   Harcourt, 1968. fc

Travel Articles

ATLANTIC
1979   Oct   On the wine-colored earth of Provence,
                    E.A. Orick - p. 10

BIKE WORLD
1980 Jan-Feb   A taste of French culture, C. Gadomski - p. 49
1979 Sep-Oct   Page from a tourist notebook while pedaling through
                  France - p. 45

BLAIR & KETCHUM'S COUNTRY JOURNAL
1979   Feb   Old Gus (French peasant), D. Behrman - p. 45

COSMOPOLITAN
1980   Aug   Marvelous Monaco - p. 246

CUISINE
1980   Nov   A visit to Roquefort: ancient caves hold the secret of
                  a noble cheese, R.A. de Groot - p. 42
1979 Jul-Aug France from the North Sea to the Alps,
                  M. Kamman - p. 12
      Nov   France—along the Seine into Normandy (cheese-
                  tasting), M. Kamman - p. 12
      Nov   Travel through Perigord, R. and J. Cattani - p. 16

ESQUIRE
1979   Apr 10 The Gentlemen's Paris, G.Y. Dryansky - p. 73
      Jun 5   Gentleman's shopping guide to Paris, B. Glinn - p. 55
      Jul 3   Eight hotels in a class by themselves, Relais et
                  Chateaux, S. Birnbaum - p. 58

ESSENCE
1979	May	Doing it my way in Paris, B.W. McCrary - p. 62
	May	Spring flings in Paris and London, J. Harris - p. 64
	Aug	A woman in Paris, J. White - p. 46

50 PLUS
| 1979 | Oct | Hail Brittany! off the beaten track in France, R. Hemming - p. 44 |

FORTUNE
| 1979 | Aug | A deep immersion in French living (sabbatical in France), M. Wellemeyer - p. 21 |

GLAMOUR
| 1979 | Oct | Paris on the cheap—travel guidelines - p. 120 |

GOURMET
1980	Jan	Paris Journal (parks and gardens), J. Wechsberg - p. 10
	Apr	Dining in Mougins (near Cannes), S. Patterson - p. 31
	Apr	Paris Journal (the French telephone system; Au Trou Gascon restaurant, a museum of locksmithing and metalwork), C.P. Reynolds - p. 10
	Jul	Paris Journal (walking tour of Marais section of Paris), C.P. Reynolds - p. 4
	Oct	Paris' Beaubourg, N. Barry - p. 48
	Oct	Paris Journal (a book store, Rostangs and Ecole Polytechnique), C.P. Reynolds - p. 16
1979	Jan	Paris Journal (Cézanne, a book store for books on gastronomy, Chiberta Restaurant), J. Wechsberg - p. 8
	Feb	Cognac (the town and the drink), J. Wechsberg - p. 32
	Mar	Provençal Hill Towns, L. Langseth-Christensen - p. 18
	Apr	Past becomes present in Paris (traditional work clothes and folk art), N. Barry - p. 30
	Apr	Paris Journal (Lanvin perfumes, French subway system), J. Wechsberg - p. 10
	May	Gourmet Holiday: old Nice, P. and F.T. Mitchell - p. 27
	Jul	In search of Victor Hugo, N. Barry - p. 33
	Jul	Paris Journal (small hotels and bistros), J. Wechsberg - p. 10
	Sep	Rue du pont-Louis Philippe, N. Barry - p. 20
	Oct	Paris Journal (Faubourg St. Germain), J. Wechsberg - p. 14
	Nov	Young chefs of Paris, N. Barry - p. 35

HARPER'S BAZAAR
1979   Sep   Spirited tour of France, W. Massee - p. 138

HOBBIES
1979   Feb   Famous Amiens Cathedral near Paris—art treasure of
                 the world - p. 144

HORIZON
1980   Jul   Museums in the Sun, M. Perlman - p. 37
       Nov   American writers in Paris, B. Yagoda - p. 25
       Nov   At Gertrude Stein's in Paris, J.R. Mellow, p. 32
       Nov   Saroyan in Paris, W. Saroyan - p. 46
       Nov   Tracking Hemingway in Paris, D. Lee - p. 42
1979   Apr   Home of the Bretons: a land of mystery, savage beauty
                 and fierce independence, J. Deweese-Wehen - p. 22

HOUSE & GARDEN
1979   Oct   Finding things for your house; linens from Cambrai,
                 N. Richardson - p. 16

HOUSE BEAUTIFUL
1980   Jan   The whole wide wonderful world of snow (skiing
                 vacations), M. Gough - p. 16
       Jun   France: Diane de Poitiers, ballooning and all that,
                 things old and new, things you shouldn't miss,
                 M. Gough - p. 30
       Aug   Six continents in search of a traveler, M. Gough - p. 24
1979   Mar   High life at the Ritz (Paris Ritz Hotel),
                 P. O'Higgins - p. 82
       Apr   Remembrance of things French, M. Gough - p. 48
       Jul   Take a wine tour: travel while you taste,
                 E. Fried - p. 47

INTERNATIONAL WILDLIFE
1980 May-Jun   My quest for the illusive black diamond of France—
                 truffles, M. Wexler - p. 12

LADIES' HOME JOURNAL
1980   Jun   Paris with a difference (La Varenne Cooking School),
                 D. Glasser - p. S 10

McCALL'S
1980   Mar   Riding the wind through France (Le Mistral, all first-
                 class train), B. Sertl - p. V-26

MADEMOISELLE
1980   Apr   How to be happy—alone—in the world's most romantic
                city, J. Shapiro - p. 108
       Jun   Honeymoon "tried and true trips" - p. 80

MONEY
1980   Feb   Barging through Europe, J.S. Coyle - p. 76
       Apr   Up and about in Paris, London and Rome,
                R. Beardwood - p. 60

NATIONAL GEOGRAPHIC
1980   Aug   Bordeaux: fine wines and fiery Gascons,
                W. Davenport - p. 32

NATIONAL GEOGRAPHIC WORLD
1980   Aug   Floating through France (on a barge) - p. 18

NATIONAL REVIEW
1980   Apr 4   The Marne sans taxis, P.L. Buckley - p. 427
1979   Apr 27   Buses in France - p. 551
       Oct 12   Latermeture annuelle (Paris in August),
                N. King - p. 298

NEW YORKER
1980   Feb 11   Revised guide to Paris (humor), M. Gallant - p. 30
1979   Aug 13   Giverny; C. Monet's garden - p. 23

N.Y. TIMES SUNDAY TRAVEL SECTION (10)
1980   Jan 20   Flea markets of Paris, C. Dreyfus - p. 1
       Jan 20   The Paris Opera opens to sightseers,
                S.H. Anderson - p. 1
       Jan 27   Inside the Boisserie, the country home of Charles
                De Gaulle - p. 3
       Feb 17   Experiencing the Riviera, A. Burgess - p. 1
       Feb 24   Off on the wind in a blue French sky, P. Maher - p. 1
       Mar 2   Downhill in the French Alps, B. Louenheim - p. 1
       Mar 9   An Old French town stubbornly defends its past,
                J. Egan - p. 7
       Mar 9   France at 14: learning and living with the language,
                D. G. Charken - p. 10
       Apr 6   A leisurely meander along the Seine and its tributaries,
                C. Gould, p. 1
       Apr 27   When an American couple tackles Corsica by moped,
                P. Keese, p. 3

SAIL
1979 Apr   Where the tides gallop like horses (sailing Brittany),
            B. Payne - p. 102

SATURDAY REVIEW
1979 May 12 Paix as you go, Cafe de la Paix, H. Sutton - p. 50
      Jun 9   Buses in France, M. Moneuse - p. 43
      Jun 23 Paris, Paris!, H. Sutton - p. 46
      Aug 4   French Line cuisine, P. Rossi and J. Wechsberg - p. 34
      Sep 1   In high spirits (winemaking in France),
              H. Sutton - p. 50
      Oct 13 Doing the Paris pas de deux, W. Terry - p. 46

SEVENTEEN
1979 Jul   Paris on a budget, K. Reading - p. 32

SKIING
1979 Feb   Alps d'Huez: la statión complète,
            A.H. Greenberg - p. 76
      Sep   Ski the Alps, P. Gordon - p. 163
      Nov   Looking in on Mont Tremblant, A. Pospisil - p. 64
      Nov   Skiing in the clouds (Le Plagne and Les Arcs),
            A. Greenberg - p. 179

SMITHSONIAN
1980 Feb   Artist's garden blooms again at Monet's Giverny,
            B. Schiff - p. 52
1979 Feb   Tatin's Museum as paradoxical as its inventor,
            R. Chelminski - p. 110
      Jun   Maegert Foundation where art is fine and the grass is
            green, W. Robert - p. 62

SUNSET
1980 Mar   Underground in Paris . . . the metro saves you time,
            francs, bother - p. 66
1979 Aug   Paris is park garden pleasures - p. 42

TENNIS
1980 Feb   A tennis vacation on the French Riviera - p. 83
      Jun   Play your way to Monaco this year,
            D. Doherty - p. 110

TOWN & COUNTRY
1980 Apr   Ballooning in Burgundy, N. Holmes - p. 83

A traveling cloak suitable for autumn weather is made of drap de soie which it is claimed is impermeable (waterproof) and made so by a process "that does not detract from its beauty."

Notes - Germany

1. Abbreviations of reference sources for novels:
   fc - Fiction Catalog, 9th Edition
   fc/s76 (77, etc.) - Supplement to 9th Edition
   fc/8ed - Fiction Catalog, 8th Edition
   brd/78 (79, etc.) - Book Review Digest for the year

2. Standard Series Guidebooks for Germany:
   Fodor
   Fodor Budget
   Frommer Dollarwise
   Michelin Green Guide (Federal Republic)
   Michelin Red Guide
   Nagel (Democratic Republic)
   Foreign Area Studies (East Germany, German
      Federal Republic, Germany)

3. See Appendix 1 for more complete data on the above.

4. See Europe, at end of country sections, for additional possible sources of reading and information for Germany.

Germany

INCLUDING: EAST GERMANY

Background Reading

Ardagh, J.   A TALE OF FIVE CITIES; LIFE IN EUROPE TODAY
   See entry under France, on page 77.
   Harper, 1980.
Bunting, J.   BAVARIA
   Description and travel.
   Hastings House, 1972.
Cole, R. and J.   EUROPE: A SECOND TIME AROUND
   "An informal guide to selected places you may have missed on your
   first trip. Off-the-beaten-track places to visit in Germany.
   Funk & Wagnall, 1971.
Deardorff, R.H.   A DAY OUTSIDE THE CITY
   Interesting and pleasant trips to take with Munich as your base.
   Holt, 1968.
Elon, A.   JOURNEY THROUGH A HAUNTED LAND
   Observations and descriptions of cities, including East and West Ber-
   lin, by an Israeli visiting Germany.
   Holt, 1967.
Feldkamp, F.   NOT EVERYBODY'S EUROPE
   A grand tour of nine unique cities including Baden-Baden.
   Harper's Magazine Press, 1976.
Gibbon, M.   WESTERN GERMANY
   A Batsford series guide.
   Batsford, 1955.

Grunfeld, F.V.   PROPHETS WITHOUT HONOUR
"A background to Freud, Kafka, Einstein and their world."
Holt, 1979.
Gunther, J.   TWELVE CITIES
See full entry under Austria—Hamburg is one of the cities.
Harper, 1969.
Hartrich, E.   THE FOURTH AND RICHEST REICH
An account of the "fortuitous circumstances, innovative thinking
and daring leadership that transformed a pariah among nations into a
stunning example of success."
Macmillan, 1980.
Hillaby, J.   A WALK THROUGH EUROPE
See entry under Belgium, on page 11.
Houghton, 1972.
Levi, C.   THE LINDEN TREES
Vivid impressions of a visit to Germany by the Italian novelist.
Knopf, 1962.
Marsden, W.   THE RHINELAND
Good armchair traveling; the Rhine River from the Neckar to Cologne
and including castles, wine, side trips to interesting places on the way.
Hastings, 1973.
Marsden, W.   WEST GERMANY
Part of the Batsford series; travel and description.
David & Charles, 1978.
Morris, J.   PLACES
Literary essays by a leading travel genre writer—"entertainment and
information are fused in imaginative prose." Includes material on
Baden-Baden.
Harcourt, 1972.
Nurge, E.   BLUE LIGHT IN THE VILLAGE:
                    DAILY LIFE IN A GERMAN VILLAGE IN 1965-66
Univ. Microfilms, 1977.
Ogrizek, D., ed.   GERMANY
History, art, literature, music, special areas of the country—many
contributors, each a specialist in his field.
McGraw-Hill, 1956.
Perl, L.   FOODS AND FESTIVALS OF THE DANUBE LANDS
World, 1969.
Rippley, L.   OF GERMAN WAYS
A bit each of history, sports, art, music, literature, food, customs
and the people—German life in both America and Germany.
Dillon 1970.
Russ, J.   CUSTOMS AND FESTIVALS IN GERMANY
Humanities, 1980.

Berlin/East Germany

Brett, Smith, R.   BERLIN '45: THE GREY CITY
   Written by an Englishman, who had served as a 22-year old member
   of the British occupation force in Berlin, between July 1945 and
   March 1946.
   Macmillan, 1967.

Collier, R.   BRIDGE ACROSS THE SKY:
                    THE BERLIN BLOCKADE AND AIRLIFT 1948-49
   Re-creation of that period when the Russians attempted to drive the
   Allies out of Berlin by preventing food and medical supplies from
   reaching Berlin; vivid and authentic.
   McGraw-Hill, 1978.

Galante, P.   THE BERLIN WALL
   "The story of the people who escaped over, under and through."
   Doubleday, 1965.

Kunze, R.   THE WONDERFUL YEARS
   Portraits and sketches of life behind the iron curtain—officials, stu-
   dents, teachers under a totalitarian political regime.
   Braziller, 1977.

Nelson, W.H.   THE BERLINERS, THEIR SAGA AND THEIR CITY
   A "cornucopia of important fact and fascinating trivia" of the post-
   Hitler period on both sides of the wall. Also a good deal of informa-
   tion and suggestions on Berlin's famed nightlife.
   David McKay, 1969.

Ryan, C.   THE LAST BATTLE
   The last three weeks of WWII and the fall of Berlin to the Soviets in
   1945.
   Simon & Schuster, 1966.

Smith, J.E.   GERMANY BEYOND THE WALL; PEOPLE,
                                 POLITICS . . .AND PROSPERITY
   Little, Brown, 1969.

Von Eckardt, W.   BERTOLT BRECHT'S BERLIN;
                            A SCRAPBOOK OF THE TWENTIES
   "A very readable course in the civilization of a decade."
   Doubleday, 1975.

History

Bramsted, E.K.   GERMANY
   Prentice-Hall, 1972.

Detwiler, D.S.   GERMANY: A SHORT HISTORY
   Southern Illinois Univ. Press, 1976.

Dill, M.   GERMANY: A MODERN HISTORY
   Succinct, streamlined history beginning with the fifth century but

concentrating on events of the twentieth century.
Univ. of Michigan Press, 1961.

Fitzgibbon, C.   A CONCISE HISTORY OF GERMANY
Viking, 1973.

Lowie, R.H.   THE GERMAN PEOPLE:
A SOCIAL PORTRAIT TO 1914
First published in 1945.
Octagon, 1980.

Maehl, W.H.   GERMANY IN WESTERN CIVILIZATION
Culture, history from pre-historic times to the seventies.
Univ. of Alabama Press, 1979.

Pachter, H.M.   MODERN GERMANY; A SOCIAL,
CULTURAL, AND POLITICAL HISTORY
Westview Press, 1978.

Russell, F.   THE HORIZON CONCISE HISTORY OF GERMANY
American Heritage, 1973.

Ryder, A.J.   TWENTIETH-CENTURY GERMANY
FROM BISMARCK TO BRANDT
Columbia Univ. Press, 1972.

Kaisers and Kings

Aronson, T.   THE KAISERS
Bobbs, 1971.

Palmer, A.W.   THE KAISER: WARLORD OF THE SECOND REICH
Scribner, 1978.

Wandruszka, A.   THE HOUSE OF HABSBURG: SIX HUNDRED
YEARS OF A EUROPEAN DYNASTY
Doubleday, 1964.

See also: Various books on the Hapsburg dynasty under Austria.

Art, Music, Literature

Adams, M.   THE GERMAN TRADITION: ASPECTS OF ART
AND CULTURE IN GERMAN-SPEAKING COUNTRIES
The German-speaking intellectual, cultural and political tradition.
John Wiley, 1971.

Bettex, A.W.   THE GERMAN NOVEL OF TODAY
"A guide to contemporary fiction in Germany."
Books for Libs., 1969.

Brody, E.   MUSIC GUIDE TO AUSTRIA & GERMANY
See entry under Austria.
Dodd, 1975.

Lohan, R.   THE GOLDEN AGE OF GERMAN LITERATURE
Ungar, 1963.

World War II

Farago, L.   THE LAST DAYS OF PATTON
The end of the war and Allied occupation.
McGraw-Hill, 1980.

Hauser, R.   A NOBLE TREASON
The story of the "White Rose" which was a group of people at a
university in Munich who carried on a resistance movement against
Hitler.
Putnam, 1979.

Lang, D.   A BACKWARD LOOK: GERMANS REMEMBER
Recalling the Nazi era is a class assignment for high school students
in a town in the Rhineland.
McGraw-Hill, 1979.

Manvell, R. and Fraenkel, H.   THE CANARIS CONSPIRACY
The secret plot to overthrow Hitler, lead by Admiral Wilhelm Canaris—the courage and sacrifice of a few men "who came close to
changing the course of history."
McKay, 1969.

Ryan, C.   A BRIDGE TOO FAR
The battle of the critical Arnhem Bridge.
Simon & Schuster, 1974.

Senger, V.   NO. 12 KAISERHOFSTRASSE
Written by a Jew whose family survived the Nazis by pretending to
be gentiles, though this was known to those living on their block. A
unique story.
Dutton, 1980.

Shirer, W.L.   THE RISE AND FALL OF THE THIRD REICH
A lengthy book, and a classic on the subject.
Simon & Schuster, 1960.

Spender, S.   EUROPEAN WITNESS
Impressions of post-WWII occupied Germany: the British army, Ger-
man intellectuals, DP's—first published in 1946.
Greenwood, 1972.

Stone, N.   THE MAKING OF ADOLPH HITLER
One of several biographies; the birth, and rise, of Nazism.
Macmillan 1977.

Switzer, E.E.   HOW DEMOCRACY FAILED
Interviews with many German people about events preceding WWII
and why Hitler succeeded in coming to power.
Atheneum, 1975.

Shears, D.   THE UGLY FRONTIER
A survey of the "858 miles of frontier and 20 miles of Berlin wall."
Knopf, 1970.

Novels

Adler, W.   BLOOD TIES
   1945 to present; greed, adventure.
   Putnam, 1979. fc/s79
Albrand, M.   RHINE REPLICA
   American journalist caught up in neo-Nazi intrigue, carnival time.
   Random House, 1969. fc
Andersch, A.   WINTERSPELT
   German army, WWII.
   Doubleday, 1978. fc/s78
Andersch, A.   MY DISAPPEARANCE IN PROVIDENCE
   1945 to present and effect of WWII; short stories.
   Doubleday, 1978. fc/s78
Arnold, E.   FORESTS OF THE NIGHT
   Neo-Nazis in Wurzburg encountered by returnee after 25 years.
   Scribner, 1971. fc
Asch, S.   THE WAR GOES ON
   Post-WWI Germany.
   Putnam, 1936.
Böll, H.   THE BREAD OF THOSE EARLY YEARS
   Love story in a Rhineland town in the post-WWII years and the trans-
   formation of a cynic.
   McGraw-Hill, 1976. fc/s77
Böll, H.   LOST HONOR OF KATHARINA BLUM
   A book that weighs the moral question of the rights of a free press
   and the right of an individual to privacy, as a young woman's life is
   ruined by a tabloid's exploitation of her private life.
   McGraw-Hill, 1975. fc/s76
Böll, H   THE CLOWN
   Bonn. Bitter experiences in Nazi Germany and post-War period.
   McGraw-Hill, 1965. fc
Böll, H.   AND NEVER SAID A WORD
   One family's story, 1945 to present.
   McGraw-Hill, 1978. fc/s78
Buckley, W.F.   STAINED GLASS
   Adventure and unsavory aspects of international politics in a "first-
   rate spy story" set in the early fifties.
   Doubleday, 1978. brd/78
Fagyas, M.   COURT OF HONOR
   Baroness wife of army officer involved in affair ending in husband's
   murder, 1900-18.
   Simon & Schuster, 1978. fc/s78

Feuchtwanger, L.   THE OPPERMANNS
    A Jewish family falls victim to the Nazis.
    Viking, 1934.

Fish, R.L.   PURSUIT
    A Nazi feigns Jewish identification and lives the lie.
    Doubleday, 1978. fc/s79

Gibbs, P.H. (Sir)   BLOOD RELATIONS
    English woman married to a German during Hitler's rise.
    Doubleday, 1935.

Glaeser, E.   THE LAST CIVILIAN
    German-American returns to Germany after WWI.
    McBride, 1935.

Handke, P.   THE LEFT-HANDED WOMAN
    1945 to present.
    Farrar, Straus, 1978. fc/s78

Kirst, H.H.   THE AFFAIRS OF THE GENERALS
    1918-45 Army and fictionalized Hitler.
    Coward, McCann, 1979. fc/s79

Kirst, H.H.   DAMNED TO SUCCESS
    Munich. Prominent businessman and a brutal murder.
    Coward, McCann, 1973. fc

Kirst, H.H.   EVERYTHING HAS ITS PRICE
    Munich. Inspector involved in murder, robbery, kidnapping.
    Coward, McCann, 1976. fc/s76

Kyle, D.   BLACK CAMELOT
    Army and WWII, 1918-45.
    St. Martin's, 1978. fc/s79

LeCarre, J.   A SMALL TOWN IN GERMANY
    Bonn. Britain must solve mystery of missing "green" file in Bonn.
    Coward, McCann, 1968. fc

Lenz, S.   AN EXEMPLARY LIFE
    Hamburg. Three educators asked to describe an "exemplary life"
    and cannot.
    Hill & Wang, 1976. fc/s76

Lenz, S.   THE GERMAN LESSON
    Schleswig-Holstein. A son undermines his police chief father's attempt
    to censor the work of a controversial artist.
    Hill & Wang, 1972. fc

MacLean, A.   WHERE EAGLES DARE
    Bavaria. Mission to rescue an American general.
    Doubleday, 1967. fc

Malraux, A.   DAYS OF WRATH
    Undercover communist working against the Nazis.
    Random House, 1936.

Mann, K.   MEPHISTO
  Weimar Republic and resulting Nazism.
  Random House, 1977. fc/s77
Mann, T.   THE BLACK SWAN
  Dusseldorf. Infatuation of widow with American tutor.
  Knopf, 1954. fc
Monteilhet, H.   MURDER AT THE FRANKFURT BOOK FAIR
  Frankfurt, at the end (starts in Paris). Mystery and deception.
  Doubleday, 1976. fc/s76
Trumbo, D.   NIGHT OF THE AUROCHS
  "Fictional autobiography of a Nazi"–unfinished.
  Viking, 1979. brd/80
Uhlman, F.   REUNION
  Stuttgart. Two friends are forced apart by Nazism.
  Farrar, Straus, 1977. fc/s77
VanRijndt, P.   THE TRIAL OF ADOLF HITLER
  Fictional version of what happened to Hitler. In this book, Hitler fails
  at suicide and he is brought to trial.
  Summit, 1978. fc/s79
Wiseman, T.   THE DAY BEFORE SUNRISE
  Diplomacy and intrigue in closing days of WWII.
  Holt, 1976. fc/s76

Berlin/East Germany

Baum, V.   GRAND HOTEL
  Two days in life of hotel guests and employees in Berlin of the 1920's.
  Doubleday, 1931. fc
Becker, J.   SLEEPLESS DAYS
  Conformity and dreariness of life in E. Germany.
  Harcourt, 1979. brd/80
Caine, J.   THE COLD ROOM
  Young girl "lives" simultaneously in 1944 and 1972, E. Berlin.
  Knopf, 1977. fc/s77
Deighton, L.   FUNERAL IN BERLIN
  Russian scientist smuggled out of E. Berlin.
  Putnam, 1965. fc
Fontane, T.   THE WOMAN IN ADULTERY, and
                                       THE POGGENPUHL FAMILY
  Bourgeoisie in Berlin and East Germany in 19th Century.
  Univ. of Chicago Press, 1979. brd/80
Hall, A.   THE QUILLER MEMORANDUM
  West Berlin. Search for a neo-Nazi.
  Simon & Schuster, 1965. fc

Heym, S.   FIVE DAYS IN JUNE
East Germany and Berlin; workers' rebellion in 1953.
Prometheus, 1978. brd/78

Higgins, J.   DAY OF JUDGMENT
East Berlin; smuggling of people from East to West and a fictional account of John F. Kennedy's visit to Berlin in 1963.
Holt, 1979. brd/79

Isherwood, C.   THE BERLIN STORIES
Stories reflecting life in Berlin in early 30's on which *I Am A Camera* and musical version, *Cabaret,* were based.
New Directions, 1954. fc

Laqueur, W.   THE MISSING YEARS
A "family's precarious existence in Berlin" during WWII.
Little, Brown, 1980. brd/80

Marlowe, S.   THE VALKYRIE ENCOUNTER
1918-45, Nazis and WWII in Berlin.
Putnam, 1978. fc/s78

Nabokov, V.   THE GIFT
Russian emigre in Berlin, originally published 1935.
Putnam, 1963. fc

Nabokov, V.   KING, QUEEN, KNAVE
Berlin, 1928; illicit romance between a bored wife and her country cousin. Originally published in 1928.
McGraw-Hill, 1968. fc

Nabokov, V.   LAUGHTER IN THE DARK
Middle-aged man leaves his wife for young mistress with disastrous consequences. First published 1938.
New Directions, 1960. fc

Nabokov, V.   MARY
Russian emigre's first love ends up in Berlin also. First published in 1926.
McGraw-Hill, 1970.fc

Pliéver, T.   BERLIN: A NOVEL
Third part of a trilogy (*Stalingrad* and *Moscow,* listed under Russia are volumes one and two). Deals with Fall of Berlin in 1945.
Doubleday, 1957. fc

Strauss, B.   DEVOTION
Berlin bookseller is jilted.
Farrar, Straus. brd/80

Strindberg, A.   THE CLOISTER
Incomplete autobiographical novel that covers a period in 1892 after the author's arrival in Berlin.
Hill & Wang, 1969. fc

Trachtenberg, I.   SO SLOW THE DAWNING
   1930's and one Jewish family's slow realization of the true nature of
   Nazism.
   Norton, 1973. fc
Uris, L.   ARMAGEDDON: A NOVEL OF BERLIN
   A saga of Berlin: defeat, occupation and the Berlin air lift.
   Doubleday, 1964. fc

Travel Articles

BETTER HOMES & GARDENS
   1980   Oct   Discovering northern Germany - p. 28

COSMOPOLITAN
   1980   Aug   Bewitching Bavaria, R. Ashley - p. 50

GLAMOUR
   1979   Oct   How to get the most from your trip (smart shopping
                      in foreign countries) - p. 121

GOURMET
   1980   Jan   Three chefs in Germany, J. Wechsberg - p. 24
          Aug   Wagner's Bayreuth, L. Langseth-Christensen - p. 17
          Dec   Nurnberg's Christmas market,
                      L. Langseth-Christensen - p. 27
   1979   Jan   King Ludwig's castles, L. Langseth-Christensen - p. 16

HORIZON
   1980   Aug   The ten-year passion (Oberammergau festival) - p. 20

HOUSE & GARDEN
   1979   Oct   Fuel-safe vacations, N. Hazelton - p. 100

HOUSE BEAUTIFUL
   1980   May   Bavaria: royal road to castles, jewels, schuhplatter,
                      M. Gough - p. 26
          Sep   Great spas: where the water works, M. Gough - p. 30
   1979   Jul   Take a wine tour: travel while you taste,
                      E. Fried - p. 47

MOTOR BOATING & SAILING
   1980   Mar   Bavaria on a budget, S. Stapleton - p. 62

NATIONAL REVIEW
1980   Nov 28   Go hang (hang gliding in East Germany) - p. 1461

N.Y. SUNDAY TIMES TRAVEL SECTION (10)
1980   Mar 30   What's doing in Dusseldorf, L. Schlein - p. 5
       Apr 27   Exploring the old city of Cologne, P. Wells - p. 1
       Jun 1   What's doing in Frankfurt, A. Riepe - p. 5
1979   Sep 2   What's doing in Munich, A. Riepe - p. 5

POPULAR MECHANICS
1980   Feb   A hundred ways to beat the border - p. 103

READER'S DIGEST
1979   Jan   Berlin beyond the wall, L. Elliott - p. 81

SATURDAY EVENING POST
1979   Apr   Burg Frankenstein: a man's house can be a castle,
                S.F. Geiser - p. 122

SATURDAY REVIEW
1979   Sep 15   Funeral in Berlin (travel in East Germany),
                A. Burgess - p. 10
       Oct 27   Overlooked city (Dusseldorf), H. Sutton - p. 53

TRAVEL & LEISURE
1980   May   Dallmage, G.S. Bush - p. 69
       May   Bavaria—Germany as you've dreamed it,
                J. Dornberg - p. 99
       May   Munich—a village for cosmopolitans,
                J. Dornberg - p. 108
       Aug   Frankfurt, P.M. Graves - p. 83
       Nov   Four small towns in Germany (Regensburg, Bamberg,
                Lübeck, Trier), J. Dornberg - p. 156
1979   Jul   The post hotels of Germany, J. Dornberg - p. 85
       Dec   Flamingos in Frankfurt at a remarkable zoo,
                B. Keating - p. 28

TRAVEL/HOLIDAY
1980   Mar   Bavaria on a budget, T.W. Traska - p. 62
1979   May   The enduring spell of German wines, p. 116
       Jun   Along Germany's romantic road, N. Lo Bello - p. 50
       Nov   Oberammergau and the passion play, T.W. Traska - p. 6

VOGUE
1979   Jul   Baden-Baden, Germany: a glorious madness
                D. Messinesi - p. 95

Notes - Greece

1. Abbreviations of reference sources for novels:
   fc - Fiction Catalog, 9th Edition
   fc/s76 (77, etc.) - Supplement to 9th Edition
   fc/8ed - Fiction Catalog, 8th Edition
   brd/78 (79, etc.) - Book Review Digest for the year

2. Standard Series Guidebooks for Greece:
   Blue Guides (Crete, Athens and Environs,
      Greece)
   Fodor
   Frommer $ Guide
   Frommer (Athens)
   Nagel (Cyprus, Greece)
   Foreign Area Studies (Cyprus, Greece)

3. See Appendix 1 for more complete data on the
   above.

4. See Europe, at end of country sections, for additional possible sources of reading and information
   for Greece.

Greece

INCLUDING: CYPRUS

Background Reading

Athas, D.   GREECE BY PREJUDICE
   Beautifully written description of a visit to Greece by the author and
   her father (who had been born there); village life, religious life and
   customs.
   Lippincott, 1963.

Barret, A.   GREECE OBSERVED
   "Athens and its environs; the history, atmosphere and people of each
   area."
   Oxford, 1974.

Beer, E.S.   MARVELOUS GREECE
   "An appreciation of the country and its people"—useful and detailed
   description by a woman who has lived there throughout the seasons.
   Walker, 1967.

Chase, I.   THE VARIED AIRS OF SPRING
   An anecdotal and informative travelogue by a writer of many travel
   books in the same lighthearted and perceptive style. This trip's itinerary included Greece, as well as Italy, Spain and a bit of Africa. See
   also her book, *Fresh from the Laundry,* under Bulgaria (page 17) which
   is an account of a trip that includes a touch of Greece.
   Doubleday, 1969.

DuBoulay, J.   PORTRAIT OF A GREEK MOUNTAIN VILLAGE
   This is a "tribute to the traditional culture" on the island of Euboea.
   Oxford, 1975.

Durrell, L.   THE GREEK ISLANDS
By one of the leading writers in the travel genre—"description, history
and myth . . . personal reminiscence." See also *Reflections on a Marine Venus* (Rhodes) and *Prospero's Cell* (Corfu). *Spirit of Place* (see
page 77) also has material on Greece.
Penguin, 1980.

Fermor, P.   ROUMELI: TRAVELS IN NORTHERN GREECE
A travelogue of "an extraordinary journey to the most remote—and
the wildest—region of Greece . . . a picturesque and learned book
with plenty of peasant comedy to lighten . . ." the description.
Harper, 1966.

Kimbrough, E.   FOREVER OLD, FOREVER NEW
An account of " . . . a visit in Greece by one who had access to . . .
eminent personages and cordial hospitality of Greek friends." Interesting and entertaining. See also her book *Water, Water Everywhere*
which begins in Greece.
Harper, 1964.

Kubly, H.   GODS AND HEROES
"A year spent touring Greece prior to the coup d'etat in 1967."
Doubleday, 1969.

McNeill, W.H.   THE METAMORPHOSIS OF GREECE
                                        SINCE WORLD WAR II
The author first visited Greece in 1947, and later in 1956, 1966 and
1976.
Univ. of Chicago Press, 1978.

Mead, R.   CRETE
History, what to see and do; part of the Batsford series.
Batsford, 1980.

Mead, R.   GREECE
A Batsford guide.
David & Charles, 1976.

Miller, H.   THE COLOSSUS OF MAROUSSI
This is a very special kind of travel book, written by Henry Miller. It
was first published in 1941—a "friendly and joyful" book.
New Directions, 1973.

Payne, R.   THE ISLES OF GREECE
"Traveler's grand tour of Greece and the Islands"—Crete, Mykonos,
Delos, and many others. A vicarious tour with a knowledgeable companion.
Simon & Schuster, 1965.

Rennell, J.   THE CUSTOMS AND LORE OF MODERN GREECE
Argonaut, 1968.

Warburton, M.   MYKONOS
Coward, 1979.

Zotos, S.   THE GREEKS
"A portrait of the manners, morals, habits, customs and defects of today's Hellenes."
Funk & Wagnall, 1969.

Cyprus

Crawshaw, N.   THE CYPRUS REVOLT
"The political and military history of the Greek-Cypriot revolt during the 1950's."
Allen & Unwin, 1978.

Decavallec, A., ed.   THE CHARIOTEER
"The voice of Cyprus; an anthology of Cypriot literature."
October House, 1966.

Durrell, L   BITTER LEMONS
Experiences as a visitor and a resident (teaching English); villages and ways of life.
Dutton, 1957.

Hill, Sir G.F.   A HISTORY OF CYPRUS
Cambridge Univ. Press, 1972.

Lee, M.   CYPRUS
Travel and description.
David & Charles, 1973.

Markides, K.C.   THE RISE AND FALL OF THE CYPRUS REPUBLIC
Historical and political analysis of the tragic recent history of Cyprus; The July 1974 coup by the Greeks and the Turkish invasion.
Yale Univ. Press, 1977.

Purcell, H.   CYPRUS
History and architecture, flora and fauna—"concise, lively and accurate."
Praeger, 1969.

History

Asimov, I.   THE GREEKS: A GREAT ADVENTURE
From earliest days to modern times, an outline of Greek history with emphasis on classical Greece.
Houghton, 1965.

Averoff-Tossizza, E.   BY FIRE AND AXE
Examination of the "development of the Greek Communist Party and its role in the Greek civil war."
Caratzas Bros., 1978.

Burn, A.R.   A TRAVELLER'S HISTORY OF GREECE
Funk & Wagnall, 1965.

Clogg, R.   A SHORT HISTORY OF MODERN GREECE
Cambridge Univ. Press, 1979.

Crow, J.A.   GREECE; THE MAGIC SPRING
"Cultural history of the main sources of Western Civilization."
Harper, 1970.

Dakin, D.   THE UNIFICATION OF GREECE 1770-1923
St. Martin's, 1972.

Dicks, B.   GREECE: THE TRAVELLER'S GUIDE
                                      TO HISTORY AND MYTHOLOGY
David & Charles, 1980

Eliot, A.   HORIZON CONCISE HISTORY OF GREECE
American Heritage, 1973.

Hopkins, A.   CRETE: ITS PAST, PRESENT AND PEOPLE
An introduction to the history, civilization and comtemporary so-
ciety of Crete for the general reader with some advice on tourism.
Faber, 1977.

Howarth, D.A.   THE GREEK ADVENTURE: LORD BYRON AND
        OTHER ECCENTRICS IN THE WAR OF INDEPENDENCE
The Greek war of independence of the 1820's enlisted the sympathy
of "well-to-do Western idealists and adventurers hoping to help Greece
revive ancient glories."
Atheneum, 1976.

Langford, E.   BYRON'S GREECE
Retraces Byron's two journeys to Greece.
Harper, 1976.

Roux, J. and G.   GREECE
Traces heritage of Greece as it is linked to Greek life today—"evocative description, scrupulous scholarship and historical and architectural knowledge."
Oxford, 1965.

Woodhouse, C.M.   A SHORT HISTORY OF MODERN GREECE
Praeger, 1968.

Ancient Greece and Antiquities

Ceram, C.   GODS, GRAVES AND SCHOLARS
                                      THE STORY OF ARCHAEOLOGY
"A popular story of the great archaeological discoveries of the last
two centuries and the men who made the discoveries." Includes ar-
chaeologic sites in Crete, Pompeii and Troy in Italy, as well as sites
in the Middle East and Central America.
Knopf, 1951.

Cook, R. and K.   SOUTHERN GREECE:
                                   AN ARCHAEOLOGICAL GUIDE
"Attica, Delphi and the Peloponnese."
Praeger, 1968.

Cotterell, L.   THE MINOAN WORLD
  Scribner, 1980.
Cotterell, L.   REALMS OF GOLD
  "A journey in search of the Mycenaens . . . evidence and theories about the (fabled) Mycenaen civilization and its bloody and violent end."
  N.Y. Graphic Soc., 1963.
Gardner, E.A.   ANCIENT ATHENS
  Haskell House, 1968.
Hale, W.H.   THE HORIZON BOOK OF ANCIENT GREECE
  American Heritage, 1965.
MacKendrick, P.   THE GREEK STONES SPEAK
  "An introduction to archaeology . . . popular without being trivial."
  St. Martin's 1962.
Meinardus, O.F.A.   ST. JOHN OF PATMOS AND THE
                 SEVEN CHURCHES OF THE APOCALYPSE
  Church history for the serious tourist, archaeological and religious.
  Caratzas Bros., 1979.
Parke, H.W.   FESTIVALS OF THE ATHENIANS
  Ceremonial occasions of Ancient Greece.
  Cornell Univ. Press, 1977.
Payne, R.   THE SPLENDOR OF GREECE
  Weaves together the arts, history, mythology of Ancient Greece; by "an expert guide and enthusiastic devotee."
  Simon & Schuster, 1965.
Pentreath, G.   HELLENIC TRAVELLER:
         A GUIDE TO THE ANCIENT SITES OF GREECE
  The author includes both the well known and lesser known sites of interest to travelers.
  Crowell, 1964.
Pomeroy, S.B.   GODDESSES, WHORES, WIVES, AND SLAVES
  "Women in classical antiquity"—an account of the status of women in Ancient Greece.
  Schocken, 1975.
Schoder, R.V.   WINGS OVER HELLAS;
         ANCIENT GREECE FROM THE AIR
  For the traveler with a particular interest in archaeology; pictures of the excavated sites of Ancient Greece.
  Oxford, 1974.
Sherrard, P., ed.   THE PURSUIT OF GREECE
  Anthology of "short pieces from Homer to Rex Warner and George Seferis"—a travelogue and a planned itinerary with literature.
  Walker, 1966.

Novels

Aiken, J.   A CLUSTER OF SEPARATE SPARKS
   Island of Dendros; mystery.
   Doubleday, 1972. fc

Aiken, J.   LAST MOVEMENT
   English girl visiting Greek island of Dendros becomes involved in ro-
   mance and mystery.
   Doubleday, 1977. fc/s77

Ambler, E.   A COFFIN FOR DIMITRIOS
   Analysis of life of a fig picker turned criminal. First published in
   1939.
   Knopf, 1975. fc

Crane, S.   ACTIVE SERVICE
   Contained in *The Complete Novels of Stephen Crane.*
   Doubleday, 1967. fc

Dickinson, P.   THE LIZARD IN THE CUP
   Suspense, drug traffic; Greek island atmosphere.
   Harper, 1972. fc

Durrell, L.   THE DARK LABYRINTH
   Crete. Post-WWII story of a group of "lost souls" on a Mediterranean
   cruise.
   Dutton, 1962. fc

Durrell, L.   TUNC
   Athens. (Also Istanbul and London.)
   Dutton, 1968. fc

Fowles, J.   THE MAGUS
   British teacher on isolated Greek island.
   Little, Brown, 1966. fc

Haviaras, S.   WHEN THE TREE SINGS
   German occupation of Greece, WWII.
   Simon & Schuster, 1979. fc/s79

Innes, H.   LEVKAS MAN
   Anthropologist searches for missing father in Ionian Sea digs.
   Knopf, 1971. fc

Jones, J.   A TOUCH OF DANGER
   An American detective and a murder involving drugs and the beat
   generation on a Greek Island.
   Doubleday, 1973. fc

Kallifatides, T.   MASTERS AND PEASANTS
   German army occupation of Ialos in 1941.
   Doubleday, 1977. fc/s77

Kazantzakis, N.   THE FRATRICIDES
    Civil wars, 1940.
    Simon & Schuster, 1964. fc

Kazantzakis, N.   ZORBA THE GREEK
    Crete. The philosophy and adventures of Zorba (a mine foreman) are
    narrated by his employer, the mine owner.
    Simon & Schuster, 1953. fc

MacInnes, H.   DECISION AT DELPHI
    Mystery with scenes from "Taormina to Sparta."
    Harcourt, 1960. fc

MacInnes, H.   THE DOUBLE IMAGE
    Mykonos. A novel of intrigue.
    Harcourt, 1966. fc

Mather, B.   WITH EXTREME PREJUDICE.
    Cyprus. British agent in Cyrpus as Turks invade.
    Scribner, 1976. fc/s76

Myrivilis, S.   LIFE IN THE TOMB
    Letters of a soldier on the front in Serbian Macedonia in 1917. First
    published in Greece in 1924.
    Univ. Press of N.E., 1977. fc/s77

Petrakis, H.M.   THE HOUR OF THE BELL
    "A Novel of the 1821 Greek War of Independence Against the Turks."
    Doubleday, 1976. fc/s76

Read, Miss   FARTHER AFIELD
    Crete. Two British ladies (one single, one married) vacation in Greece
    and return to England better able to cope with their chosen lives.
    Houghton, 1975.

Rumanes, G.N.   THE MAN WITH THE BLACK WORRY BEADS
    Piraeus. Intrigue and the German occupation of Greece, WWII.
    Arthur Fields, 1973. fc

Sarton, M.   JOANNA AND ULYSSES
    Young woman on holiday rescues a little gray donkey from being ill
    treated.
    Norton, 1963. fc

Stewart, M.   MY BROTHER MICHAEL
    Delphi. Romance and mystery.
    Morrow, 1960. fc

Stewart, M.   THE MOON SPINNERS
    Crete. English girl involved in mystery while on vacation.
    Morrow, 1963. fc

Stewart, M.   THIS ROUGH MAGIC
    Corfu. Romance and mystery.
    Morrow, 1964. fc

Stewart, J.I.M.   VANDERLYN'S KINGDOM
   Novel set in rural Greece; "hypnotic sense of place."
   Norton, 1968. fc
Vassilikos, V.   Z
   Twentieth-century politics in Salonika and assassination of socialist
   deputy.
   Farrar, Straus, 1968. fc

Ancient Greece

Bryher   THE COIN OF CARTHAGE
   Novel of ordinary life and the Second Punic War.
   Harcourt, 1963. fc
Bryher   GATE TO THE SEA
   Greek temples and ancient city of Paestum (south of Naples).
   Pantheon, 1958. fc
Caldwell, T.   GLORY AND THE LIGHTNING
   Sex, violence and women's lib.
   Doubleday, 1974. fc
Graves, R.   HERCULES, MY SHIPMATE
   Novel built around Jason and the Argonauts' quest for the golden
   fleece.
   Creative Age, 1945. fc
Powell, R.P.   WHOM THE GODS DESTROY
   Mycenaean civilization and the Trojan Wars.
   Scribner, 1970.
Renault, M.   THE BULL FROM THE SEA
   Adventures of Theseus; sequel to *The King Must Die.*
   Pantheon, 1962. fc
Renault, M.   THE KING MUST DIE
   Novel based on the legend of Theseus.
   Pantheon, 1958. fc
Renault, M.   FIRE FROM HEAVEN
   Story of Alexander the Great.
   Pantheon, 1969. fc
Renault, M.   THE LAST OF THE WINE
   Student of Socrates relates every day life in Athens.
   Pantheon, 1956. fc
Renault, M.   THE MASK OF APOLLO
   An actor's life in Syracuse and Athens, 4 B.C.
   Pantheon, 1966. fc
Renault, M.   THE PRAISE SINGER
   Novel based on historical figure Simonides.
   Pantheon, 1978. fc/s79

Rofheart, M.   MY NAME IS SAPPHO
    Novel based on life of Sappho and Alchaeus.
    Putnam, 1974. fc
Schmitt, G.   ELECTRA
    Retelling of the Electra story.
    Harcourt, 1965. fc
Sutcliff, R.   THE FLOWERS OF ADONIS
    Story of Athenian general in Poloponnesian War, 431 B.C.
    Coward, McCann, 1970. fc
Wilder, T.   THE WOMAN OF ANDROS
    In *The Cabala and The Woman of Andros;* Island of Brynos. First
    published in 1930.
    Harper, 1968. fc

Travel Articles

COSMOPOLITAN
    1980 Jun   Greek Odyssey, S.F. Enos - p. 266
            Oct   From here to antiquity, R. Ashley - p. 116
    1979 Apr   Greek Island odyssey - p. 126

CRUISING WORLD
    1980 Nov   Island hopping in the moody Aegean, C. Day - p. 69

ESQUIRE
    1979 Jun 5   This summer in Europe, T. Theodoracopulos - p. 9
            Sep   September's Island (Mykonos),
                      T. Theodoracopulos - p. 9

GEO
    1980 Oct   My father's Greece: a young American looks
                      back - p. 66

GLAMOUR
    1980 Mar   There's more than just islands to Greece - p. 114

GOURMET
    1980 Apr   Aspects of Athens, D. Beal - p. 24
    1979 Sep   Gourmet holidays (Crete), D. Beal - p. 24

HOUSE BEAUTIFUL
    1980 Mar   A backpack trip for adults, A. Keefe - p. 72

LADIES' HOME JOURNAL
1980   Apr   Cruising the Greek Isles in a learning adventure (Smithsonian foreign study cruise), L. Carpenter - p. S34

MADEMOISELLE
1980   Sep   Island hopping in the Aegean (Crete) - p. 144

MS
1980   Jan   Travel in the footsteps of Harriet Boyd Hawes: uncovering Minoan ruins at the turn of the century, J. Silverman - p. 13

NATIONAL GEOGRAPHIC
1980   Mar   "To be indomitable, to be joyous," P. White - p. 360

NEW REPUBLIC
1980   Sep 20   Report from Saloniki (art), J. Canaday - p. 27

N.Y. TIMES SUNDAY TRAVEL SECTION (10)
1980   Mar 2   Settling in with year-rounders on Greece's Syme, E.L. Ranelagh - p. 3
       Apr 6   The closely kept land of the Mani, A. Jones - p. 3
       Jul 6   Living with history in Greek villages, P. Anastasi - p. 1
       Aug 31   Far from the crowd, a sun-filled holiday on Cyprus, C. Wren - p. 1
       Oct 5   The pleasures of learning by touring, J. Keller - p. 1
       Oct 26   Chapels recall Byzantine era in Athens, R.D. Kaplan - p. 20
1979   Apr 29   Ancient Sparta: a warrior city in retirement, R.J. Walton - p. 1
       Jun 17   What's doing in Cyprus, A. Borowiec - p. 11
       Aug 5   Back of beyond in the Peloponnese, A. Jones - p. 1
       Oct 28   Greece calls time on revelers, P. Anastasi - p. 3
       Dec 9   Wintering mildly in Greece, P. Anastasi - p. 1

SAIL
1979   Nov   In Greece, the flotilla was half the fun, R. Robinson - p. 67

SATURDAY EVENING POST
1979   Jul/Aug   Greece's best kept island secret (Corfu).- p. 98

SATURDAY REVIEW
1979   Mar 17   The far-out traveler's guide to places you never thought of, P. Brooks - p. 46

Jul 7   Star-studded festivities - p. 37
Aug 4   Adrift on the Aegean, L. Dennis - p. 30

SMITHSONIAN
1979   Aug   Around the mall and beyond: tour with R.H. Howland,
               E. Park - p. 22

SUNSET
1980   May   To Greek island villages by speedy hydrofoil - p. 58

TOWN & COUNTRY
1980   Feb   The five faces of Corfu, L. Gwinn - p. 47

TRAVEL & LEISURE
1980   May   Delphi—where the spirit of the oracle survives,
               A. Eliot - p. 76
       Aug   A fresh look at the Acropolis, J. Morris - p. 38
       Dec   Small hotels of Athens, I. Keown - p. 39
1979   Apr   Corfu: the essential island, H. Ehrlich - p. 115
       Jun   Islands off Athens, H. Koenig - p. 89

TRAVEL/HOLIDAY
1980   Sep   The Aegean islands—ferry shopping in the fall,
               B. Kraus - p. 85
1979   Feb   Greek Island of Kos, C. Adelson and H. Angelo-
               Castrillon - p. 14
       Aug   Athens: the number one tourist crossroads in the
               world, G. and H. Koenig - p. 40

VOGUE
1980   Feb   Athens: 1980's sophistication in Greece's timeless
               capitol, R. Alleman - p. 166
       Feb   Northern Greece: discovering new joys in an antique
               land, L. Davis - p. 174
1979   Jun   Corfu—the lushest Greek Island of all,
               J.S. Roberts - p. 140

WORKING WOMAN
1979   Traveling easy, A. Schwartz - p. 90

WORLD PRESS REVIEW (formerly Atlas)
1980   Sep   Rhodes' Gallery—Greek island of Rhodes,
               J. Holloway - p. 63

Notes - Hungary

1. Abbreviations of reference sources for novels:
   fc - Fiction Catalog, 9th Edition
   fc/s76 (77, etc.) - Supplement to 9th Edition
   fc/8ed - Fiction Catalog, 8th Edition
   brd/78 (79, etc.) - Book Review Digest for the year

2. Standard Series Guidebooks for Hungary:
   Nagel
   Foreign Area Study

3. See Appendix 1 for more complete data on the above.

4. See Europe, at end of country sections, for additional possible sources of reading and information for Greece.

Hungary

Background Reading

Blunden, G.   EASTERN EUROPE: CZECHOSLOVAKIA,
                                         HUNGARY, POLAND
    Description and travel.
    Time, Inc., 1965.
Boldizsar, I.   HUNGARY;
                                A COMPREHENSIVE GUIDEBOOK
    "For visitors and armchair travellers."
    Hastings House, 1969.
Chase, I.   FRESH FROM THE LAUNDRY
    See entry under Bulgaria on page 17.
    Doubleday, 1967.
Dornberg, J.   EASTERN EUROPE:
                                A COMMUNIST KALEIDOSCOPE
    See entry under Bulgaria on page 17.
    Dial, 1980.
Farago, L.   STRICTLY FROM HUNGARY
    Lighthearted "goulash."
    Wallace, 1962.
Garas, K.   THE BUDAPEST GALLERY
                        PAINTINGS IN THE MUSEUM OF FINE ARTS
    IPS, 1977.
Gero, L.   CASTLES IN HUNGARY
    IPS, 1969.

Granasztoi, P.   BEAUTIFUL HUNGARIAN TOWNS
   Seen through the eyes of an architect.
   IPS, 1978.
Halasz, Z.   HUNGARY: A GUIDE WITH A DIFFERENCE
   Many aspects of Hungary—history, literature, music, theatre.
   Corvina, 1978.
Hofer, T.   HUNGARIAN FOLK ART
   "Basically photographs of buildings, furniture, clothes and other ob-
   jects from public and private collections."
   Oxford Univ. Press, 1979.
Kovago, J.   YOU ARE ALL ALONE
   A harrowing account of the author's experiences in a communist pri-
   son; he was the last elected mayor of Budapest.
   Praeger, 1960.
McNair-Wilson, D.   HUNGARY
   A Batsford guide.
   Batsford, 1976.
Manga, J.   HERDSMEN'S ART IN HUNGARY
   IPS, 1972.
Mann, P. and Hersh, G.   "GIZELLE, SAVE THE CHILDREN"
   Personal narratives of the persecution of Jews in Hungary.
   Beaverbrooks, 1980.
Pap, M. and Szekely, L.   BUDAPEST: A GUIDE
                                   TO THE CAPITAL OF HUNGARY
   IPS, 1970.
Perl, L.   FOODS AND FESTIVALS OF THE DANUBE LANDS
   World, 1969.
Sarfalvi, B. ed.   CHANGING FACE OF THE GREAT
                                              HUNGARIAN PLAIN
   IPS, 1971.
Starkie, W.   RAGGLE TAGGLE
   An unconventional and adventurous travel memoir of pre-WWII Hun-
   gary. A professor-vagabond "fiddles" his way across Hungary living
   with peasants and gypsies. Adventure, travel and music.
   Dutton, 1933.

History

Ignotus, P.   HUNGARY
   Praeger, 1972.
Kann, R.A.   HISTORY OF THE HABSBURG EMPIRE
   1526-1918.
   Univ. of California Press, 1974.
Lengyel, E.   1,000 YEARS OF HUNGARY; A SHORT HISTORY
   John Day, 1958.

Lukinich, I.   A HISTORY OF HUNGARY
IN BIOGRAPHICAL SKETCHES
    Books for Libraries, 1968.
Macartney, C.A.   HUNGARY: A SHORT HISTORY
    From ninth century (the beginning of definable Hungarian history)
to 1956 and the revolution.
    Aldine, 1962.
May, A.J.   THE HAPSBURG MONARCHY
    Harvard Univ. Press, 1951.

The 1956 Revolution

Barber, N.   SEVEN DAYS OF FREEDOM
    Stein & Day, 1974.
Lomax, B.   HUNGARY 1956
    Fresh perceptions and new materials on the revolution.
    St. Martin's, 1976.
Marton, E.   THE FORBIDDEN SKY;
INSIDE THE HUNGARIAN REVOLUTION
    Repertorial account of the events by a Hungarian citizen who was
a correspondent for Associated Press.
    Little, Brown, 1971.
Michener, J.A.   THE BRIDGE AT ANDAU
    A first hand account of the revolt against the Soviets and of the
Hungarian refugees in Vienna.
    Random House, 1957.
Mikes, G.   LEAP THROUGH THE CURTAIN
    A ballet dancer and her husband defect to the west. A second book
by Mr. Mikes gives impressions of Hungary on a return visit several
years later—*Any Souvenirs? Central Europe Revisited* (Gambit, 1972).
    Dutton, 1956.
Pryce-Jones, D.   THE HUNGARIAN REVOLUTION
    Horizon, 1970.

Novels

Blackstock, C.   THE KNOCK AT MIDNIGHT
    Scottish girl in Hungary who stays to rescue a Jewish girl.
    Coward, McCann, 1967. fc
Bridge, A.   THE TIGHTENING STRING
    Pre-WWII Budapest.
    McGraw-Hill, 1962 fc

Elman, R.M.   THE RECKONING
   1944. One man's diary before the Germans move in (sequel to *Lilo's
   Diary*).
   Scribner, 1965. fc
Elman, R.M.   LILO'S DIARY
   Looking back at WWII.
   Scribner, 1968. fc
Holland, C.   RAKÓSSY
   Sixteenth-century Hungary during Turkish incursions.
   Atheneum, 1967. fc
Konrád, G.   THE CASE WORKER
   Budapest, twentieth century.
   Harcourt, 1974. fc
MacLean, A.   THE SECRET WAYS
   British agent in Hungary.
   Doubleday, 1959. fc/8ed
Pearson, D.   CSARDÁS
   An aristocratic family's fall to world wars and communism.
   Lippincott, 1975. fc/s76
Sjöwall, M.   THE MAN WHO WENT UP IN SMOKE
   Set in Budapest; this is the story of a missing Swedish journalist.
   Random House, 1976. fc/8ed
Wiesel, E.   THE TOWN BEYOND THE WALL
   Survivor of a concentration camp returns to his birthplace.
   Holt, 1967. fc
Zilahy, L.   CENTURY IN SCARLET
   Saga of a noble Hungarian family from 1815 to WWI.
   McGraw-Hill, 1965. fc
Zilahy, L.   THE DUKAYS
   The effect of WWI and WWII on the Dukays family.
   Prentice-Hall, 1949. fc

Travel Articles

HISTORY TODAY
   1980   Aug   Dependent independence? Eastern Europe, 1918-1956,
                    L.P. Morris - p. 38

N.Y. TIMES SUNDAY TRAVEL SECTION (10)
   1980   May 25   Cross-country riding tour in Hungary, C. Miller - p. 1

1979   Apr 1   Family echoes on a Budapest street, G. Vecsey - p. 3

SMITHSONIAN
1979   Aug   Matzoh, wine, salami and piety still flavor this war-
                 time ghetto; Jewish community (Budapest)
                 H. Sochurek - p. 64

WEIGHTWATCHERS
1979   May   Staying slender in Budapest, J.H. Silverman - p. 46

Notes - Iceland

1. Abbreviations of reference sources for novels:
   fc - Fiction Catalog, 9th Edition
   fc/s76 (77, etc.) - Supplement to 9th Edition
   fc/8ed - Fiction Catalog, 8th Edition
   brd/78 (79, etc.) - Book Review Digest for the year

2. Standard Series Guidebooks for Iceland:
   Fodor (Scandinavia)
   Frommer $ Guide (Scandinavia)
   Nagel

3. See Appendix 1 for more complete data on the above.

4. See Europe, at end of country sections, and items with an asterisk under Denmark, for additional possible sources of reading and information for Iceland.

Iceland

Background Reading

Auden, W.H. and MacNeice, L.   LETTERS FROM ICELAND
"Two young poets on a trip to Iceland record their impressions in prose and verse . . . ." First published in 1937.
Random House, 1969.

Bardarson, H.R.   ICELAND: ICE AND FIRE
Heinman, 1972.

Berry, E.   THE LAND AND PEOPLE OF ICELAND
Lippincott, 1959.

Foote, P.G. and Wilson, D.M.   THE VIKING ACHIEVEMENT
"A comprehensive survey of the society and culture of early medieval Scandinavia."
Praeger, 1970.

Hamar, H.J.   ICELAND; THE UNSPOILED LAND
Iceland Review, 1972.

Jones, G.   NORSE ATLANTIC SAGA
"Being the Norse voyages of discovery and settlement to Iceland, Greenland, America." A dramatic narrative history of the settlements along with analysis of the literary evidence.
Oxford, 1964.

Kjaran, B.   ICELAND NATIONAL PARKS
Vanous, 1972.

Linklater, E.   THE ULTIMATE VIKING
An informal history of the Viking heroes of the Orkney Islands and

Iceland—" . . . a fascinating epic . . . in heroic prose, peppered with dry witticisms." The author is noted in reviews for his superior writing style. See entries under Scotland, on page 210.
Harcourt, 1956.

Magnusson, M.   VIKINGS!
Based on ten-part public television series; Viking culture, religion, mythology, literature and a reconstruction of origins.
Dutton, 1980.

Magnússon, S.   NORTHERN SPHINX
Popular, readable history that includes literature, music, art, commerce, industry, and communications. The book begins with the settlement of Iceland and goes on through to the present.
McGill Queens Univ. Press, 1977.

Magnusson, S.   STALLION OF THE NORTH
A pictorial and written account of a unique breed of horse used in Iceland but it is also about "a land, a people and a way of life that co-exists easily with nature."
Longship Press, 1979.

Morris, J.   PLACES
Literate essays by a leading travel writer—"entertainment and information are fused in imaginative prose." Includes material on Iceland.
Harcourt, 1972.

Scherman, K.   DAUGHTER OF FIRE
Evocative travel book telling of a series of leisurely trips made by the author; much description of nature and of birds.
Little, 1976.

Simpson, C.   THE VIKING WORLD
" . . . authentic and vivid picture of life in Viking times."
St. Martin's, 1980.

Stefansson, V.   ICELAND: THE FIRST AMERICAN REPUBLIC
"A history and contemporary study (1939) of an island that was a republic in 930 A.D., and once had peasants who spoke fluent Latin" from settlement to contemporary times. The book was originally published in 1939.
Greenwood, 1971.

Novels

Bagley, D.   RUNNING BLIND
British intelligence agent involved in intrigue in Iceland.
Doubleday, 1971. fc

Cooper, D.   MEN AT AXLIR
Violent family feud in eighteenth-century Iceland—a story of "harsh passions in a harsh land."
St. Martin's, 1980.

Falkirk, R.   THE CHILL FACTOR
A British agent, investigating suspected Russian sympathizers in Iceland, uncovers a group whose aim it was to gain a foothold for Hitler in the country.
Doubleday, 1971. fc

Gunnarson, G.   THE GOOD SHEPHERD
A shepherd and his dog, and their heroic rescue of sheep in the isolated and rugged mountains of Iceland. A classic picture of a way of life; first published in 1910.
Bobbs, 1940. fc/8ed

Gunnarson, G.   THE BLACK CLIFFS
This is a book that is based on an actual nineteenth-century murder. First published in 1929.
Univ. of Wisconsin Press, 1967. fc/8 ed

Holland, C.   TWO RAVENS
An historic novel set in the twelfth century. It involves family feuds and conflicts between those converted to Christianity and those who remained loyal to Icelandic pagan beliefs.
Knopf, 1977. fc/s77

Laxness, H.   INDEPENDENT PEOPLE
Laxness is a major Icelandic writer and has won a Nobel prize for his literature. This is a story of sheepraising and rural life set in contemporary Iceland.
Knopf, 1946. fc/8ed

Laxness, H.   PARADISE RECLAIMED
Story of a man's pilgrimage to Utah from Iceland. He is a Mormon convert, and is impelled to make the pilgrimage but reflects also on the life he has left behind. Set in the nineteenth century.
Crowell, 1962. fc

Laxness, H.   WORLD LIGHT
The novel is based on the life of the Iceland poet Magnusson.
Univ. of Wisconsin Press, 1969. fc/8ed

Laxness, H.   FISH CAN SING
The novel contrasts the simple lifestyle and unworldly values of fishermen in Iceland, with those who have come in contact with a more sophisticated world.
Crowell, 1967.

Roberts, D.J.   FIRE IN THE ICE
Medieval tale of a disastrous love.
Little, Brown, 1961. fc

Seton, A.   AVALON
    Tenth-century Viking romance.
    Houghton, 1965. fc

Travel Articles

FIELD & STREAM
    1979   Oct   Land of fire and ice (fishing in Iceland),
                            B. Wright - p. 32

GEO
    1980   Dec   From Sagas to riches, M. Orshefsky - p. 110

N.Y. TIMES SUNDAY TRAVEL SECTION (10)
    1979   Feb 24   Icelandic saga: geysers, glaciers, millions of birds,
                            S. Brown - p. 11

SIERRA CLUB BULLETIN
    1980 Jan/Feb   Iceland, J. Russell Boulding - p. 48

SOUTHERN LIVING
    1979   Feb   Icelandic way to go - p. 21

SUNSET
    1979   Jul   Iceland stopover . . . it's easier cheaper than you might
                            guess - p. 52

TOWN & COUNTRY
    1980   Apr   Salmon fishing in Iceland, S. Wilding - p. 81

A traveling cloak, large enough to envelop the dress beneath it, is of dust-repelling satin.

Notes - Ireland

1. Abbreviations of reference sources for novels:
   fc - Fiction Catalog, 9th Edition
   fc/s76 (77, etc.) - Supplement to 9th Edition
   fc/8ed - Fiction Catalog, 8th Edition
   brd/78 (79, etc.) - Book Review Digest for the year

2. Standard Series Guidebooks for Ireland:
   Blue Guide
   Fodor
   Frommer $ Guide
   Michelin Red Guide (Great Britaian and Ireland)
   Nagel (Great Britain and Ireland)

3. See Appendix 1 for more complete data on the above.

4. See Europe, at end of country sections, and items with an asterisk under Great Britain, for additional possible sources of reading and information for Ireland.

Ireland

Background Reading

Atkinson, O.   THE SOUTH AND WEST OF IT; IRELAND AND ME
"The author's account of her journey across Ireland combines description of the land and the people with anecdotes, folklore and history."
Random House, 1956.

Bence-Jones, M.   THE REMARKABLE IRISH
"Chronicle of a land, a culture, a mystique—and the coming of a new sophistication to a traditionalist people."
McKay, 1966.

Böll, H.   IRISH JOURNAL
Impressions of a distinguished German novelist from a visit made in the fifties.
McGraw-Hill, 1967.

Colum, P.   CROSS ROADS IN IRELAND
Travel essays by an Irish poet.
Macmillan, 1930.

Connery, D.S.   THE IRISH
A quick look at the past, present and the economic standing of Ireland—"a reasoned, objective study of contemporary Ireland . . . lively journalistic style."
Simon & Schuster, 1968.

Craig, M.   CLASSIC IRISH HOUSES OF THE MIDDLE SIZE
Architectural Books, 1977.

DeBreffny, B.   THE LAND OF IRELAND
A photo book combined with history, description and travel.
Abrams, 1979.

DeBreffny, B., ed.   THE IRISH WORLD: THE ART AND CULTURE
                                        OF THE IRISH PEOPLE
". . . chronicle of Ireland compiled by eleven superb scholars of Irish
history, art, archaeology, architecture and religion."
Abrams, 1977.

Deal, W.   A GUIDE TO FOREST HOLIDAYS
                                  IN GREAT BRITAIN AND IRELAND
See entry under England on page 47.
David & Charles, 1976.

Delaney, M.M.   OF IRISH WAYS
Social life and customs.
Dillon, 1973.

Feldkamp, F.   NOT EVERYBODY'S EUROPE
A grand tour of nine unique cities and towns, including Tralee and
the Dingle Peninsula.
Harper's Magazine Press, 1976.

Forbes, A.   TOWNS OF NEW ENGLAND AND OLD ENGLAND
                              IRELAND AND SCOTLAND
See entry under England on page 47.
Putnam, 1921.

Gray, T.   THE IRISH ANSWER
Written by a former Dubliner—food and drink, law and order, sport
and leisure, the language, censorship, the Church, love and marriage,
tourism—orientation for the potential traveler.
Little, Brown, 1966

Morris, J.   PLACES
Literate essays by a leading travel genre writer—"entertainment and
information are fused in imaginative prose"—includes material on
Ireland.
Harcourt, 1972.

Murphy, M.   TRAVELLER'S GUIDE TO IRELAND
Written by a native: information on history, culture and practical
matters.
Hastings, 1977.

Newby, E. and Petry D.   WONDERS OF IRELAND
"A personal choice of 484" sites, some with pictures.
Stein & Day, 1969.

O'Brien, E.   MOTHER IRELAND
The "mystique of Ireland"—history, mythology, the land, the people,
books and plays, religion, Dublin.
Harcourt, 1976.

O'Brien, M. and C.C.   THE STORY OF IRELAND
  "Historical survey from the earliest times to the present."
  Viking, 1972.

Dublin

Byrne, D.   THE STORY OF IRELAND'S NATIONAL THEATRE;
                          THE ABBEY THEATRE, DUBLIN
  Haskell, 1971.
Chiang, I.   THE SILENT TRAVELLER IN DUBLIN.
  Photos and observations of a traveler, "silent" because he is Chinese
  and not proficient in English.
  Day, 1953.
Deardorff, R.A.   A DAY OUTSIDE THE CITY
  Pleasant and interesting day trips using Dublin as a base.
  Holt, 1968.
Kenny, H.A.   LITERARY DUBLIN
  A history—"Survey and appreciation of Irish writers and writing
  from Celtic origins."
  Taplinger, 1974.
Lottman, H.   DETOURS FROM THE GRAND TOUR
  "Off-beat, overlooked and unexpected Europe"—travel writing that
  includes material on Dublin.
  Prentice-Hall, 1970.
Pritchett, V.S.   DUBLIN, A PORTRAIT
  Photographs and text; the text "is delightful and extremely percep-
  tive."
  Harper, 1967.
Ryan, J.   REMEMBERING HOW WE STOOD:
              BOHEMIAN DUBLIN AT THE MID-CENTURY
  Nostalgic literary memoir of the period 1945-55; anecdotes of many
  Irish authors—Donleavy, Patrick Kavenagh, Brendan Behan, etc.
  Taplinger, 1975.
Somerville-Large, P.   DUBLIN
  For the general reader; artistic and architectural achievements, social
  history and general history and observations.
  Hamilton, 1979.

Islands and Waterways

Delany, R.   THE GRAND CANAL OF IRELAND
  David & Charles, 1973.
Gibbings, R.   LOVELY IS THE LEE
  River Lee country.
  Dutton, 1945.

Kimbrough, E.   TIME ENOUGH
  A River Shannon holiday cruise with a group of friends described by
  the writer of many such narratives.
  Harper, 1974.

Mason, T.H.   THE ISLANDS OF IRELAND
  Scenery, people, life and antiquities.
  Batsford, 1950.

Mullen, P.   MAN OF ARAN
  An account of the making of the classic film of the same name. Also
  an autobiography of one of the local people who played a chief char-
  actor in the film and tells ". . . more of the ways of life on the Islands
  than was possible to include in the film."
  Dutton, 1935.

Shaw, Ruth   JOHN M. SYNGE'S GUIDE TO THE ARAN ISLANDS
  Devin-Adair, 1974.

Wibberley, L.   THE SHANNON SAILORS
  A "light hearted family adventure" down the Shannon River.
  Morrow, 1972.

History

Curtis, E.   HISTORY OF IRELAND
  A classic, standard history of Ireland from pre-historic times to 1922,
  by a Dublin University professor of history.
  Van Nostrand, 1937.

Inglis, B.   THE STORY OF IRELAND
  A readable text—"A popular history of Ireland with a relatively un-
  biased point of view . . . well-conceived structure."
  Faber, 1958.

Kee, R.   THE GREEN FLAG; THE TURBULENT HISTORY
                           OF THE IRISH NATIONAL MOVEMENT
  The book begins with events leading up to the rebellion of 1798 and
  continues on to 1922, and the civil war that created the Irish Free
  State, and a separate Northern Ireland.
  Delacorte, 1972.

Lyons, F.S.L.   IRELAND SINCE THE FAMINE:
                                          1850 TO THE PRESENT
  Scribners, 1971.

MacManus, S.   THE STORY OF THE IRISH RACE;
                                  POPULAR HISTORY OF IRELAND
  First published in 1921, this is a revised edition.
  Devin-Adair, 1968.

Neill, K.   AN ILLUSTRATED HISTORY
                                          OF THE IRISH PEOPLE
  Mayflower Books, 1980.

Woodham-Smith, C.   THE GREAT HUNGER
"The story of the famine of the 1840's which killed a million Irish peasants, sent hundreds of thousands to the New World, and influenced history down to the present day." Also *Out of the Lion's Paw: Ireland Wins Her Freedom.*
Harper, 1962.

The Irish People

Millman, L.   OUR LIKE WILL NOT BE THERE AGAIN
"Notes from the West of Ireland"—recorded conversations with local people and storytellers.
Little, Brown, 1977.

O'Faolain, S.   THE IRISH: A CHARACTER STUDY
By one of Ireland's leading story writers.
Devin-Adair, 1956.

O'Hanlon, T.J.   IRISH
(full subtitle) "Sinners, saints, gamblers, gentry, priests, Maoists, rebels, Tories, Orangemen, dippers, heroes, villains, and other proud natives of the fabled isle."
Harper, 1975.

Smith, J.C.   THE CHILDREN OF MASTER O'ROURKE;
AN IRISH FAMILY SAGA
One family's saga—"a microcosm of contemporary Ireland and US problems" as the O'Rourke family of fifteen children live out their lives and times; follows the fortunes of those who stay in Ireland and those who emigrate to America.
Holt, 1977.

Somerville-Large, P.   IRISH ECCENTRICS: A SELECTION
Eccentric figures from the fifteenth to the twentieth centuries.
Harper, 1975.

The I.R.A. and the Partition

Bell, J.B.   THE SECRET ARMY: THE I.R.A. 1816-1979
This is a revised and updated edition of a book originally published in 1970.
MIT Press, 1980.

Coogan, T.P.   THE I.R.A.
History and activities, internal dissensions, foreign links (particularly with the U.S.); comprehensive, fully detailed account that captures the "dilemmas of violence and politics" and intransigence of the movement.
Praeger, 1970.

Dangerfield, G.   THE DAMNABLE QUESTION:
A STUDY IN ANGLO-IRISH RELATIONS
Little, Brown, 1976.

Fitzgerald, R.   CRY BLOOD, CRY ERIN
    The Sinn Fein rebellion in 1916.
    Potter, 1966.

Drama, Literature, Music

Brody, E.   MUSIC GUIDE TO GREAT BRITAIN;
                                    ENGLAND, SCOTLAND, WALES, IRELAND
    See full annotation under Austria (Brody) on page 1.
    Dodd, 1975.
Cahill, S. and T.   A LITERARY GUIDE TO IRELAND
    Scribner, 1979.
Carpenter, A.   PLACE, PERSONALITY
                                    AND THE IRISH WRITER
    Barnes & Noble, 1977.
Cronin, J.   THE ANGLO-IRISH NOVEL
    Barnes & Noble, 1980.
Daiches, D.   LITERARY LANDSCAPES OF THE
                                    BRITISH ISLES: A NARRATIVE ATLAS
    See entry under England (Literary Guides for Travelers) on page 45.
    Paddington, 1975.
ÓhAodha, M.   THEATRE IN IRELAND
    Theatre, dramatists, actors, in Ireland's history.
    Rowman & Littlefield, 1974.

Tinkers

Gmelch, S.   TINKERS AND TRAVELLERS
    "As relatively little has been published on the tinkers, this book can
    serve as a useful primer." (See also the book *Irish Tinkers*, published
    by St. Martin's Press, which is predominantly photographs but in-
    cludes quotes by the tinkers.)
    McGill-Queens Univ. Press, 1976.

Novels

Boyle, P.   AT NIGHT ALL CATS ARE GREY
                                    AND OTHER STORIES
    Grove, 1966. fc
Christopher, J.   THE LITTLE PEOPLE
    Girl inherits a castle, turns it into a hotel and then "the little people"
    arrive—chiller.
    Simon & Schuster, 1967. fc

Colum, P.   CASTLE CONQUER
   Story of political independence.
   Macmillan, 1923.
Crane, S.   THE O'RUDDY
   In *The Complete Novels of Stephen Crane.*
   Doubleday, 1967. fc
Donleavy, J.P.   THE DESTINIES OF
                DARCY DANCER, GENTLEMAN
   "Irish Tom Jones."
   Delacorte, 1977. fc/s77
DuMaurier, D.   HUNGRY HILL
   Family chronicle of mine owners in nineteenth century.
   Bentley, 1971. fc
Edgeworth, M.   CASTLE RACKRENT AND THE ABSENTEE
   Tenants and absentee owners; first published in 1800.
   Dutton, 1960. fc
Flanagan, T.   THE YEAR OF THE FRENCH
   Historical novel of the County Mayo revolt in 1798 and assis-
   tance of French revolutionists.
   Holt, 1979. brd/79
Garrity, D.A., ed.   44 IRISH SHORT STORIES
   Devin-Adair, 1955. fc
Gill, B.   MCGARR ON THE CLIFFS OF MOHER
   A mystery that involves a woman journalist, from America, and the
   I.R.A.
   Scribner, 1978. fc/s78
Gill, B.   MCGARR AND THE SIENESE CONSPIRACY
   An ex-secret service man is involved in a mystery that moves from
   Ireland, to London, to Italy.
   Scribner, 1977. fc/s78
Hanly, D.   IN GUILT AND GLORY
   An American TV crew on location in Ireland and a picture of present
   day Ireland.
   Morrow, 1979. brd/79
Holland, C.   THE KINGS IN WINTER
   Eleventh century. Attempts to unify Ireland.
   Atheneum, 1968. fc
Jeal, T.   A MARRIAGE OF CONVENIENCE
   Nineteenth-century Victorian romance.
   Simon & Schuster, 1979. fc/s79
Lavin, M.   COLLECTED STORIES
   Houghton, 1971. fc
Lavin, M.   THE SHRINE, AND OTHER STORIES
   Houghton, 1977. fc/s77

McGahern, J.   THE PORNOGRAPHER
  Man dealing with love and death.
  Harper, 1979. brd/80
Macken, W.   SEEK THE FAIR LAND
  Priest, merchant and clansman under rule of Oliver Cromwell in the
  seventeenth century.
  Macmillan, 1959. fc
Moore, B.   THE MANGAN INHERITANCE
  A poet's attempt to establish a family photograph as the poet James
  Clarence Mangan.
  Farrar, Straus, 1979. brd/80
O'Brien, E.   GIRLS IN THEIR MARRIED BLISS
  Last of a trilogy about sisters "growing up Irish and female" from
  early life through convent school in Dublin, their search for husbands
  and marriage. *The Country Girls* (1960) and *The Lonely Girl* (1962)
  precede this book.
  Simon & Schuster, 1968. brd/68
O'Faolain, S.   THE FINEST STORIES OF SEAN O'FAOLAIN
  Little, Brown, 1957. fc
O'Faolain, S.   A NEST OF SIMPLE FOLK
  1854-1916; three generations of poverty and revolution, set in south-
  west Ireland.
  Viking, 1934.
O'Faolain, S.   SELECTED STORIES OF SEAN O'FAOLAIN
  Stories of the twentieth century by one of the leading contemporary
  writers of Ireland.
  Little, Brown, 1978. fc/s78
Pollard, M.A.   SABRINA
  Upper middle class Catholics; poignant love story.
  Delacorte, 1979. fc/s79
Stephens, J.   THE CROCK OF GOLD
  "Fairy tale for adults"—first published in 1912.
  MacMillan, 1960. fc
Tracy, H.   IN A YEAR OF GRACE
  Amusing story of politico and his family.
  Random House, 1975. fc/s76
Uris, L.   TRINITY
  1840-1916 from viewpoint of "trinity"—British, Irish-Catholic and
  Protestant-Ulster families.
  Doubleday, 1976. fc/s76
Wahl, B.   RAFFERTY & CO.
  Irish-American historian returns to Ireland on leave and, in the end,
  "goes native."
  Farrar, Straus, 1969. fc

Dublin

Beckett, S.   MORE PRICKS THAN KICKS
First published in 1934.
Grove, 1970. fc

Behan, B.   THE SCARPERER
Thugs arrange a murder to protect one of their own.
Doubleday, 1964. fc

Brown, C.   DOWN ALL THE DAYS
Dublin slums and a large family; story is told from point of view of
one of its members.
Stein & Day, 1970. fc

Donleavy, J.P.   THE BEASTLY BEATITUDES OF BALTHAZAR B.
Part of hero's adventures take place in Trinity College in Dublin
(the rest in Paris and England).
Delacorte, 1968. fc

Donleavy, J.P.   THE DESTINIES OF
DARCY DANCER, GENTLEMAN
Life of a gay blade in early twentieth century.
Delacorte, 1977. brd/78

Donleavy, J.P.   THE GINGER MAN
Picaresque novel of ex-G.I. begins in Dublin, moves on to London.
Delacorte, 1965. fc

Gill, B.   McGARR AT THE DUBLIN HORSE SHOW
Murder of an old woman involves crooked veterinarian and a horse
show.
Scribner, 1979. brd/80

Johnston, J.   THE OLD JEST
Young girl in Ireland of 1920's and Irish Republican terrorism.
Doubleday, 1980. brd/80

Joyce, J.   THE DUBLINERS
Short Stories first published in 1914.
Modern Library. fc

Joyce, J.   PORTRAIT OF THE ARTIST AS A YOUNG MAN
First published in 1914.
Autobiographical novel.
Viking. fc

Joyce, J.   STEPHEN HERO. . . .
Earlier version of *Portrait of the Artist As A Young Man.*
New Directions, 1955. fc

Joyce, J.   ULYSSES
First published in 1922; "thoughts and actions of a group of people
in Dublin through a single day."
Random House, fc

McMullen, M.   DEATH BY REQUEST
   Heroine inherits antiques and fortune hunters start closing in; set in
   Dublin and New York.
   Doubleday, 1977. fc/s78
Murdoch, I.   THE RED AND THE GREEN
   Anglo-Irish family in 1916.
   Viking, 1965. fc
O'Flaherty, L.   THE INFORMER
   Irish revolutionary betrays his former comrades.
   Knopf, 1925. fc
Plunkett, J.   FAREWELL COMPANIONS
   Life of young men companions between two wars.
   Coward, McCann, 1978. brd/78
Plunkett, J.   STRUMPET CITY
   Early twentieth-century labor movement.
   Delacorte, 1969. fc

Rural Settings

Bridge, A.   JULIA IN IRELAND
   West of Ireland; country life and interlopers who try to change it.
   McGraw-Hill, 1973. fc
Gaskin, C.   EDGE OF GLASS
   Combination of mystery, romance and setting.
   Doubleday, 1967. fc
Johnston, J.   HOW MANY MILES TO BABYLON?
   Two boys go off to WWI.
   Doubleday, 1974. fc
Lockley, R.   SEAL-WOMAN
   Based on true but fantastic incident on the Irish coast.
   Bradbury Press, 1974. fc/s76
Macken, W.   RAIN ON THE WIND
   Galway. Story of a poor and disfigured fisherman who finds love.
   Macmillan, 1950. fc
Macken, W.   THE SCORCHING WIND
   Set in Galway in 1916; story of two brothers in the Anglo-Irish civil
   wars.
   Macmillan, 1964. fc
Macken, W.   THE SILENT PEOPLE
   Nineteenth-century potato famine and exodus to America.
   Macmillan, 1962. fc
Manning, M.   THE LAST CHRONICLES OF BALLY FUNGUS
   Irish market town threatened by industrialization; black humor.
   Little, Brown, 1978. brd/79

O'Brien, F.   THE POOR MOUTH: A BAD STORY
ABOUT THE HARD LIFE
  Comic novel of exaggerated bad times.
  Viking, 1974. fc/s76

O'Connor, F.   THE STORIES OF FRANK O'CONNOR
  Knopf, 1952. fc

O'Connor, F.   MORE STORIES
  Knopf, 1954. fc

O'Flaherty, L.   FAMINE
  Irish peasant life in the 1840's.
  Random House, 1937. fc

Power, R.   THE HUNGRY GRASS
  An undistinguished priest's story.
  Dial, 1969. fc

Tracy, H.   THE FIRST DAY OF FRIDAY
  Mother and son try vainly to hold on to ancestral home. Humor and sadness.
  Random House, 1963. fc

Tracy, H.   THE QUIET END OF EVENING
  An English brother and sister live in Ireland. The brother tries to unload their old house on another Englishman "almost as besotted about Ireland" as the sister is. Honor Tracy writes often of the contrast between the Irish and the English in a humorous fashion.
  Random House, 1972. fc

Tracy, H.   THE STRAIGHT AND NARROW PATH
  Small Irish village is setting for varying views of "the straight and narrow path"—humorous satire.
  Random House, 1956. fc

Aran Islands

O'Flaherty, L.   THE STORIES OF LIAM O'FLAHERTY
  Devin-Adair, 1956. fc

Wibberley, L.   THE HANDS OF CORMAC JOYCE
  Storm strikes the lives of an Island family.
  Morrow, 1967. fc

Travel Articles

ANTIQUES JOURNAL
  1980   Mar   Irish silver, M. Holland - p. 12

BACKPACKER
1979 Oct/Nov Hill walking Ireland (trails to take), D. Ford - p. 28

COSMOPOLITAN
1980 Apr The magic of Ireland, E. Levine & J. Mackey - p. 300

CRUISING WORLD
1980 Oct Through the Irish mist (sailing in Ireland),
B. LeCompte - p. 125

GEO
1980 Apr The long memories of May T. Flanagan - p. 56

GLAMOUR
1979 Jul Where to go, what to do in Ireland - p. 98

GOLF
1979 Nov Dromoland Castle (Newmarket-on-Ferus, County
Clare) - p. 47

GOURMET
1980 Feb Dublin Dining, I.C. Kuhn - p. 18
1979 Aug Two castles in Ireland; Dromoland Castle and Ashford Castle, L. Cox - p. 30

HORIZON
1980 Apr Irish voices, M. Stitt - p. 60

MADEMOISELLE
1980 Mar Europe: special places and bargains to know about,
the best things to see, to do - p. 124
      Jun Honeymoon! (11 tried and true trips) - p. 88

MODERN BRIDE
1980 Jun/Jul Ireland (honeymoon vacation), P. Brooks - p. 224

NEW YORKER
1980 Jun 2 A walk along the Boyne (River), A. Bailey - p. 92

N.Y. TIMES SUNDAY TRAVEL SECTION (10)
1980 May 18 In praise of Ireland's giants on a literary tour of Dublin, W. Borders - p. 1
      Jul 27 Genealogy and sentiment enhance a visit to Ireland,
R. Halloran - p. 1
      Sep 28 A walking tour in the rugged hills of Ireland,
R. Robinson - p. 1

1979   Mar 11   Buying a Shillelagh in Shillelgah, R.J. Dunphy - p. 11
        Mar 25   A quiet retreat on the Irish coast, R.J. Dunphy - p. 4
        Sep 23   A medieval Irish town, M.Z. Gray - p. 1

POPULAR PHOTOGRAPHY
1979   May   Irish odyssey (visual equivalent of Yeats, Joyce and
                 Synge), D. Kaufman - p. 112

SATURDAY REVIEW
1979   Apr 28   Bewley's Oriental Cafe, J.P. Donleavy - p. 50

SPINNING WHEEL
1980   Sep/Oct Irish patchwork quilts, J. Bamford - p. 34

TRAVEL & LEISURE
1980   Mar   Ireland's Ashford Castle, J. Wilson - p. 51
        Apr   A Dublin pub crawl, D. Hanly - p. 21
        Nov   Ireland's Connemara, J. Coyne - p. 143

TRAVEL/HOLIDAY
1980   May   Discovering Dublin, H. and G. Koenig - p. 56
        Jul   A pearl of a pub in Galway, J.H. Silverman - p. 8
1979   Jul   And maybe even Leprechauns, D. Waldron - p. 68
        Oct   Blooms (new hotel in Dublin), J.H. Silverman - p. 6

Notes - Ireland (Northern)

1. Abbreviations of references sources for novels:
   fc - Fiction Catalog, 9th Edition
   fc/s76 (77, etc.) - Supplement to 9th Edition
   fc/8ed - Fiction Catalog, 8th Edition
   brd/78 (79, etc.) - Book Review Digest for the year

2. Standard Series Guidebooks for Northern Ireland
   Check all guides for Great Britain and Ireland
   listed under England and Ireland

3. See Appendix 1 for more complete data on the
   above.

4. See Europe, at end of country sections, and items
   with an asterisk under England, for additional
   possible sources of reading and information for
   Northern Ireland.

Ireland, Northern

Background Reading

Bailey, A.   ACTS OF UNION; REPORTS ON IRELAND
Six "slice of life" essays which originally appeared in New Yorker,
Quest and The Observer, on contemporary Northern Irish life
Random House, 1980.

Bell, J.B.   THE SECRET ARMY: THE I.R.A. 1816-1979
See entry under Ireland (The I.R.A. and the Partition).
MIT Press, 1980.

Brown, R.H.   I AM OF IRELAND
The "human side" of the Irish conflict.
Harper, 1974.

Coogan, T.P.   THE I.R.A.
See entry under Ireland (The I.R.A. and the Partition).
Praeger, 1970.

Darby, J.   CONFLICT IN NORTHERN IRELAND;
                    THE DEVELOPMENT OF A POLARIZED COMMUNITY
"Deals primarily and in great detail with the many aspects of social
life in Northern Ireland that keep two religiously labeled ethnic groups
invidiously distinct."
Harper, 1976.

Devlin, B.   THE PRICE OF MY SOUL
Autobiography of Bernadette Devlin who is a leading activist both in
women's rights and the IRA.
Knopf, 1969.

Fitzgibbon, C.   RED HAND: THE ULSTER COLONY
"Northern Ireland religious, political and economic history from the
time of William of Orange . . . to the establishment of the Irish Free
State.
Doubleday, 1971.

Fraser, M.   CHILDREN IN CONFLICT
Poignant analysis of ". . . the effects of severe pressure, and fear, of
approval gained through violence, of engendered hatred at an early
age."
Basic Books, 1977.

McCreary, A.   CORRYMEELA: HILL OF HARMONY
                                          IN NORTHERN IRELAND
This is a radical Christian community begun in 1964. The book tells
of its history and reactions to the conflicts and Community efforts at
reconciliation between Catholics and Protestants.
Hawthorne, 1976.

Murphy, D.   A PLACE APART
Woman's reflections on bicycle trips to Northern Ireland—"far more
illuminating . . . than the impersonal studies."
Devin-Adair, 1979.

Stevens, P.B.   GOD SAVE IRELAND!
        THE IRISH CONFLICT IN THE TWENTIETH CENTURY
Struggle for a peaceful and united Ireland.
Macmillan, 1974.

Uris, L. and J.   IRELAND: A TERRIBLE BEAUTY;
                                  THE STORY OF IRELAND TODAY
The conflict in Ireland from the viewpoint of a New York liberal; a
word and picture portrait.
Doubleday, 1975.

Novels

Atwater, J.D.   TIME BOMB
Belfast; IRA bombings and plot to counteract them.
Viking, 1977. brd/78

Breslin, J.   WORLD WITHOUT END, AMEN
American gets involved in Catholic/Protestant confrontation on visit
to see his father.
Viking, 1973. fc

Dillon, E.   BLOOD RELATIONS
Novel of a Protestant/Catholic couple in 1916.
Simon & Schuster, 1978. fc/s78

Gallie, M.   YOU'RE WELCOME TO ULSTER
  Two parts: first a woman's story of love and sex; the second concerns
  Catholic/Protestant conflict.
  Harper, 1970. fc
Herron, S.   THROUGH THE DARK AND HAIRY WOOD
  Border conflicts between Catholics and Protestants in present day
  troubles.
  Random House, 1972. fc
Johnston, J.   SHADOWS ON OUR SKIN
  Londonderry; young teacher befriended by two young Catholics is
  later attacked when they feel she has betrayed their trust.
  Doubleday, 1978. fc/s78
Moore, B.   THE DOCTOR'S WIFE
  Belfast doctor's wife and love affair with a younger American.
  Farrar, Straus, 1976. fc/s76
Moore, B.   THE EMPEROR OF ICE CREAM
  Young Catholic joins air raid protection group in WWII.
  Viking, 1965. fc
Moore, B.   THE LONELY PASSION OF JUDITH HEARNE
  Lonely, middle-aged spinster, in Belfast.
  Little, Brown, 1956. fc
Seymour, G.   HARRY'S GAME
  British secret agent tracks down killer of cabinet minister.
  Random House, 1975. fc/s76

Travel Articles

YANKEE
  1979   Nov   Visit to free Derry, K. Kilgore - p. 148

Notes - Italy

1. Abbreviations of reference sources for novels:
   fc - Fiction Catalog, 9th Edition
   fc/s76 (77, etc.) - Supplement to 9th Edition
   fc/8ed - Fiction Catalog, 8th Edition
   brd/78 (79, etc.) - Book Review Digest for the year

2. Standard Series Guidebooks for Italy:
   Blue Guides (Malta, Northern Italy, Rome and
        Environs, Southern Italy)
   Fodor
   Frommer Dollarwise
   Frommer (Rome)
   Michelin Green Guides (Italy, Rome)
   Michelin Red Guide
   Nagel (Fr. and Italian Riviera, Italy, Malta,
        Rome)
   Foreign Area Study

3. See Appendix 1 for more complete data on the
   above.

4. See Europe, at end of country sections, for additional possible sources of reading and information
   for Italy.

Italy

INCLUDING: MALTA
SAN MARINO
VATICAN

Background Reading

Ardagh, J.　　A TALE OF FIVE CITIES; LIFE IN EUROPE TODAY
See entry under France on page 77.
Harper, 1980.

Baker, P.R.　　　　　　　　THE FORTUNATE PILGRIMS;
AMERICANS IN ITALY, 1800-1860
Harvard Univ. Press, 1964.

Barzini, L.　　　　　　　　　　　　THE ITALIANS
Full-length portrait which touches on many aspects of Italian life:
virtues and vices, achievements and failures, past and future. An en-
joyable, indispensible introduction to Italy. Also by Barzini, *From
Caesar to the Mafia, Sketches of Italian Life* (Library Press, 1971).
Atheneum, 1964.

Chase, I　　　　　　　　THE VARIED AIRS OF SPRING
An anecdotal and informative travelogue by a writer of many travel
books in the same lighthearted, and perceptive style. The trip's itinerary includes Greece as well as Italy, Elba, Sardinia and Corsica.
Doubleday, 1969.

Cole, R. and James, T.　　EUROPE: A SECOND TIME AROUND
"An informal guide to selected places you may have missed on your
first trip. Off-the beaten track places to visit in Italy.
Funk & Wagnall, 1971.

Deardorff, R.H.　　　　　　A DAY OUTSIDE THE CITY
Pleasant and interesting day trips out of a city used as a base. In the

case of Italy, there are several base cities to choose from—Florence,
Genoa, Milan, Naples, Rome or Venice.
Holt, 1968.

Hillaby, J.   A WALK THROUGH EUROPE
See entry under Belgium on page 11.
Houghton, 1972.

James, H.   ITALIAN HOURS
An old book, reissued in 1968, by the American writer who wrote
several novels with European settings. See also entries under Novels.
Horizon, 1968.

Kubly, H.   AMERICANS IN ITALY
"Chatty, anecdotal account of the author's fourteen-month sojourn
in Italy and Sicily on a Fulbright grant."
Simon & Schuster, 1955.

Lawrence, D.H.   TWILIGHT IN ITALY
First published in 1916. Also *Etruscan Places.*
Viking, 1958.

Lottman, H.   DETOURS FROM THE GRAND TOUR
"Off-beat, overlooked and unexpected Europe"—in this case the off-
beat suggestions include Asolo, Calabria, Sicily, Venice.
Prentice-Hall, 1970.

Menen, A.   SPEAKING THE LANGUAGE LIKE A NATIVE
Memoir, and autobiography, of one who has lived in Italy for many
years.
McGraw-Hill, 1962.

Morris, J.   PLACES
Literate essays by a leading travel genre writer (Capri and Malta).
Harcourt, 1972.

Morton, H.V.   A TRAVELLER IN ITALY
A classic travel book written by a writer considered among the best.
Dodd, 1964.

Nichols, P.   ITALIA, ITALIA
Written by a professional journalist who lives in and loves Italy but
wishes to strike a balance between unfair dislike of the way of life
and sentimental adoration; "well guided peregrination up and down
the Peninsula."
Little, Brown, 1974.

O'Faolain, S.   AN AUTUMN IN ITALY
Writing by the noted Irish author on Naples, Capri, Calabria, WWII
landmarks, Palermo.
Devin-Adair, 1953.

Shaw, I.   IN THE COMPANY OF DOLPHINS
Story of the Shaw family on a six-week cruise of the Mediterranean
with visits to such places as Portofino, Elba, Ischia, Amalfi—the ful-

fillment of a lifelong dream of this prominent American novelist.
Geis, 1964.

Simon, K.   THE PLACES IN BETWEEN
Leads the sightseer "to those less known but no less fascinating towns
and villages . . . the book proceeds around and between the major urban centers" and down the Adriatic Coast.
Harper, 1970.

Streeter, E.   ALONG THE RIDGE
See entry under France on page 79.
Harper, 1964.

Rome

Bowen, E.   A TIME IN ROME
An essay rather than a travel book; impressions of Rome, past and
present.
Knopf, 1960.

Clark, E.   ROME AND A VILLA
Travel notes and impressions of Rome by a leading travel writer.
Random House, 1974.

Elling, C.   ROME: THE BIOGRAPHY OF HER ARCHITECTURE
                         FROM BERNINI TO THORVALDSEN
For people who love buildings.
Westview Press, 1976.

Gunther, J.   TWELVE CITIES
See full entry under Austria; Rome is one of the twelve.
Harper, 1969.

Menen, A.   ROME FOR OURSELVES
A pictorial portrait with text by a novelist; unconventional point of
view and a provocative examination of aspects of Roman history.
McGraw-Hill, 1973.

Mertz, R. and B.   TWO THOUSAND YEARS IN ROME
"A chronological guide to the Eternal City—placing its works of art,
its monuments, its turbulent history through the ages in lucid perspective for the modern traveler."
Coward, McCann, 1968.

Morton, H.V.   A TRAVELLER IN ROME
Classic travel writing by a leading travel writer.
Dodd, 1964.

Simon, K.   ROME PLACES & PLEASURES
Ideal companion to Simon's *The Places in Between* (see above).
Knopf, 1972.

Stendahl   A ROMAN JOURNAL
Journal of a tour of Rome by Stendahl and a group of friends.
Orion, 1957.

Florence

Barret, A.   FLORENCE OBSERVED
"Arranged so that each chapter can form an itinerary for one day."
History, artists, description, many photographs.
Oxford Univ. Press, 1974.

McCarthy, M.   STONES OF FLORENCE
A book combining photographs and first-rate text. See also this author's book on Venice, page 162.
Harcourt, 1976.

Nencini, F.   FLORENCE: THE DAYS OF THE FLOOD
Account of the disastrous flood in 1966 and its effects on the buildings and art of Florence.
Stein & Day, 1967.

Malta

Balls, B.   TRAVELLER'S GUIDE TO MALTA
T. Cox, 1978.

Blouet, B.   A SHORT HISTORY OF MALTA
Praeger, F.A., 1967.

Cox, T.   TRAVELLER'S GUIDE TO MALTA
"A concise guide to the Mediterranean Islands of Malta, Gozo and Comino."
Hastings, 1969.
(See also essay in *Places* by James Morris)

Southern Italy, Sicily, Sardinia

Coates, R.M.   SOUTH OF ROME
"A spring and summer in Southern Italy and Sicily"—history, architecture, travel at a leisurely pace. The book is written by an art critic and novelist.
Morrow, 1965.

Cornelisen, A.   TORREGRECA: LIFE, DEATH, MIRACLES
An American protestant sets up a nursery in a poor town in Southern Italy; fascinating account of the culture and the people. Also *Women of the Shadows* (Little, Brown, 1976).
Atlantic Monthly, 1969.

Cronin, V.   GOLDEN HONEYCOMB
"A most fascinating account of Sicily . . ."—not really a travel book.
Dutton, 1954.

Durrell, L.   SICILIAN CAROUSEL
Lighthearted and humorous tour of Sicily on a carousel bus, by the noted author. Also: *Sea and Sardinia* (Viking, 1972).
Viking, 1977.

Feldkamp, F.   NOT EVERYBODY'S EUROPE
A grand tour of nine unique places, including Sicily.
Harper's Magazine Press, 1976.

Fernandez, D.   MOTHER SEA: TRAVELS IN SOUTH ITALY,
SARDINIA AND SICILY
Fulfills a "literary, instead of self-help" function. Critical, highly readable.
Hill & Wang, 1967.

Kubly, H.   EASTERN SICILY
Scenery and legends, ancient and modern; ". . . a delightful reading experience."
Simon & Schuster, 1956.

Levi, C.   CHRIST STOPPED AT EBOLI
Story of a year spent by the author (a physician) amongst the people of a poverty sticken area in Southern Italy.
Farrar, 1947.

Morton, H.   A TRAVELLER IN SOUTHERN ITALY
The third of a trio of excellent books on Italy by this leading writer of travel literature (see also pages 158 and 159).
Dodd, 1969.

Newby, E.   WHEN THE SNOW COMES
THEY WILL TAKE YOU AWAY
A British airman escaping from the Germans in 1942 hides out with peasants; "ordinary people who helped prisoners of war at great personal risk." Also a love story as the airman marries an Italian girl he meets during the experience.
Scribner, 1971.

Trieste

Morris, Jan   DESTINATIONS
Impressionistic essays, originally published in Rolling Stones Magazine; includes essays on Trieste and London.
Oxford/Rolling Stone, 1980.

Vatican

Calvesi, M.   TREASURES OF THE VATICAN
"Museums of the Vatican and the churches and palaces."
World, 1962.

Lipinski, A.   THE VATICAN
Doubleday, 1968.

Menen, A.   UPON THIS ROCK
"A study of the Vatican, specifically St. Peter's Cathedral."
Sat. Review Press, 1972.

Pucci, E.   THE VATICAN CITY
"A complete guide for a visit to the Papal State, to St. Peter's and
the Vatican Museums."
IPS, 1971.
(No author given)   THE VATICAN OF CHRISTIAN ROME
Libreria Editrice, 1974.
(No author given)   VATICAN CITY
Plurigraf, 1975.

Venice

Cole, T., ed.   VENICE: A PORTABLE READER
"An anthology of selections on the art, history and civilization of
Venice." Enjoyable, and a good introduction to a fabulous city.
Hill, 1979.
Combray, R. de   VENICE, FRAIL BARRIER
Kenneth Clark calls it "the most accurate picture of Venetian life I
have ever read."
Doubleday.
Feist, A.   THE LION OF ST. MARK
"Venice: the story of a city from Attila to Napoleon."
Bobbs, 1971.
Honour, H.   THE COMPANION GUIDE TO VENICE
Contains half and full-day walking tours, arranged to a degree chron-
ilogically and by periods of art history.
Harper, 1966.
Lauritzen, P.   PALACES OF VENICE
For the general reader; 45 of the palaces are photographed and de-
scribed in terms of the families who built them, the architecture, and
changes that have been made.
Viking, 1978.
Lauritzen, P.   VENICE; A THOUSAND YEARS OF CULTURE
                                                          AND CIVILIZATION
Atheneum, 1978.
McCarthy, M.   VENICE OBSERVED
A photography book, with text that reflects the author's "searching
observations and astonishing comprehension of Venetian taste and
character."
Harper, 1963.
Morris, J.   THE WORLD OF VENICE
A classic on the city.
Harcourt, 1973.
Salvadori, A.   ONE HUNDRED ONE BUILDINGS
                                                          TO SEE IN VENICE
Harper, 1972.

History

Alexander, S.   LIONS AND FOXES; MEN AND
IDEAS OF THE ITALIAN RENAISSANCE
Macmillan, 1974.
Balsdon, J.P.V.D.   ROME: THE STORY OF AN EMPIRE
McGraw, 1970.
Balsdon, J.P.V.D.   ROMAN WOMEN: THEIR HISTORY
AND HABITS
Women, and the family lives of women, of all classes, and from the virtuous to the demi-monde. Also: *Life and Leisure in Ancient Rome* (McGraw-Hill, 1969).
Day, 1963.
Cassels, A.   FASCIST ITALY
Crowell, 1968.
Casson, L.   THE HORIZON BOOK OF DAILY LIFE
IN ANCIENT ROME
American Heritage, 1975.
Chamberlin, E.R.   THE FALL OF THE HOUSE OF BORGIA
Pope Alexander VI and the Borgia family ". . . the embodiment of Renaissance evil."
Dial, 1974.
Cronin, V.   HORIZON CONCISE HISTORY OF ITALY
American Heritage, 1972.
Cronin, V.   THE FLOWERING OF THE RENAISSANCE
Dutton, 1969.
Cunliffe, B.   ROME AND HER EMPIRE
The roots of Roman culture, social and political structure, daily life in Rome, history and disintegration of the Empire.
McGraw-Hill, 1978.
Gallo, M.   MUSSOLINI'S ITALY;
TWENTY YEARS OF THE FASCIST ERA
Macmillan, 1973.
Giacosa, G.   WOMEN OF THE CAESARS
THEIR LIVES AND PORTRAITS ON COINS
The history of ancient Rome with a very unique point of departure— the women whose portraits appear on early coins. "A brief, and non-traditional, introduction to Imperial history. . . ."
Edizioni Arte E Moneta, 1977.
Grant, M.   HISTORY OF ROME
A narrative history; "happy selection of material, organization and felicitous expression . . ." and covering Roman history from the beginnings to the sixth century A.D.
Scribner, 1978.

Hadas, M.   GIBBON'S THE DECLINE AND FALL OF THE
                                                      ROMAN EMPIRE
     A modern abridgement.
     Putnam, 1962.
Mack Smith, D.   ITALY: A MODERN HISTORY
     Also: *Mussolini's Roman Empire* (Viking, 1976).
     Univ. of Michigan Press, 1959.
Prescott, O.   PRINCES OF THE RENAISSANCE
     "Private lives and public careers of the kings, popes and despots who
     ruled Italy in the fifteenth century."
     Random House, 1969.
Seton-Watson, C.   ITALY FROM LIBERALISM
                                                 TO FASCISM, 1870-1925
     Methuen, 1967.
Trease, G.   THE ITALIAN STORY:
                   FROM THE ETRUSCANS TO MODERN TIMES
     The author's intention is "to provide the traveler . . . with an outline
     of the significant events in the Peninsula's history." Readable style,
     "crisply compressed."
     Vanguard, 1964.

Archaeology

Ceram, C.W.   GODS, GRAVES AND SCHOLARS;
                                         THE STORY OF ARCHAEOLOGY
     See entry under Greece on page 118.
     Knopf, 1951.
MacKendrick, P.   THE MUTE STONES SPEAK
     Archaeology in Italy with emphasis on post-WWII findings and how
     they illuminate the history of Italy.
     St. Martin's, 1961.

Arts and Architecture

Berenson, B.   THE PASSIONATE SIGHTSEER
     "From the diaries 1947-1956"—a diary of travels, with pictures, in
     Italy, Sicily and North Africa by the renowned art critic and collec-
     tor ". . . to consider and reconsider works of art."
     Simon & Schuster, 1960.
Fregnac, C., ed.   GREAT HOUSES OF ITALY
     Published in conjunction with Réalités Magazine.
     Putnam, 1968.
Wall, B.   ITALIAN ART, LIFE AND LANDSCAPE
     A perceptive book ". . . by one of the most instructed and instructive
     observers of European affairs . . . that tells you what you are looking
     at, how to look at it." In the author's words, "a description of the

places at which travelers in Italy may some day find themselves."
William Sloane, 1956.

Music and Literature

Brody, E.   MUSIC GUIDE TO ITALY
See entry under Austria. on page 1.
Dodd, 1978.

Schauffler, R.H.   THROUGH ITALY WITH THE POETS
An anthology of poetry about Italy, ancient to early twentieth century, originally published in 1908.
Books for Libs., 1972.

Wright, N.   AMERICAN NOVELISTS IN ITALY;
                        THE DISCOVERERS: ALLSTON TO JAMES
Univ. of Pennsylvania Press, 1965.

Novels

Avery, I.   THE MIRACLE OF DOMMATINA
Crippled boy expects a healing miracle; American couple (and the Pope) provide a solution.
Putnam, 1978. fc/s78

Berto, G.   THE SKY IS RED
Gang of children in post-WWII Italy
Greenwood, 1971. fc

Crichton, E.   THE SECRET OF SANTA VITTORIA
Italian and German conflict at end of WWII.
Simon & Schuster, 1966. fc

DeWohl, L.   THE JOYFUL BEGGAR
St. Francis of Assisi.
Lippincott, 1958. fc

Gallico, P.   THE SMALL MIRACLE
A war orphan and his donkey.
Doubleday, 1952. fc

Godden, R.   THE BATTLE OF THE VILLA FIORITA
Two English children in "battle" to force their mother to return home to England.
Viking, 1963. fc

Guareschi, G.   THE LITTLE WORLD OF DON CAMILLO
This is the first in a series of humorous books about the on-going "war" between Don Camillo, a local village priest, and the Communist mayor. This, and the five books that follow, listed individually,

recount various contretemps involving local villagers, social activist younger priests, flower children. They give a highly readable and insightful account of a country that can have a large Communist party and yet remain very Catholic.
Pellegrini, 1950 fc

Guareschi, G.   DON CAMILLO AND HIS FLOCK
Pellegrini, 1952. fc

Guareschi, G.   DON CAMILLO'S DILEMMA
Farrar, Straus, 1954. fc

Guareschi, G.   DON CAMILLO TAKES THE DEVIL BY THE TAIL
Farrar, Straus, 1957. fc

Guareschi, G.   COMRADE DON CAMILLO
Farrar, Straus, 1964. fc

Guareschi, G.   DON CAMILLO MEETS THE FLOWER CHILDREN
Farrar, Straus, 1969. fc

Heller, J.   CATCH-22
American bombing squadron stationed in Italy in WWII.
Simon & Schuster, 1961. fc

Hemingway, E.   A FAREWELL TO ARMS
WWI story and doomed love affair between an American and an English nurse.
Scribner, 1929. fc

James, H.   PORTRAIT OF A LADY
Scribner, 1936.

James, H.   DAISY MILLER
Scribner, 1937.

Lem, S.   THE CHAIN OF CHANCE
Murder of middle-aged foreigners in southern Italy involves espionage and science fiction.
Harcourt, 1978. fc/s78

Michaels, B.   WINGS OF THE FALCON
Gothic romance and Italian politics in mid-1800's.
Dodd, 1977. fc/s78

Rosenblum, R.   THE GOOD THIEF
Murder of a priest, with Mafia involvement—investigator is an ex-cop from N.Y.
Doubleday, 1974. fc

Silone, L.   BREAD AND WINE
Peasants under Fascism.
Atheneum, 1962, fc

Silone, L.   FONTAMARA
Peasant life in Italy and disillusionment with communism. First published in 1934; revised in 1949 to make it "more universal in theme."
Atheneum, 1960. fc

Silone, L.   THE SEED BENEATH THE SNOW
Sequel to *Bread and Wine.* Abruzzi during Ethiopian conflict.
Atheneum, 1965. fc

Styron, W.   SET THIS HOUSE ON FIRE
U.S. government employee passing through Italian village encounters
death and rape.
Random House, 1960. fc

Vivante, A.   RUN TO THE WATERFALL
Series of stories portraying a life at various ages—time is WWII.
Scribner, 1979. brd/80

West, M.   DAUGHTER OF SILENCE
Contemporary novel set in Tuscany; murder trial of a young woman.
Morrow, 1961. fc

West, M.   THE DEVIL'S ADVOCATE
English priest in Italy.
Morrow, 1959. fc

West, M.   THE SALAMANDER
Left and right politics in contemporary Italy.
Morrow, 1973. fc

Capri

Douglas, N.   SOUTH WIND
Capri is fictional isle "Nepenthe" in this classic; novel of the effect
of the Capri lifestyle on visitors. First published in 1917.
Scholarly Press, 1971. fc

Ferrara

Bassani, G.   FIVE STORIES OF FERRARA
Harcourt, 1971. fc

Bassani, G.   THE HERON
An Italian-Jew marries a Catholic and the book relates the hostility
the couple experience.
Harcourt, 1970. fc

Bassani, G.   THE GARDEN OF THE FINZI-CONTINIS
The story of a wealthy Italian-Jewish family in the 1920's and 1930's
as their world begins to change.
Atheneum, 1965. fc

Bassani, G.   THE SMELL OF HAY
Stories of the Jewish families in Ferrara and their sufferings under
the Fascists.
Harcourt, 1975. fc/s76

Briggs, J.   THE FLAME OF THE BORGIAS
Historical novel of the Borgias in the sixteenth century.
Harper, 1975. fc

Florence

Anthony, F.   MISSION TO MALASPIGA
American woman visiting as a tourist is actually government agent
investigating a drug ring.
Coward, McMann, 1974. fc

DuMaurier, D.   THE FLIGHT OF THE FALCON
Tour guide becomes involved when he finds his former nurse has been
murdered.
Doubleday, 1965. fc

DuMaurier, D.   MY COUSIN RACHEL
A romantic mystery that begins in Cornwall, but much of the plot
takes place in Italy.
Bentley, 1972. fc

Forster, E.M.   A ROOM WITH A VIEW
The "room with a view" occupied by upper class English woman
causes profound changes in her view of life. First published in 1908.
Knopf, 1923. fc

Howells, W.D.   INDIAN SUMMER
A story of American colony in Florence in nineteenth century. First
published in 1886.
Univ. of Indiana Press, 1972. fc

LaMure, Pierre   THE PRIVATE LIFE OF MONA LISA
Fifteenth-century historical novel.
Little, Brown, 1976. fc/s76

Lawrence, D.H.   AARON'S ROD
Florence and London.
Seltzer, 1922. fc

Maugham, W.S.   THEN AND NOW
The leading novelist has written a book based on the sixteenth-century
Italian statesman, and writer, Machiavelli.
Doubleday, 1948, 1975.

Spencer, E.   THE LIGHT IN THE PIAZZA
The slightly retarded, but lovely, daughter of an American is wooed
by a young Italian and her mother decides to let her marry him. You
can still catch the movie version on late night TV.
McGraw-Hill, 1960. fc

Stone, I.   THE AGONY AND THE ECSTASY
A fictional account of the life of Michelangelo, the Renaissance ar-
tist, sculptor and poet.
Doubleday, 1961. fc

Yarbro, C.Q.   THE PALACE
"An historical horror novel" of the fifteenth century.
St. Martin's Press, 1978. fc/s79

Malta

Dunnett, D.   THE DISORDERLY KNIGHTS
  Historical romance shifts between Malta, Tripoli and Scotland.
  Putnam, 1966. fc
Monsarrat, N.   THE KAPPILLAN OF MALTA
  German-Italian siege of Malta, 1940-42.
  Morrow, 1974. fc

Milan

Manzoni, A.   THE BETROTHED "I PROMESSI SPOSI"
  "A Tale of XVII-Century Milan"—and insight into the life and culture
  of the period.
  Dutton, 1956. fc
Tagliavia, S.   THE HERITAGE
  Right-wing student agrees to his being kidnapped for political pur-
  poses only to find that the Mafia has taken control.
  Harper, 1977. fc/s77

Naples

Bulwer-Lytton, Sir E.   THE LAST DAYS OF POMPEII
  Eruption of Vesuvius. First published in 1834.
  Dodd, 1946. fc
Bryher   GATE TO THE SEA
  Historical novel of ancient Greek city of Paestum, south of Naples.
  Pantheon, 1958. fc
Giovene, A.   THE BOOK OF SANSEVERRO
  Autobiographical novel of Neapolitan aristocrat, 1904-34.
  Houghton, 1970. fc
Giovene, A.   THE DILEMMA OF LOVE
  Sequel to *The Book of Sanseverro.* Main character moves to remote
  village just before outbreak of WWII. (In the third volume of the
  series, *The Dice of War,* WWII has come and he is stationed in Alps.)
  Houghton, 1973. fc
Griffin, G.   A LAST LAMP BURNING: A NOVEL
  Novel of the aristocracy, new rich and the poor.
  Putnam, 1966. fc
Hazzard, S.   THE BAY OF NOON
  An English girl "grows up" in Naples through example of an older
  woman.
  Little, Brown, 1970. fc
Hodge, J.A.   SHADOW OF A LADY
  Naples during war between England and Napoleon.
  Coward, McCann, 1973. fc

Silone, L.   A HANDFUL OF BLACKBERRIES
Ex-communist engineer returns to mountain village near Naples.
Harper, 1953. fc

Steegmuller, F.   SILENCE AT SALERNO
Island in the Bay of Naples is setting for this "comedy of intrigue."
Holt, 1978. fc/s78

Rome

Bedford, S.   A FAVOURITE OF THE GODS
Before and during WWI; story of a girl of Italian-American parents in
Rome and London.
Simon & Schuster, 1963. fc

Broughton, T.A.   WINTER JOURNEY
Mother and son spend a year in Rome in the mid-1950's redirecting
their lives.
Dutton, 1980. brd/80

Burgess, A.   ABBA ABBA
Fictional speculation on John Keats' meeting with Giuseppe Belli
(poet) in Rome during last months of Keats' life and how this would
affect each (includes Belli sonnets in translation).
Little, Brown, 1979. brd/79.

Burgess, A.   BEARD'S ROMAN WOMEN
"Dead" wife returns.
McGraw-Hill, 1976. fc/s76

Hayes, A.   GIRL ON THE VIA FLAMINIA
An affair between an American soldier and a Roman girl in the last
year of WWII.
Harper, 1949.

Linzee, D.   DISCRETION
Art theft from a gallery in Rome.
Seaview, 1978. fc/s78

MacInnes, H.   NORTH FROM ROME
Communist trafficking in narcotics through Italy and destined for
the U.S.
Harcourt, 1958. fc

Marsh, N.   WHEN IN ROME
Mystery—a blackmailing entrepeneur, and a love affair.
Little, Brown, 1971. fc

Moravia, A.   THE WOMAN OF ROME
A widow and her daughter and their ordeal in the closing days of
WWII. Other novels by Moravia include: *Roman Tales, More Roman
Tales, Mistaken Ambitions.*
Farrar, 1949. fc

Peters, E.   THE SEVENTH SINNER
Art history student involved in a murder.
Dodd, 1972. fc

Peters, E.   STREET OF THE FIVE MOONS
Mystery with (again) a beautiful art historian involved.
Dodd, 1978. fc/s78

Tucci, N.   THE SUN AND THE MOON
A recent book, but set in pre-WWI (1902)—". . . the writing is filled
with descriptive grandeur."
Knopf, 1977. brd/78

Williams, T.   THE ROMAN SPRING OF MRS. STONE
Mrs. Stone is a fading beauty of 50 who meets a gigolo.
New Directions, 1950. fc

Sicily

Brancati, V.   BELL' ANTONIO
Italian fascism, 1930's and 40's.
Ungar, 1978. fc/s78

Hersey, J.   A BELL FOR ADANO
Pulitzer Prize novel of American in post-WWII Italy.
Knopf, 1944. fc

Lampedusa, G.   THE LEOPARD
A prince and his family, 1860-1910 as feudal era crumbles.
Pantheon, 1960. fc

Seton, C.P.   A FINE ROMANCE
Two American families meet on a bus tour in Italy with changes in
their lives a result; an amusing book.
Norton, 1976.

Zeno   THE FOUR SERGEANTS
British paratroopers during invasion of Sicily by British and Ameri-
can troops.
Atheneum, 1977. fc/s77

Trieste

Svevo, I.   A LIFE
Novel of a "non-hero" in turn-of-the-century Trieste. Originally pub-
lished in 1893.
Knopf, 1963. fc

Turin

Pavese, C.   THE SELECTED WORKS OF CESARE PAVESE
Four novels published in 1942-49; middle class characters.
Farrar, Straus, 1968. fc

Vatican

Cleary, J.   PETER'S PENCE
  The pope is kidnapped.
  Morrow, 1974. fc
Holland, C.   CITY OF GOD
  Fifteenth-century papal intrigue.
  Knopf, 1979.
Romans, J.   MISSION TO ROME
  In *Death of a World,* Book 3; the mission is that of the French government to the Papacy, pre-WWII.
  Knopf, 1938. fc
West, M.L.   THE SHOES OF THE FISHERMAN
  Fictional account of a new pope who comes from the Ukraine.
  Morrow, 1963. fc

Venice

Briggs, J.   THE FLAME OF THE BORGIAS
  Sixteenth-century Venice.
  Harper, 1975. fc
Byrne, D.   MESSER MARCO POLO
  Based on the life of Marco Polo.
  Century, 1921. fc
Habe, H.   PALAZZO
  A woman, struggling financially to save her palazzo from collapse, deals in fraudulent art to raise some money.
  Putnam, 1977. fc/s77
Healey, B.   THE VESPUCCI PAPERS
  Suspense novel involving authenticity of a Botticelli painting.
  Lippincott, 1972. fc
Hemingway, E.   ACROSS THE RIVER AND INTO THE TREES
  American colonel and his love in post-WWII Venice.
  Scribner, 1950. fc
James, H.   THE AMBASSADORS
  Scribner, 1937.
James, H.   THE ASPERN PAPERS
  In *The Complete Tales of Henry James, Vol. 6.*
  Lippincott, 1975. fc
MacInnes, H.   THE VENETIAN AFFAIR
  Venice and Paris in 1961 and a plot to assassinate DeGaulle.
  Harcourt, 1963. fc
Mann, T.   DEATH IN VENICE
  Originally published in 1913.
  Knopf, 1965. fc

Pasinetti, P.   **VENETIAN RED**
   Two families' lives, 1938-41.
   Random House, 1960. fc
Powell, A.   **TEMPORARY KINGS**
   Meeting of academics and the story of those who attend.
   Little, Brown, 1973. fc
Shellabarger, S.   **LORD VANITY**
   Eighteenth-century Venice is setting for historical novel.
   Little, Brown, 1953. fc
Shellabarger, S.   **PRINCE OF FOXES**
   Renaissance and the Borgias.
   Little, Brown, 1947. fc
Sheridan, A.M.   **SUMMONED TO DARKNESS**
   Nineteenth-century adventure story.
   Simon & Schuster, 1978. fc/s78
Spark, M.   **TERRITORIAL RIGHTS**
   Hilarious encounters with male prostitute, Bulgarian refugee, aging
   male lover, father, father's mistress, etc.
   Coward, McCann, 1979. brd/79
Wallace, I.   **THE PIGEON PROJECT**
   Venice espionage.
   Simon & Schuster, 1979. fc/s79
Weiss, D.   **THE VENETIAN**
   Biographical novel of Titian.
   Morrow, 1976. fc/s77
Wharton, E.   **THE CHILDREN**
   First published in 1928.
   Scribner, 1971. fc

Travel Articles

APARTMENT LIFE
   1980 Apr   Chianti classic: Italy's undiscovered wine country,
                   M. Hodgson - p. 28
   1979 Jun   Business (and pleasure) tripper's guide to
                   Rome - p. 24

COSMOPOLITAN
   1980 Nov   Open road: Italian style, R. Ashley - p. 116
   1979 Sep   Exploring the Italian islands, L.B. Eisenberg - p. 128

1979   Dec   Taking the waters at Salsomaggiore, K. Olson - p. 116

CUISINE
  1980 Jan-Feb   Tastes of Northern Italy (cheese), G. Bugiali - p. 10
         Apr   Cheeses of Southern Italy: mozzarella and provolone,
                     G. Bugiali - p. 10
         May   Cheeses of Lombardy: gorgonzola to taleggio,
                     G. Bugiali - p. 14
         Nov   Exploring Italian wines - p. 8

CYCLE
  1980   Mar   Racer as tourist, K. Cameron - p. 110

FORTUNE
  1979   Mar 26   Dining where the Archduke lodged; Saint George
                     Premier Restaurant, Monza, W. Galling - p. 23

GOLF
  1979   Nov   Cala de Volpe (Costa Smeralda, Sardinia) - p. 45

GOURMET
  1980   Jul   Venezia in Campagna, N. Barry - p. 17
         Dec   Caterina Cornaro's Asolo, V. and G. Elbert - p. 43
  1979   Feb   Gourmet holidays: skiing in Cortina, P.J. Wade - p. 24
         Jun   Gourmet holidays: Gozo (Calypso's isle),
                     S. Paterson - p. 34

HARPER'S BAZAAR
  1980   Sep   Tuscany: the connoisseur's choice, P. Brooks - p. 72
         Nov   Watering down your worries (spa in Italy) - p. 212
  1979   Jun   Stars of Venice, N. Barry - p. 122

HOUSE BEAUTIFUL
  1980   Apr   Italy: pasta, Puccini and other pure pleasures,
                     M. Gough - p. 20
         Aug   Six continents in search of a traveler, M. Gough - p. 24
  1979   Jul   Take a wine tour: travel while you taste,
                     E. Fried - p. 47

MADEMOISELLE
  1980   Mar   Europe: special places and bargains to know about,
                     the best things to see, to do - p. 124

MONEY
  1980   Apr   Up and about in Paris, London & Rome- p. 60

NATIONAL REVIEW
1979   Sep 14   Pergo: summer 1979, N. Hazelton - p. 1167
          Oct 12   Notes from Tuscany, N. Hazelton - p. 1313

NATURAL HISTORY
1979   Apr   Pompeii A.D. 79, A.M. Cunningham - p. 37

NEW YORKER
1980   Sep 15   Letter from Rome, W. Murray - p. 16
          Dec 29   Rapido. (Traveling by train from Switzerland to Italy),
                   B. Rorieche - p. 45

N.Y. SUNDAY TIMES TRAVEL SECTION (10)
1980   Jan 27   Getting to know Malta, J. Markham - p. 1
          Feb 17   Experiencing the Riviera, A. Burgess - p. 1
          Mar 16   The cheaper, sunnier face of the Alps, C. Wren - p. 1
          Mar 23   The Eternal City's new subway line, P. Hofmann - p. 3
          Mar 30   Splendid survivors of the Renaissance:
                   Palladio's villas - p. 28
          Apr 20   A sea voyage to the Lipari, land of the Aeolus,
                   D. Yeadon - p. 1
          May 25   Be sure to keep your check after dining out in Italy,
                   P. Hofmann - p. 14
          Aug 3   What's doing in Trieste, P. Hoffman - p. 7
          Aug 31   The little known charms within Luca's old walls,
                   Bernard D. Nossiter - p. 1
          Aug 31   New Swiss tunnel cuts driving time - p. 8
          Nov 2   What's doing in Nice, S. Anderson - p. 11
1979   Jan 14   What's doing in Florence, N. Lo Bello - p. 11
          Feb 11   When in Rome, how to attend a Papal audience,
                   P. Hofman - p. 1
          Feb 11   What's doing in Verona, N. Lo Bello - p. 15
          Feb 18   The scenic overkill of Taormina, R. Packard - p. 1
          Apr 8   The many steps of Rome, J. Ferris - p. 3
          Apr 15   What's doing in Palermo, P. Hofmann - p. 9
          May 20   Italy without fear: how to avoid crime and terrorism,
                   P. Hofmann - p. 3
          Jun 3   There's more to Pisa than a tower, R. Packard - p. 1
          Aug 5   Travel notes: the golden horses of Venice.- p. 5
          Sep 16   A second look at Merano, R. Corman - p. 1
          Oct 28   What's doing in Rome, P. Hofmann - p. 11
          Nov 11   Pompeii past and present, P. Hofmann - p. 1
          Dec 2   The vanishing wine taverns of Rome, C. Lord - p. 3
          Dec 9   What's doing in Venice, P. Hofmann - p. 7

POPULAR PHOTOGRAPHY
1979   Sep   Traveler's camera, Rome (in recording Rome's gran-
                  deur, take time to find good angles for shooting its
                  monuments), C. Purcell - p. 42

SATURDAY REVIEW
1980   Feb 16   The old-stone fancier's urban checklist, H. Sutton

SKIING
1980   Jan   Solo at Val Senales, A. Pospisil - p. 100
        Oct   The sunny side of the Matterhorn, A. Pospisil - p. 136
1979   Sep   Ski the Alps, P. Gordon - p. 163

SUNSET
1980   Feb   Crossing the Grand Canal . . . 20 cents - p. 18
1979   Mar   Through Italy's chianti country . . . into castles, villas,
                  monasteries - p. 40

TOWN & COUNTRY
1980   Apr   Mud, glorious mud (Italian resort),
                      R. Hollander - p. 42
        May   The Italians have a word for it (Hotel Pace in
                      Florence), A. Loos - p. 88
        Jun   The variety of Venice, N.T. Birmingham - p. 112
        Jun   The vivacious Venetians - p. 107
        Jul   Pleasures of Positano, L. Ashland - p. 75
1979   Apr   Le Grand Hotel, L. Gwinn - p. 134
        Jul   Princely Sardinia, L. Ashland - p. 38

TRAVEL & LEISURE
1980   Feb   The romance of travel, Venice, P. Fiori - p. 47
        Feb   A reluctant romantic in Capri, C. Trillin - p. 100
        Mar   The small hotels of Florence, J. Friedberg - p. 106
        May   Peck-Milano, E. and M. Greenberg - p. 71
        May   Torcello, B.D. Colen - p. 120
        May   Diminutive domains (San Marino), H. Koenig - p. 90
        Jun   The world around Rome, J. Shapiro - p. 87
        Jul   Rome in the shade, S. Joslin - p. 22
        Aug   The small hotels of Rome, J. Friedberg - p. 76
        Nov   Opera, Italian style, W. Weaver - p. 6
1979   Mar   Roman holiday, R.S. Kane - p. 16
        Apr   Resorting to the high life—Italian style,
                      R.S. Kane - p. 62
        Jun   Reflections on Venice, G. Lang - p. 12

	Jun	Siena in the sun, K. Simon - p. 82
	Sep	When in Rome, G. Lang - p. 12

TRAVEL/HOLIDAY
1980	Apr	Roaming southern Italy, C. Adelson and H. Angelo-Castrillon - p. 24
	Sep	Roman holiday, Chef L. Szathmary - p. 18
	Nov	Rome—the eternal vacation, S. and J. Elmore - p. 83
	Dec	Montecatini: Italy's grand old spa, T.W. Traska - p. 20
1979	Feb	Il Burchiello: along the Brenta Canal from Padua to Venice, B.H. Matthiessen - p. 34
	May	Pompeii A.D. 79, S.A. Maguire - p. 16

VOGUE
1979	Aug	See Italy free-style—on a money-saving tour, D. Messinesi - p. 156
	Oct	Learning to cook in Italy—a delicious adventure, L. Hackett - p. 169

WINE WORLD
1980	Mar/Apr	Touring the vineyards of Italy - p. 28

WORLD PRESS REVIEW (formerly Atlas)
1980	Dec	Renaissance on Italy's Riviera: the rich and regal return to Portofino, C. Beria - p. 57

YACHTING
1980	Sep	Malta: a winter haven, A. Carl - p. 148

Notes - Netherlands

1. Abbreviations of reference sources for novels:
   fc - Fiction Catalog, 9th Edition
   fc/s76 (77, etc.) - Supplement to 9th Edition
   fc/8ed - Fiction Catalog, 8th Edition
   brd/78 (79, etc.) - Book Review Digest for the year

2. Standard Series Guidebooks for Netherlands:
   Blue Guide (Holland)
   Fodor (Holland)
   Michelin Red Guide (Benelux)
   Nagel (Holland)

3. See Appendix 1 for more complete data on the above.

4. See Europe, at end of country sections, for additional possible sources of reading and information for Netherlands.

Netherlands

Background Reading

Bailey, A.   REMBRANDT'S HOUSE
  Rembrandt's House (now a museum) is the point of departure for
  this account of his life and the customs and life of the seventeenth
  century.
  Houghton, 1978.

Bailey, A.   THE HORIZON CONCISE HISTORY
                                                   OF THE LOW COUNTRIES
  American Heritage, 1974.

Barnouw, A.   THE PAGEANT OF NETHERLANDS HISTORY
  An "intimate and heartwarming introduction to the people of the
  Netherlands . . ."–culture, mores, history, from earliest days to time
  of publication.
  Longmans, 1952.

Brody, E.   THE MUSIC GUIDE TO BELGIUM, LUXEMBOURG,
                                       HOLLAND, AND SWITZERLAND
  See entry under Belgium on page 11.
  Dodd, 1977.

Cotterell, G.   AMSTERDAM, THE LIFE OF A CITY
  A traveler's history. The book outlines the history of Amsterdam,
  but with special attention to the past four hundred years, and empha-
  sizing works of art, buildings, and places that still may be seen by
  tourists.
  Little, Brown, 1972.

Deardorff, R.H.   A DAY OUTSIDE THE CITY
 Pleasant and interesting day trips with Amsterdam as a base.
 Holt, 1968.
Feldkamp, F.   NOT EVERYBODY'S EUROPE
 A grand tour of nine unique cities, including Maastricht in Holland.
 Harper's Magazine Press, 1976.
Frank, A.   DIARY OF A YOUNG GIRL
 The experiences of a Jewish family, living in hiding in Amsterdam
 during the Nazi occupation.
 Doubleday, 1952.
Haley, K.H.D.   THE DUTCH IN THE SEVENTEENTH CENTURY
 Holland at the height of its power and influence, 1579 to the begin-
 ning of the eighteenth century "decline."
 Thames & Hudson, 1972.
Hillaby, J.   A WALK THROUGH EUROPE
 See entry under Belgium on page 11.
 Houghton, 1972.
Hoffmann, A.   THE DUTCH
 "How they live and work."
 Praeger, 1971.
Hoffman, W.   QUEEN JULIANA: THE STORY OF THE
                             RICHEST WOMAN IN THE WORLD
 Harcourt, 1979.
Kossmann, E.H.   THE LOW COUNTRIES, 1780-1940
 Oxford Univ. Press, 1978.
Lecaldano, P., ed.   THE RIJKSMUSEUM OF AMSTERDAM
 Arco, 1974.

Novels

Albrand, M.   NO SURRENDER
 Five spy novels, originally published in 1942, about a Dutchman
 who is a Nazi double agent.
 Doubleday, 1962. fc
Braider, D.   AN EPIC JOY
 Novel based on the life of Rubens.
 Putnam, 1971. fc
Camus, A.   THE FALL
 Amsterdam. Successful lawyer bares his soul to a stranger.
 Knopf, 1957. fc

Dumas, A.   THE BLACK TULIP
Seventeenth-century romance originally published in 1850.
Dutton, 1961. fc

Freeling, N.   CRIMINAL CONVERSATION
Inspector Van der Valk mystery; neurologist involved in murder of
a painter.
Harper, 1966. fc

Freeling, N.   DOUBLE BARREL
Poison pen letters and murder in a provincial town.
Harper, 1965. fc/8ed

Freeling, N.   THE LOVELY LADIES
Seemingly senseless murder in Amsterdam leads to Dublin for an
answer.
Harper, 1971

Hartog, J. de   THE CAPTAIN
The time is 1942, as an escapee from the Nazis becomes commander
of a Dutch tug.
Atheneum, 1966. fc

Hartog, J. de   THE INSPECTOR
1946; story of a young Dutch-Jewish girl.
Atheneum, 1960. fc

Hartog, J. de   THE LITTLE ARK
The 1953 hurricane in the Netherlands, and its aftermath, in this
country so vulnerable to the sea.
Atheneum, 1970. fc

Hartog, J. de   THE LOST SEA
Kidnap of a Dutch orphan to serve aboard a fishing ship, and his
escape.
Atheneum, 1966. fc

Hutchinson, R.C.   JOHANNA AT DAYBREAK
Post WWII, woman's story.
Harper, 1969. fc

Lambert, D.   TOUCH THE LION'S PAW
Amsterdam jewel heist.
Sat. Review Press, 1975. fc/s76

MacLean, A.   PUPPET ON A CHAIN
British narcotics agent on assignment in Amsterdam.
Doubleday, 1969. fc

Morgan, C.   THE FOUNTAIN
WWI British officer's stay at castle, love triangle.
Knopf, 1932. fc

Schmitt, G.   REMBRANDT
Novel based on the life of the seventeenth-century painter.
Random House, 1961. fc

Schoonover, L.   KEY OF GOLD
Three novellas of physicians set in fifteenth to seventeenth centuries.
Little, Brown, 1968. fc

Simenon, G.   MAIGRET ABROAD
Inspector Maigret involved in a double mystery.
Harcourt, 1940. fc/8ed

Vesaas, T.   PALACE OF ICE
Story of two young girls—one dies, the other assumes the dead girl's
personality; vivid landscape.
Morrow, 1968. fc

Wetering, J.W. van de   THE BLOND BABOON
Murder of a former chanteuse.
Houghton, 1978. fc/s78

Wetering, J.W. van de   THE CORPSE IN THE DIKE
Amsterdam's colorful Dike community is setting for this murder
mystery.
Houghton, 1976. fc/s76

Wetering, J.W. van de   THE JAPANESE CORPSE
Smuggling in Amsterdam and Japan.
Houghton, 1977. brd/78

Wetering, J.W. van de   TUMBLEWEED
Murder on an Amsterdam houseboat.
Houghton, 1976. fc/s76

Williams, J.A.   THE MAN WHO CRIED I AM
Dying American black man in Amsterdam discovers plot to wipe out
black organizations in America.
Little, Brown, 1967. fc

Travel Articles

ANTIQUES
1980   Jan   Dutch royal collections, S.B. Sherrill - p. 108

CUISINE
1979   Apr   Holland: a memorable feast, R.A. de Groot - p. 26

GOURMET
1980   May   Holland's spring flowers,
                          L. Langseth-Christensen - p. 25
1979   Nov   The Willet-Holthuysen kitchen,
                          L. Langseth-Christensen - p. 42

HORIZON
1979   Jan   Culture shock (Holland festival) - p. 14

HOUSE & GARDEN
1980   Oct   When it's tulip time in Holland, J. Fanning - p. 275

MODERN BRIDE
1980   Feb/Mar   Holland (honeymoon) - p. 330

N.Y. TIMES SUNDAY TRAVEL SECTION (10)
1979   Jul 29   Barging through the Netherlands, R. Bendiner - p. 1

ROAD & TRACK
1980   Apr   Driving tours of the Netherlands, J. Scalzo - p. 163

SATURDAY EVENING POST
1979   Jan/Feb   Frisian spoken here, B. Burrows - p. 130

SOUTHERN LIVING
1980   Aug   Finding Holland's bargains - p. 20

SUNSET
1980   May   Pedal across Holland, six to nine days, your rooms
                  reserved - p. 50
1979   Apr   Dutch still dress up for the fairs (market town
                  festivals) - p. 58
       Sep   Cows and a cow museum, handicrafts, little traffic . . .
                  it's pastoral Friesland - p. 44

TOWN & COUNTRY
1979   Apr   Hotel de L'Europe, L. Gwinn - p. B2
       Apr   Cruisin' down the canal (travel by barge in Europe),
                  S. Anderson - p. 18

TRAVEL & LEISURE
1980   Apr   Antiquing in Amsterdam, I. Keown - p. 58
       Sep   Rotterdam, J.B. Farber - p. 121
       Dec   Airports: Amsterdam, S. Wilkinson - p. 121

TRAVEL/HOLIDAY
1980   Feb   Afloat in Holland, B.H. Matthiessen - p. 44
1979   Apr   Holland culture card, H. Fisher - p. 8
       Jun   Walking tour of Amsterdam, L. Foster - p. 42

WORLD PRESS REVIEW (formerly Atlas)
1979   Nov   Amsterdam's houseboat culture, S. Klein - p. 60

Notes - Norway

1. Abbreviations of reference sources for novels:
   fc - Fiction Catalog, 9th Edition
   fc/s76 (77, etc.) - Supplement to 9th Edition
   fc/8ed - Fiction Catalog, 8th Edition
   brd/78 (79, etc.) - Book Review Digest for the year

2. Standard Series Guidebooks for Norway:
   Fodor (Scandinavia)
   Frommer $ Guide (Scandinavia)

3. See Appendix 1 for more complete data on the above.

4. See Europe, at end of country sections, and items with an asterisk under Denmark, for additional possible sources of reading and information for Norway.

Norway

Background Reading

Baden-Powell, D. PIMPERNEL GOLD; HOW NORWAY
FOILED THE NAZIS
A suspenseful, true story of the race to evacuate the gold supply following the German invasion in 1940, written in such a way that the " . . . reader's heart and head are equally entranced."
St. Martin's Press, 1978.

Caraman, P. NORWAY
An account of the three-year stay of a Jesuit priest in Norway; contacts and conversations with all classes of people, and a long journey from Oslo to the Norwegian-Russian border.
Paul S. Erikson, 1969.

Dahl, G.K. FAMILY DIARY: EVERYDAY LIFE IN NORWAY
IPS, 1971.

Davis, P. AN EXPERIENCE OF NORWAY
A trip via motor caravan.
David & Charles, 1974.

Deardorff, R.A. A DAY OUTSIDE THE CITY
Interesting and pleasant day trips with Oslo as a base city.
Holt, 1968.

Foote, P.G. and Wilson, D.M. THE VIKING ACHIEVEMENT
"A comprehensive survey of the society and culture of early medieval Scandinavia."
Praeger, 1970.

Hopp, Z.   NORWEGIAN FOLKLORE
Grieg, 1974.
Larsen, K.   A HISTORY OF NORWAY
A standard history with a text "lively enough (for the) intelligent
tourist."
Princeton Univ. Press, 1948.
Lottman, H.   DETOURS FROM THE GRAND TOUR
"Off-beat, overlooked, and unexpected Europe"—travel writing that
includes material on the Scandinavian capital city of Oslo.
Prentice-Hall, 1980.
Magnusson, M.   VIKINGS!
Based on ten-part public television series; Viking culture, religion,
mythology, literature, and a reconstruction of origins.
Dutton, 1980.
Midgaar, J.   A BRIEF HISTORY OF NORWAY
Tanum, 1971.
Miller, M.M.   NORWEGIAN ROSEMALING
This is the art of decorative painting on wood which is a traditional
folk art in Norway.
Scribner, 1974.
Petrow, R.   THE BITTER YEARS
"The invasion and occupation of Denmark and Norway, April/40-
May/45."
Morrow, 1979.
Popperwell, R.G.   NORWAY
Praeger, 1972.
Sansom, W.   THE ICICLE AND THE SUN
Four essays on Scandinavia by a gifted travel writer. First published
in 1959.
Greenwood, 1976.
Simpson, C.   THE VIKING WORLD
". . . an authentic and vivid picture of life in Viking times."
St. Martin's, 1980.
Streeter, E.   SKOAL SCANDINAVIA
Perceptive and pleasant account of author's trip by car through Scan-
dinavia with his wife and another couple.
Harper, 1952.
Taylor, S.   YOUNG AND HUNGRY: A COOKBOOK
                                  IN THE FORM OF A MEMOIR
This is a charming book, based on the author's childhood memories
of summering in Norway with her grandparents, and including recipes
for many of the memorable meals. The visits combined the city of
Stavanger, and a mountain cottage.
Houghton, 1970.

Vanberg, B.   OF NORWEGIAN WAYS
"Lighthearted and irreverent" account of manners and mores.
Dillon, 1970.

Novels

Balzac, H. de   SERAPHITA
Eighteenth-century Norway; philosophical novel.
Books for Libs., 1970. fc

Bojer, J.   THE GREAT HUNGER
One man's life, education, loves, etc.
Moffat, 1919. fc

Buchan, J.   THE THREE HOSTAGES
Third volume of *Adventurers All*. . . . A twentieth-century mystery
by a Briton.
Houghton, 1924. fc

Francis, D.   SLAYRIDE
A mystery involving horseracing in Norway; written by an English-
man who is an ex-jockey and has written many stories of this milieu.
Harper, 1974. fc

Frison-Roche, R.   THE RAID
Girl runs away from Norwegian school to save her reindeer flock.
Descriptive of "sub arctic" rural ways.
Harper, 1964. fc

Gulbranssen, T.   BEYOND SING THE WOODS
Story of a proud family in eighteenth-century Norway.
Putnam, 1936. fc

Gulbranssen, T.   THE WIND FROM THE MOUNTAINS
Sequel to *Beyond Sing the Woods;* 1809 and on.
Putnam, 1937. fc

Hamsun, K.   GROWTH OF THE SOIL
Won Nobel prize for literature in 1920. Novel of peasant life.
Knopf, 1968. fc

Hamsun, K.   HUNGER
Story of struggling writer longing to create. First published in 1890.
Farrar, Straus, 1967. fc

Hamsun, K.   MYSTERIES
Rambling monolog of young man who drowns himself. First pub-
lished in 1892.
Farrar, Straus, 1971. fc

Hamsun, K.   PAN; FROM LT. THOMAS GLAHN'S PAPERS
    Love triangle, first published in 1894.
    Farrar, Straus, 1956. fc
Hamsun, K.   VICTORIA; A LOVE STORY
    Story of a miller and the woman he loves. First published in 1898.
    Farrar Straus, 1969. fc
Hamsun, K.   THE WANDERER: UNDER THE AUTUMN STAR
                                        AND ON MUTED STRINGS
    Two novels first published in 1906 and 1909; rural life.
    Farrar, Straus, 1975. fc/s76
Hamsun, K.   WAYFARERS
    The author is a leading Norwegian writer, and winner of a Nobel prize
    for literature in 1920. This is the latest of his novels to be translated
    and thus made more accessible to American readers. It is a picaresque
    novel of the itinerant life of two friends.
    Farrar, Straus, 1980. brd/80
Reeman, D.   SURFACE WITH DARING
    WWII story of British soldiers in Norway with much action in and
    description of the Norwegian countryside.
    Putnam, 1977. fc/s77
Trew, A.   THE ZHUKOV BRIEFING
    International intrigue.
    St. Martin's, 1976. fc/s76
Undset, S.   THE FAITHFUL WIFE
    Unfaithful husband is reunited with faithful wife.
    Knopf, 1937. fc
Undset, S.   FOUR STORIES
    Short stories about four lonely people.
    Knopf, 1959. fc
Undset, S.   KRISTIN LAVRANSDATTER
    Three novels, originally published singly as *The Bridal Wreath, The
    Mistress of Husaby* and *The Cross.* "From her happy childhood and
    later romance as wife and mother on a great estate, to her old age
    and loneliness . . . forms one of the most realistic stories of a woman's
    life ever written . . . set in medieval Norway, vivid and true." By one
    of Norway's leading writers and considered a masterpiece.
    Knopf, 1953. fc
Undset, S.   THE MASTER OF HESTVIKEN
    Portrait of Norwegian life, in thirteenth and fourteenth centuries.
    Published originally in four volumes, 1925-27, as follows:*The Axe,
    The Snake Pit, In the Wilderness, The Son Avenger.* Series ends in
    1814.
    Knopf, 1952. fc

Travel Articles

GOURMET
1979   Dec   Cross country skiing in Norway; Lillehammer,
                      P.J. Wade - p. 32

N.Y. SUNDAY TIMES TRAVEL SECTION (10)
1980   Jun 8   The Nordic flavor of Bergen, D. Wolfer - p. 1
          Sep 20   A Fjord-country feast of mountains, lakes, and water-
                      falls, R.W. Apple, Jr. - p. 1
1979   Nov 25   Oslo honors the Vikings, old and new, P.Lewis - p. 1

SATURDAY EVENING POST
1980   Jan/Feb   Norway's Stave churches, B. Jenkins - p. 110

SKIING
1980   Jan   The Holmenkollen (ski jump in Norway),
                      J.H. Auran - p. 58

TRAVEL & LEISURE
1979   Dec   Ski touring in Norway, H. Ehrlich - p. 20

TRAVEL/HOLIDAY
1979   Aug   Winter weekends in Norway at reduced rates - p. 21

Notes - Poland

1. Abbreviations of reference sources for novels:
   fc - Fiction Catalog, 9th Edition
   fc/s76 (77, etc.) - Supplement to 9th Edition
   fc/8ed - Fiction Catalog, 8th Edition
   brd/78 (79, etc.) - Book Review Digest for the year

2. Standard Series Guidebooks for Poland:
   Nagel
   Foreign Area Study

3. See Appendix 1 for more complete data on the above.

4. See Europe, at end of country sections, for additional possible sources of reading and information for Poland.

Poland

Background Reading

Benes, V.L.   POLAND
   Praeger, 1970.
Blunden, G.   EASTERN EUROPE:
                          CZECHOSLOVAKIA, HUNGARY, POLAND
   Description and travel.
   Time, Inc., 1965.
Dornberg, J.   EASTERN EUROPE: A COMMUNIST KALEIDOSCOPE
   See description under Bulgaria on page 17.
   Dial, 1980.
Dziewanowski, M.K.   POLAND IN THE TWENTIETH CENTURY
   Triumphs and sufferings of the Poles; a survey of pre-1914 history
   followed by a detailed account of the twentieth century.
   Columbia Univ. Press, 1977.
Eisner, J.   THE SURVIVOR
   Survival of a thirteen-year old as Poland falls to the Nazis, from im-
   prisonment in the ghetto to concentration camp, to liberation by the
   Americans six years later, at nineteen. A remarkable story.
   Morrow, 1980.
Gunther, J.   TWELVE CITIES
   See entry on page 2—Warsaw is one of the twelve.
   Harper, 1969.
Halecki, O.   A HISTORY OF POLAND
   McKay, 1976.

Heine, M.E.   POLAND
A guidebook written by an American-educated author, with Anglo-Americans in mind. Emphasizes places tourists most wish to see along with general information on history, food, etc.
Hippocrene, 1980.

Heine, M.E.   POLES: HOW THEY LIVE AND WORK
Introduction to the country—history, government, economics, how the average people live plus some advice for foreign tourists.
Praeger, 1976.

Hotchkiss, C.   HOME TO POLAND
Visit of an American, born in Poland, during the time of the "quiet revolution" when the Poles succeeded in securing a measure of freedom from Russia.
Farrar, 1958.

Jazdzewski, K.   POLAND
Ancient Poland; antiquities and archaeology, cultural history.
Praeger, 1965.

Korbonski, S.   FIGHTING WARSAW
"The story of the Polish underground." Also *Polish Underground State* (Hippocrene Books, 1980).
Macmillan, 1956.

Kurzman, D.   THE BRAVEST BATTLE
"The twenty-eight days of the Warsaw ghetto uprising," against the Nazis—April 19 to May 16, 1943.
Putnam, 1976.

Newman, B.   THE NEW POLAND
Hale, 1968.

Watt, R.M.   BITTER GLORY: POLAND AND ITS FATE
                                                          1918-1939
Poland has had a long struggle to establish itself as an independent country between two giants—Russia and Germany. This is the story of that brief period, 1918-1939, when they succeeded.
Simon & Schuster, 1979.

Novels

Agnon, S.Y.   THE BRIDAL CANOPY
Early nineteenth-century Galicia; Jew must find dowries for three daughters. Published originally in 1922.
Schocken, 1967. fc

Agnon, S.Y.   A GUEST FOR THE NIGHT
  Galicia, post-WWI. Palestinian returns to his home town. First pub-
  lished in 1939.
  Schocken, 1968. fc

Barash, A.   PICTURES FROM A BREWERY
  Rural Jewish family.
  Bobbs, 1974. fc

Epstein, L.   KING OF THE JEWS
  Holocaust, WWII. Based on life of Chaim Rumkowski.
  Coward, McCann, 1979. brd/79.

Gogol, N.   TARAS BULBA
  Cossack struggle, 1572-1763. First published in 1834.
  Crowell, 1886. fc

Grass, G.   DOG YEARS
  Danzig and villages along the Vistula, WWII and after.
  Harcourt, 1963. fc

Grass, G.   THE TIN DRUM
  Danzig. Twelfth-century dwarf sees the past and the future.
  Pantheon, 1963. fc

Grass, G.   CAT AND MOUSE
  Danzig, WWII. Boy's struggle to become a hero.
  Harcourt, 1963. fc

Karmel-Wolfe, H.   THE BADERS OF JACOB STREET
  Krakow, WWII. Effect of the War on young Jewish girl.
  Lippincott, 1970. fc

Kosinski, J.   THE PAINTED BIRD
  Child's wanderings in Eastern Poland, WWII.
  Houghton, 1976. fc/s76

Kuniczak, W.S.   THE THOUSAND-HOUR DAY
  First thousand hours of WWII; Polish surrender.
  Dial, 1967. fc

Lustig, A.   A PRAYER FOR KATERINA HOROVITZOVA
  Jews captured in Italy, with American passports, sent to a Polish
  concentration camp and given option to "buy" their freedom. First
  published in 1964.
  Harper, 1973. fc

Read, P.P.   POLONAISE
  This novel involves " . . . the lives of a brother and sister . . . when
  their father, a Polish aristocrat, goes bankrupt . . . brilliant, sophisticated . . ." novel of Poland 1914 to late 1950's.
  Lippincott, 1976. fc/s76

Reymont, L.   THE PEASANTS
  Four volumes; peasants under old Russian rule, daily life.
  Knopf, 1924. fc

Singer, I.B.   THE BROTHERS ASHKENAZI
   Lodz. Laboring class struggle, nineteenth-century Polish life.
   Knopf, 1936. fc
Singer, I.B.   THE ESTATE
   Sequel to *The Manor* (see below).
   Farrar, Straus, 1969. fc
Singer, I.B.   THE MAGICIAN OF LUBLIN
   Nineteenth-century circus performer. First published in 1960.
   Farrar, Straus, 1975. fc
Singer, I.B.   THE MANOR
   1863 Polish insurrection, Russians take over one family's estate.
   Farrar Straus, 1967. fc
Singer, I.B.   SATAN IN GORAY
   1572-1763, Chmielnicki massacres. First published in 1955.
   Farrar, Straus. fc
Singer, I.B.   THE SEANCE AND OTHER STORIES
   Short stories set in Poland of 1870.
   Farrar, Straus, 1968. fc
Singer, I.B.   SHOSHA
   The " . . . life and times of a young journalist and budding novelist,
   rabbi's son and skeptic . . ."–by a Nobel prize winning writer known
   for his colorful characters and universality of theme.
   Farrar, Straus, 1978. brd/78
Singer, I.B.   THE SLAVE
   1572-1763. Jew driven from home by Cossack becomes slave to a
   peasant; love story of hero and peasant's daughter.
   Farrar, Straus, 1962. fc
Singer, I.J.   STEEL AND IRON
   1915. Russian deserter in Poland working for the Germans. First pub-
   lished in 1927.
   Funk, 1969. tc
Singer, I.J.   YOSHE KALB
   Boy's wanderings after he leaves an arranged marriage and infatua-
   tion with wife's mother. First published in 1933.
   Vanguard, 1974. fc

Warsaw

Asch, S.   MOTTKE, THE THIEF
   Underworld adventures. First published in 1917.
   Greenwood Press, 1970.
Hall, A.   THE WARSAW DOCUMENT
   Cold war spy story involving Polish underground and British secret
   agent.
   Doubleday, 1971. fc

Hersey, J.   THE WALL
    A ghetto is walled in by the Nazis; story of horrors and escape of many.
    Knopf, 1950. fc

Hlasko, M.   THE EIGHTH DAY OF THE WEEK
    A family's struggle, set in Warsaw of 1956. Reflects Polish contemporary life.
    Dutton, 1958. fc

Kirst, H.H.   THE NIGHT OF THE GENERALS
    Late WWII period; murder and conspiracy against Hitler.
    Harper, 1963. fc

Schaeffer, S.F.   ANYA
    Girl from wealthy family experiences horrors of WWII and concentration camps.
    Macmillan, 1974. fc

Singer, I.B.   THE FAMILY MOSKAT
    End of nineteenth century to the beginning of WWII. One family's story and the customs of Jewish life. First published in 1950.
    Farrar, Straus, 1965. fc

Uris, L.   MILA 18
    WWII and the resistance movement of the Jews.
    Doubleday, 1961. fc

Travel Articles

BICYCLING
    1980   Mar   Cycling in eastern Europe, H.T. Lyon - p. 60

COSMOPOLITAN
    1979   Jul   Marvelous middle Europe, R. Ashley - p. 58

HISTORY TODAY
    1980   Aug   Dependent Independence? Eastern Europe 1918-1856, L.P. Morris - p. 38

NATIONAL REVIEW
    1980   Oct 17   What makes the Poles different, E. Kuehnelt-Leddin - p. 1262

N.Y. TIMES SUNDAY TRAVEL SECTION (10)
    1979   Mar 4   What's doing in Warsaw, D.A. Andelman - p. 11

Mar 25   Following the route of the faithful in historic Poland,
D.A. Andelman - p. 1

POPULAR PHOTOGRAPHY
1979   Jul   Poland (yes!) surprises photographers; Vienna
unsurprisingly, is great too, K. Poli - p. 9

SATURDAY REVIEW
1979   Mar 17   The far out traveler's guide to places you never
thought of, P. Brooks - p. 46

TRAVEL/HOLIDAY
1979   Nov   Malbork, Poland: amber collection, C.E. Andelson
and H. Angelo-Castrillon - p. 38

WORLD PRESS REVIEW (formerly Atlas)
1980   Dec   Where the Pope skied: the pleasures of a pilgrimage to
Zakopane, J. Reiter - p. 63

This is a dress considered perfect for vacationing at a "watering place" or at the seaside. It is white lace trimmed with rose-pink ribbons and foulard.

Notes - Portugal

1. Abbreviations of reference sources for novels:
   fc - Fiction Catalog, 9th Edition
   fc/s76 (77, etc.) - Supplement to 9th Edition
   fc/8ed - Fiction Catalog, 8th Edition
   brd/78 (79, etc.) - Book Review Digest for the year

2. Standard Series Guidebooks for Portugal:
   Fodor
   Frommer Dollarwise
   Frommer (Lisbon-Madrid-Costa del Sol)
   Michelin Green Guide
   Michelin Red Guide (Spain and Portugal)
   Nagel (Portugal plus Madeira and Azores)
   Foreign Area Study

3. See Appendix 1 for more complete data on the above.

4. See Europe, at end of country sections, for additional possible sources of reading and information for Portugal.

Portugal

Background Reading

Bell, C.   PORTUGAL AND THE QUEST FOR THE INDIES
Voyages of exploration in 1385-1498.
Harper, 1974.

Bridge, A. and Lowndes, S. SELECTIVE TRAVELLER IN PORTUGAL
Both authors have lived in Portugal for many years, so they write
with authority; manners, customs, art, architecture, history and the
countryside.
McGraw-Hill, 1968.

Bruce, N.   THE LAST EMPIRE
An "interim appraisal of a continuing revolution"—summarizes the
events leading to the revolution of 1974 in Portugal and in Portuguese
Africa.
Wiley, 1975.

Bryans, R.   THE AZORES
The mid-Atlantic archipelago belonging to Portugal; "a vivid picture
of the Azores in all their strange and wide variety."
Faber, 1963.

Dos Passos, J.   THE PORTUGAL STORY: THREE CENTURIES
OF EXPLORATION AND DISCOVERY
An account by the novelist of the extraordinary explorations of the
Portuguese sailors and the establishment of the first extensive over-
seas empire of the age.
Doubleday, 1969.

Figueiredo, A. de   PORTUGAL
  Portugal under Salazar, 1932-1968.
  Holmes & Meier, 1976.
Gribble, F.A.   .   THE ROYAL HOUSE OF PORTUGAL
  Kennikat, 1970.
Kempner, M.J.   INVITATION TO PORTUGAL
  Combines elements of a guidebook, a history, a day-to-day journey.
  Atheneum, 1969.
Kimbrough, C.   PLEASURE BY THE BUSLOAD
  Trip in a Volkswagen bus with four good traveling companions, in
  the typically pleasant, perceptive style of Miss Kimbrough.
  Harper, 1961.
Livermore, H.V.   A NEW HISTORY OF PORTUGAL
  Cambridge Univ. Press, 1976.
MacKendrick, P.L.   THE IBERIAN STONES SPEAK
  Introduction to archaeology and cultural history based on archaeo-
  logical findings.
  Funk & Wagnall, 1969.
Mailer, P.   PORTUGAL: THE IMPOSSIBLE REVOLUTION?
  "Well written . . . thorough delight as it moves from first-person ac-
  counts of the street demonstrations through . . . political movements"
  with a large and complicated cast of politicians, military officers, peas-
  ant and worker councils. Concerns the events of April 1974 when
  the country moved from a dictatorship to moderation.
  Free Life Eds., 1977.
O'Callaghan, J.F.   HISTORY OF MEDIEVAL SPAIN
  A history of the entire peninsula and all aspects of it—Islamic, Jewish,
  Christian, Portuguese, Catalonian, Castilian—from the fifth century
  to Ferdinand and Isabella.
  Cornell Univ. Press, 1975.
Read, J.   MOORS IN SPAIN & PORTUGAL
  The emphasis is on "heightening the interest of the visitor or arm-
  chair traveler . . . to see Spain and Portugal of today in historic per-
  spective" and to discern present-day effects of the Moors' presence
  on the peninsula in 710-1614.
  Rowman & Littlefield, 1975.
Salter, C.   ALGARVE AND SOUTHERN PORTUGAL
  Hastings House, 1974.
Tuohy, F.   PORTUGAL
  Viking, 1970.
Wibberley, L.   NO GARLIC IN THE SOUP
  An American family's stay in Portugal for several months—daily life
  and experiences, and their travels throughout Portugal.
  Washburn, 1959.

Novels

Bridge, A.   EPISODE AT TOLEDO
  Espionage in a country setting.
  McGraw-Hill, 1966. fc/8ed
Bridge, A.   THE MALADY IN MADEIRA
  "Mild suspense and travelogue."
  McGraw-Hill, 1969. fc
Cadell, E.   THE FRIENDLY AIR
  Lady's companion on trip to Portugal has change of heart in respect
  to her own life.
  Morrow, 1971. fc
Cadell, E.   THE GOLDEN COLLAR
  British visitor to Portugal falls in love with landowner's niece.
  Morrow, 1969. fc
Canning, V.   BIRD CAGE
  Ex-nun's love story; thriller.
  Morrow, 1979. fc/s79
Eça de Queiroz   THE MAIAS
  Set in turn-of-the-century Lisbon; a novel of the aristocratic society
  of the period by a leading Portuguese author.
  St. Martin's, 1965. fc/8ed
Hodge, J.A.   MARRY IN HASTE
  Regency England, and Portugal.
  Doubleday, 1970. fc
Hodge, J.A.   THE WINDING STAIR
  Early nineteenth-century gothic.
  Doubleday, 1969. fc
L'Engle, M.   THE LOVE LETTERS
  Contemporary woman learns to deal with her own marriage in read-
  ing a packet of old love letters.
  Farrar, Straus, 1966. fc
Rathbone, J.   ¡CARNIVAL!
  See entry on page 242, under Spain.
  St. Martin's 1976. fc/s77

Travel Articles

COSMOPOLITAN
  1980 Nov   Lisbon & Madeira, K. Olson - p. 138

ESQUIRE
1979   Mar 13   Prainha (hotel), Faro, S. Birnbaum - p. 88

GLAMOUR
1980   Oct   The Europe where summer lasts longer - p. 170

MADEMOISELLE
1980   Jun   Honeymoon! (11 tried and true trips) - p. 88

MONEY
1979   Apr   Portugal: Europe at half price, J. Gooding - p. 54

NATIONAL GEOGRAPHIC
1980   Dec   After an empire . . . Portugal, W. Graves
             and B. Barney - p. 804

N.Y. SUNDAY TIMES TRAVEL SECTION (10)
1980   Feb 10   What's doing in Lisbon, J.M. Markham - p. 7
       Mar 23   A skeptic catches Madeira's bouquet, R. Packard - p. 1
       Aug 10   Near Lisbon, a trio of treats, R. Packard - p. 1
       Nov 2   Savoring the flavor of fine old porto, R. Packard - p. 1
1979   Aug 26   Recalling Prince Henry in Sagres, S. August - p. 9
       Dec 2   What's doing in the Algarve, V. Lewis - p. 9

TOWN & COUNTRY
1979   Apr   Hotel Ritz, L. Gwinn - p. 134

TRAVEL & LEISURE
1979   Jul   Portugal: Europe's secret bargain, H.B. LIvesey - p. 40

TRAVEL/HOLIDAY
1980   Feb   Charm of Madeira, L. and L. Dennis - p. 60
1979   Feb   Portugal's Algarve, G. Trotta - p. 42
       Sep   Lisbon, Portugal, J. Vokala - p. 85

VOGUE
1980   Sep   Portugal: a strange and secret beauty,
             A. Roiphe - p. 383

WINE WORLD
1980 Sep/Oct   The changing scene in porto, R. auf der Heide - p. 12

*Bathing costumes of the 1870's for women and children. They are
made of (l. to r.) blue flannel, light gray serge, red flannel trimmed with
black braid.*

Notes - Romania

1. Abbreviations of reference sources for novels:
   fc - Fiction Catalog, 9th Edition
   fc/s76 (77, etc.) - Supplement to 9th Edition
   fc/8ed - Fiction Catalog, 8th Edition
   brd/78 (79, etc.) - Book Review Digest for the year

2. Standard Series Guidebooks for Romania:
   Nagel
   Foreign Area Study

3. See Appendix 1 for more complete data on the above.

4. See Europe, at end of country sections, for additional possible sources of reading and information for Romania.

Romania

Background Reading

Berciu, D.   ROMANIA
    Pre-history of Romania until the time of Christ.
    Praeger, 1968.

Chase, I.   FRESH FROM THE LAUNDRY
    See entry under Bulgaria on page 17.
    Doubleday, 1967.

Crelzianu, A., ed.   CAPTIVE RUMANIA: A DECADE
                                  OF SOVIET RULE
    Praeger, 1956.

Dornberg, J.   EASTERN EUROPE: A COMMUNIST KALEIDOSCOPE
    See description under Bulgaria on page 17.
    Dial, 1980.

Fischer-Galati, S.A.   RUMANIA
    "The new Rumania: from people's democracy to socialist republic."
    Also *Twentieth Century Rumania* (Columbia Univ. Press, 1970).
    MIT Press, 1967.

MacKendrick, P.   THE DACIAN STONES SPEAK
    Archaeology and history based on archaeological sites in the Roman
    province of Dacia, now roughly the country of Romania.
    Univ. of North Carolina Press, 1975.

Matley, I.M.   ROMANIA: A PROFILE
    Highly readable overview for the foreign traveler.
    Praeger, 1970.

Perl, L.   FOODS & FESTIVALS OF THE DANUBE LANDS
    Romania along with other countries on the Danube.
    World, 1969.
Perl, L.   YUGOSLAVIA, ROMANIA, BULGARIA;
                              NEW ERA IN THE BALKANS
    History, government, culture and people.
    Nelson, 1970.
Pilon, J.G.   NOTES FROM THE OTHER SIDE OF NIGHT
    An account of the author's return to Romania in 1975, having emi-
    grated from the country as a child. The book ". . . illuminates (better
    than many scholarly approaches) the drabness, boredom and monot-
    ony . . ." of daily existence in a communist country.
    Regnery/Gateway, 1979.
Seton-Watson, R.W.   A HISTORY OF THE ROUMANIANS:
            FROM ROMAN TIMES TO THE COMPLETION OF UNITY
    Archon, 1963.
Steinberg, J.   INTRODUCTION TO RUMANIAN LITERATURE
    Twayne, 1966.
Stillman, E.   THE BALKANS
    Time, Inc.1964.

Novels

Dorian, M.   RIDE ON THE MILKY WAY
    An evocative story of childhood in Bucharest.
    Crown, 1967. brd/67
Dorian, M.   THE SEASONS
    Upper class Jewish family in pre-WWII Bucharest and the effect of a
    new servant girl on the young daughter of the house.
    Macmillan, 1977. fc/s77
Dorian, M.   THE YEAR OF THE WATER BEARER
    Recreates a period in the author's great grandmother's life in 1860's
    in a small Romanian village setting.
    Macmillan, 1976. fc/s76
Eliade, L.   THE FORBIDDEN FOREST
    Devastated worlds of Europe and Romania from 1936 to 1948.
    Univ. of Notre Dame Press, 1978. fc/s78
Horia, V.   GOD WAS BORN IN EXILE
    In the form of a journal; a fictional account of the Roman poet Ovid

and his exile in a garrison town in Dacia (approximately modern-day Romania).

St. Martin's, 1961.

Stancu, Z.   **BAREFOOT**

Reprint of a novel about the peasant uprising in the early 1900's which has become a Romanian national classic.

Twayne, 1972.

Travel Articles

CUISINE
1980   Oct   Travels in Transylvania, P. Kovi - p. 14

HISTORY TODAY
1980   Aug   Bucharest: historical perspectives of the Romanian
                       capital, D. Turnock - p. 14

N.Y. SUNDAY TIMES TRAVEL SECTION (10)
1979   Jul 1   Exploring the Danube delta, D. Binder - p. 1
        Dec 23   What's doing in Bucharest, D.A. Andelman - p. 3

TOWN & COUNTRY
1979   Feb   Rumania: between Gerovital and Dracula,
                       L. Gwinn - p. 134

Notes - Scotland

1. Abbreviations of reference sources for novels:
   fc - Fiction Catalog, 9th Edition
   fc/s76 (77, etc.) - Supplement to 9th Edition
   fc/8ed - Fiction Catalog, 8th Edition
   brd/78 (79, etc.) - Book Review Digest for the year

2. Standard Series Guidebooks for Scotland:
   Blue Guide
   Frommer Dollarwise (England and Scotland)
   Guides to Great Britain (under England)

3. See Appendix 1 for more complete data on the above.

4. See Europe, at end of country sections, and items with an asterisk under England, for additional possible sources of reading and information for Scotland.

Scotland

Background Reading

Brody, E.   MUSIC GUIDE TO GREAT BRITAIN;
                          ENGLAND, SCOTLAND, WALES, IRELAND
    See full annotation for this series under Austria (Brody), page 1.
    Dodd, 1975.

Campbell, G.   HIGHLAND HERITAGE
    A Canadian Scot's journey, and description of the Scottish clans.
    Duell, Sloan, 1962.

Craig, D.   SCOTTISH LITERATURE & THE SCOTTISH PEOPLE
    1680-1830.
    Chatto &Windus, 1961.

Daiches, D.   EDINBURGH
    A chronical of the city from origins to present.
    H. Hamilton, 1979.

Daiches, D.   SIR WALTER SCOTT AND HIS WORLD
    Viking, 1971.

Dunnett, A., ed.   ALISTAIR MACLEAN INTRODUCES SCOTLAND
    A group of essayists have each contributed to this book on a variety
    subjects :: ties to England, history, political thought, sport, character
    of the people, etc. Alistair MacLean writes the opening essay, hence
    the title.
    McGraw-Hill, 1972.

Finlay, I.   THE HIGHLANDS
    Part of the Batsford series—" . . . no better introduction to this wild

and lovely land need be sought." See also Finlay's *The Lowlands*
(Hastings, 1967).
Hastings, 1964.
Forbes, A.   TOWNS OF NEW ENGLAND AND OLD ENGLAND,
                            IRELAND AND SCOTLAND
See entry under England (Intriguing Miscellany), page 45.
Putnam, 1921.
Glover, J.R.   THE STORY OF SCOTLAND
History from medieval times—"... best available introduction to
the current state of affairs in Scotland."
Faber, 1977.
Harting, E.C. LITERARY TOUR GUIDE TO ENGLAND & SCOTLAND
See entry under England (Literary Guides for Travelers), page 43.
Morrow, 1976.
Linklater, E.   THE SURVIVAL OF SCOTLAND
"A survey of Scottish history from Roman times to the present day."
A narrative history for the general reader (as well as the specialist)
by an author who "brings to the writing of history the clarity, ele-
gance and wit of a Churchill ...."
Doubleday, 1968.
Linklater, E.   THE ULTIMATE VIKING
An informal history of the Viking heroes of the Orkney Islands and
Iceland—"... a fascinating epic ... in heroic prose, peppered with
dry witticisms."
Harcourt, 1956.
MacGregor, G.   SCOTLAND FOREVER HOME
"An introduction to the homeland for American and other Scots."
Written by a Scottish-American who was educated in Scotland—great
introductory reading for potential traveler.
Dodd, 1980.
McLaren, M., ed.   THE WISDOM OF THE SCOTS
An anthology of Scottish writing from generally unavailable sources,
including anonymous proverbs—"... strikes the reader with surpris-
ing force."
St. Martin's, 1962.
MacLean, Sir F.   A CONCISE HISTORY OF SCOTLAND
Untangles "... the incredibly complicated skein of Scottish history
... an excellent primer on Scottish history."
Viking, 1970.
Maxwell, G.   RING OF BRIGHT WATER
Description of remote and lovely area of coastal (Highlands) Scotland
and the author's unique relationship with a variety of fauna includ-
ing two sea otters. For anyone who loves nature and animals.
Dutton, 1965.

Prebble, J.   THE LION IN THE NORTH
History from Roman times to 1854; many photos and illustrations.
Coward, McCann, 1971.
Smout, T.C.   A HISTORY OF THE SCOTTISH PEOPLE, 1560-1830
Scribner, 1970.

The Hebrides & Shetland Islands

Banks, N.   SIX INNER HEBRIDES
David & Charles, 1977.
Beckwith, L.   THE HILLS IS LONELY
Experiences of an English ex-schoolteacher as a visitor to a small
Hebridian village. A follow-up book, *The Sea for Breakfast,* is an ac-
count of the author buying a cottage of her own and living there per-
manently (Dutton, 1963).
Dutton, 1959.
McPhee, J.   THE CROFTER AND THE LAIRD
Colonsay Island—its terrain, its history, its legends and gossip; written
by an American (and staff writer for the New Yorker) whose ances-
tors once lived on the Island.
Farrar, 1970.
Redfern, R.A.   RAMBLES IN THE HEBRIDES
Hale, 1966.
Shepherd, S.   LIKE A MANTLE THE SEA
"Depicting a way of life that . . . seems both rare and refreshing" by
a woman who lived on one of the Shetland Islands for eight years.
Ohio Univ. Press, 1971.
Simpson, W.D.   PORTRAIT OF SKY AND THE OUTER HEBRIDES
IPS, 1967.

Novels

Aiken, J.   CASTLE BEREBANE
Remote setting in Scotland for a novel of terror.
Viking, 1976. fc/s76
Barrie, J.M.   LITTLE MINISTER
The classic.
Scribner, 1951. fc
Black, L.   GLENDRACO
Nineteenth-century gothic.
St. Martin's 1977. fc/s77

Blackstock, C.   A HOUSE POSSESSED
  Loch Ness setting, exorcism is the subject.
  Lippincott, 1962. fc
Caird, J.   THE LOCH
  Town is flooded, when the waters recede much past life is revealed.
  Doubleday, 1969. fc/s79
Caird, J.   IN A GLASS DARKLY
  Modern gothic that begins with murder in a museum.
  Morrow, 1966. fc/s79
Crichton, R.   THE CAMERONS
  Social novel of a mining town in the early twentieth century, and
  the heroine's desire to escape from it.
  Knopf, 1972. fc
Cronin, A.J.   THE GREEN YEARS
  Orphan boy and growing up in small Scottish village.
  Little, Brown, 1944. fc
Cronin, A.J.   SHANNON'S WAY
  Sequel to *The Green Years.*
  Little, Brown, 1948. fc
Cronin, A.J.   HATTER'S CASTLE
  Ambitious man in small town setting.
  Little, Brown, 1931. fc
Cronin, A.J.   A SONG OF SIXPENCE
  Catholic youngster growing up in Protestant Scotland. (Sequel to it
  is *A Pocketful of Rye* set in Switzerland.)
  Little, Brown, 1964. fc
Gibbon, L.G.   A SCOTS QUAIR
  Three novels: *Sunset Song, Cloud How, Grey Granite*—published as a
  trilogy in 1946 and tell the life of Christine Guthrie in small Scottish
  village.
  Schocken, 1977. fc/s77
Hardwick, M.   CHARLIE IS MY DARLING
  Historic novel of Bonnie Prince Charlie, eighteenth century.
  Coward, McCann, 1977. fc/s78
Howatch, S.   APRIL'S GRAVE
  "A pleasantly spooky tale. . ."
  Fawcett, 1978. fc
Innes, M.   THE SECRET VANGUARD
  One of three tales in *Appleby Intervenes.* Nazi fifth column in Scot-
  land.
  Dodd, 1965. fc
Marshall, B.   THE WORLD, THE FLESH AND FATHER SMITH
  A priest's tales in Scotland.
  Houghton, 1945. fc

Peters, E.   LEGEND IN GREEN VELVET
    Contemporary murder and romance in archaeological digs.
    Dodd, 1976. fc/s76
Plaidy, J.   THE CAPTIVE QUEEN OF SCOTS
    Mary Stuart's last eighteen years ending in execution.
    Putnam, 1970. fc
Plaidy, J.   ROYAL ROAD TO FOTHERINGAY
    Precedes *The Captive Queen of Scots.*
    Putnam, 1968. fc
Sayers, D.L.   THE FIVE RED HERRINGS
    Peter Wimsey mystery in Scottish village.
    Harper, 1958. fc/s76
Skelton, C.L.   THE MACLARENS
    Beginning of a new saga to be called *The Regiment Quartet.* Traces a
    family and the 148th Regiment.
    Dial, 1978. fc/s78
Stevenson, D.E.   THE BAKER'S DAUGHTER
    A baker's daughter leaves London to cook for an artist in small Scot-
    tish border village. First published in 1938.
    Holt, 1976. fc/s76
Stevenson, D.E.   CELIA'S HOUSE
    Scottish border county; forty years in the life of a family starting in
    1905.
    Holt, 1977. fc/s77
Stevenson, D.E.   MRS. TIM CHRISTIE
    British officer's wife's life in Scottish town during early days of WWII.
    First published in 1940.
    Holt, 1973. fc
Stevenson, D.E.   MRS. TIM CARRIES ON
    Sequel to *Mrs. Tim Christie.* Series goes on with *Mrs. Tim Gets A
    Job* (move with husband to a post in Egypt) and *Mrs. Tim Flies
    Home* (spends summer with children in England).
    Holt, 1973. fc
Stevenson, D.E.   VITTORIA COTTAGE
    First of a family trilogy. The heroine is the widowed mistress of Vit-
    toria Cottage and mother of a family—". . . quiet stories of really
    nice people." First published in 1949.
    Holt, 1971. fc
Stevenson, D.E.   MUSIC IN THE HILLS
    Second of above trilogy. First published in 1950.
    Holt, 1972. fc
Stevenson, D.E.   SHOULDER THE SKY
    Third of the above trilogy. First published in 1951.
    Holt, 1972. fc

Webster, J.   COLLIER'S ROW
   Saga of nineteenth century in "whiskey-sotted town in Lanarkshire."
   Lippincott, 1977. fc/s77

Edinburgh

Brett, S.   SO MUCH BLOOD
   Murder mystery in the theatre.
   Scribner, 1977. fc/s77
Douglas, C.   THE HOUSEMAN'S TALE
   An "inside" hospital story written by a doctor—a comedy.
   Taplinger, 1978. fc/s79
Douglas, C.   THE GREATEST BREAKTHROUGH
                                           SINCE LUNCHTIME
   Doctors and hospital scene, comedy.
   Taplinger, 1979. fc/s79
Spark, M.   THE PRIME OF MISS JEAN BRODIE
   Spinster school teacher who profoundly affects her students; 1930's.
   Lippincott, 1962. fc

Glasgow

Bermant, C.   THE SECOND MRS. WHITBERG
   Pakistani influence on Jewish neighborhood.
   St. Martin's 1976. fc/s76
Jenkins, R.   FERGUS LAMONT
   Illegitimate son living in Glasgow discovers he is son of aristocrat and
   finally moves to Hebrides, site of the family home.
   Taplinger, 1979. brd/80
Knox, B.   LIVE BAIT
   Drugs and gangs involved in murder.
   Doubleday, 1979. fc/s79
Knox, B.   WITCHROCK
   Fishery Protection Cruiser encounters mystery in off-shore islands.
   Doubleday, 1978. fc/s78
Knox, B.   PILOT ERROR
   Mystery.
   Doubleday, 1977. fc/s77
Quigley, J.   QUEEN'S ROYAL
   Victorian times and adultery in the whiskey dynasty.
   Coward, McCann, 1977. fc/s77

Highlands

Buchan, J.   ADVENTURERS ALL
   Three mysteries (originally published separately in 1925).
   Houghton, 1942. fc

Canning, V.   FLIGHT OF THE GREY GOOSE
   Adventure tale.
   Morrow, 1973. fc
Elgin, M.   HIGHLAND MASQUERADE
   Gothic romance—"Mary Stewart" type. Has same locale and some of
   the same characters as *A Man From the Mist* (below).
   Mill, 1966. fc
Elgin, M.   A MAN FROM THE MIST
   Contemporary gothic.
   Mill, 1965. fc
Fraser, A.   THE WILD ISLAND
   Mystery; a TV personality on holiday in a cottage in the highlands,
   ". . . intermingles history with local folklore . . . a unique setting."
   Norton, 1978. brd/79
Gaskin, C.   A FALCON FOR A QUEEN
   Return of heroine from China, in early twentieth century, to high-
   land home.
   Doubleday, 1972. fc/s76
Herron, S.   ALADALE
   About clans in nineteenth century.
   Summit, 1979. fc/s79
Hubbard, P.M.   THE GRAVEYARD
   Mystery in remote highlands.
   Atheneum, 1975. fc
Johnston, V.   I CAME TO THE HIGHLANDS
   Set in pre-American Revolution era; Scotch girl is forced to return to
   ancestral castle and ends up as servant girl.
   Dodd, 1974. fc
MacKintosh, M.   HIGHLAND FLING
   Mystery that moves from antique auction rooms to the highlands.
   Delacorte, 1980.
MacLean, A.   WHEN EIGHT BELLS TOLL
   Secret service adventure.
   Doubleday, 1975. fc
Ostrow, J.   IN THE HIGHLANDS SINCE TIME IMMEMORIAL
   "Uncomplicated" life in the highlands.
   Knopf, 1970. fc
Pilcher, R.   WILD MOUNTAIN THYME
   Story with two threads, one in London the other involving inheri-
   tance of an estate in the highlands.
   St. Martin's 1979. fc/s79
Skelton, C.L.   THE REGIMENT
   Army life in the nineteenth century.
   Dial, 1979. fc/s79

Stevenson, D.E.   THE HOUSE OF THE DEER
   Sequel to *Gerald and Elizabeth* (set in London). Vacation in Scot-
   land leads to danger and love.
   Holt, 1971. fc
Stevenson, D.E.   SMOULDERING FIRE
   Romance and mystery. Originally published in 1938.
   Holt, 1972. fc

Island and Coastal Settings

Beckwith, L.   THE SPUDDY
   Orphan and a stray dog find each other.
   Delacorte, 1976. fc/s76
Black, G.   A BIG WIND FOR SUMMER
   Isle of Arran; art intrigue
   Harper, 1976. fc/s76
Brown, G.   GREENVOE
   Farmers, weavers, lobstermen in an Orkney Island village.
   Harcourt, 1972. fc
Caird, J.   MURDER REMOTE
   Mystery and romance in remote fishing village in West Scotland.
   Doubleday, 1973. fc
Cass, Zoe   THE SILVER LEOPARD
   Argyllshire, "romance and terror" on Scottish coast.
   Random House, 1976. fc/s76
Garnett, D.   UP SHE RISES
   Woman's life with man married to the sea—late eighteenth century.
   St. Martin's, 1977. brd/78
Howatch, S.   THE WAITING SANDS
   Island mystery off west coast of Scotland.
   Stein & Day, 1972. fc
Hubbard, P.M.   THE CAUSEWAY
   A suspense story for devotees of sailing and the sea.
   Doubleday, 1978. brd/78
Innes, H.   ATLANTIC FURY
   The Island of Laerg in the Hebrides is the setting for this mystery.
   Knopf, 1962. fc
Knox, B.   STORMTIDE
   Isle of Skye setting; one of a series of police mysteries involving the
   Fisheries Protection Cruisers. See also books by Knox under Glasgow.
   Doubleday, 1973. fc
Knox, B.   WHITEWATER
   Mystery involving the Fisheries Protection arm of the police, in the
   Hebrides. Also *Hellspout* (Doubleday, 1976) by the same author.
   Doubleday, 1973. fc

Stafford, C.   MOIRA
     Murder mystery on the Scottish coast.
     Simon & Schuster, 1976. fc/s77
Stewart, M.   WILDFIRE AT MIDNIGHT
     Isle of Skye, romantic mystery.
     Morrow, 1961. fc
West, M.L.   SUMMER OF THE RED WOLF
     Hebrides love story.
     Morrow, 1971. fc
Woolf, V.   TO THE LIGHTHOUSE
     The classic, intellectual novel, written in 1927 and set in a summer
     house on the Scottish coast.
     Harcourt, 1949. fc

Travel Articles

AMERICAN FORESTER
     1980   Mar   Wandering the west highlands - p. 41

FIELD & STREAM
     1980   May   Monarch of the glen, A. Oglesby - p. 68

GOLF
     1979   Nov   Gleneagles (hotel), Auchterarder; Perthshire - p. 44

GOURMET
     1980   Jul   Gourmet holiday: the western isles of Scotland,
                         Part I, D. Beal - p. 26
             Aug   Gourmet holiday: the western isles of Scotland,
                         Part II, D. Beal - p. 22

HISTORY TODAY
     1979   Mar   General George Washington: a roadmaker in the High-
                         lands, R.L. Brown - p. 147

HOUSE & GARDEN
     1979   Jul   Living in a pineapple: how to rent a national monu-
                         ment for a vacation week in Britain; the pineapple
                         in Stirlingshire, Scotland, D. Guimaraes - p. 48
             Nov   Edinburgh and the Isle of Skye in six satisfying days,
                         D. Hardle - p. 104

LADIES' HOME JOURNAL
1979 Jul   Rites of summer (festivals), P. Funke - p. 56

NATIONAL WILDLIFE
1980 Dec   The joys of curling - p. 11

N.Y. TIMES SUNDAY TRAVEL SECTION (10)
1980 Jan 6   Close to nature in the Orkneys, E. Mednick - p. 1
       Feb 10 The adventures of a student at a Scottish fishing
                 school, C.L. Cooper - p. 5
       Jun 15 Playing a round at old St. Andrews, where it (golf) all
                 began, R.D. Hershey, Jr. - p. 3
1979 Apr 15 A two-day tour of Edinburgh's history-rich hinterland,
                 R.W. Apple, Jr. - p. 1
       Jul 15 What's doing in Edinburgh, R.D. Hershey, Jr. - p. 7
       Sep 30 Shooting grouse on Scotland's heathered moors,
                 M. Sterne - p. 1

SAIL
1979 May   Cruising with a wild card, W. Stewart - p. 98

SMITHSONIAN
1980 Jun   St. Kildans had harsh but good life on world's edge
                 (Hebrides), C. MacLean - p. 143

TRAVEL & LEISURE
1980 Apr   Edinburgh, F. Ferretti - p. 57
1979 Mar   Scotland's western isles, B. Gale - p. 126
       Jun   The bonnie inns of Scotland, I. Keown - p. 113

TRAVEL/HOLIDAY
1979 Feb   Golf in Scotland, C. Bernard - p. 40
       Sep   My heart's in the highlands, B.H. Matthiessen - p. 40

A shirt-waist and tweed skirt for golfing in the 1890's.

Notes - Soviet Union

1. Abbreviations of reference sources for novels:
   fc - Fiction Catalog, 9th Edition
   fc/s76 (77, etc.) - Supplement to 9th Edition
   fc/8ed - Fiction Catalog, 8th Edition
   brd/78 (79, etc.) - Book Review Digest for the year

2. Standard Series Guidebooks for Soviet Union:
   Fodor
   Nagel (Leningrad and Environs, Moscow and
      Environs)
   Foreign Area Study

3. See Appendix 1 for more complete data on the
   above.

4. See Europe, at end of country sections, for additional possible sources of reading and information
   for the Soviet Union.

Soviet Union

Background Reading

Brokhin, Y.   HUSTLING ON GORKY STREET
"Sex and crime in Russia today . . . entertaining rogues' gallery of . . . the socialist underworld." Unfortunate this title is alphabetically the first, but nevertheless interesting for the potential tourist.
Dial, 1975.

Dornberg, J.   EASTERN EUROPE: A COMMUNIST KALEIDOSCOPE
See entry under Bulgaria, page 17.
Dial, 1980.

Feldkamp, F.   NOT EVERYBODY'S EUROPE
A grand tour of nine unique cities including Leningrad.
Harper's Magazine Press, 1976.

Fisher, L. and W.   MOSCOW'S GOURMET: DINING OUT
IN THE CAPITAL OF THE U.S.S.R.
Ardis, 1974.

Gerhart, G.   THE RUSSIAN'S WORLD; LIFE AND LANGUAGE
Description of "what every Russian knows"—every day life.
Harcourt, 1974.

Gross, E.H. and J.   THE SOVIET UNION;
A GUIDE FOR TRAVELERS
Harper, 1977.

Gunther, J.   TWELVE CITIES
See full entry under Austria—Moscow is one of the cities.
Harper, 1969.

Hingley, R.   THE RUSSIAN MIND
An analysis of Russian life and "what makes the Russians tick."
Scribner, 1977.

Keller, W.   EAST MINUS WEST=ZERO
A provocative title; premise is that without what it has taken or absorbed from the West, Russia would be a "zero."
Putnam, 1961.

Louis, V.E. and J.M.   THE COMPLETE GUIDE
                                                  TO THE SOVIET UNION
Travel and description.
St. Martin's, 1976.

MacLean, F.   HOLY RUSSIA
"An historical companion to European Russia"—history, walking
tours of cities. It is a history for travelers.
Atheneum, 1979.

Perl, L.   FOODS & FESTIVALS OF THE DANUBE LANDS
The Soviet Union along with other countries on the Danube.
World, 1969.

Smith, D.   SMITH'S MOSCOW
For Western visitors: ". . . going beyond the routine itinerary and
gaining a basic knowledge of historical and cultural heritage." Also
includes off-beat tips, like where to get a tooth fixed, etc.
Knopf, 1974.

Struve, N.   CHRISTIANS IN CONTEMPORARY RUSSIA
Scribner, 1967.

Wechsberg, J.   IN LENINGRAD
Story of the fascinating city that was St. Petersburg—beautifully written with many photographs.
Doubleday, 1977.

Siberia

Botting, D.   ONE CHILLY SIBERIAN MORNING
Travelogue of the remote places in Siberia and Asia; well-written,
at times humorous, introduction to one of the unique and less known
areas of the world.
Macmillan, 1968.

Mowat, F.   THE SIBERIANS
An account of two lengthy visits in 1966 and 1969. The author challenges "the myth of Siberia as . . . a desolate wilderness." He writes
of it as a "teeming and productive country" and makes Siberia and
the Siberians come alive for the reader.
Little, Brown, 1970.

Servadio, G.   A SIBERIAN ENCOUNTER
Written by a woman journalist of Italian birth " . . . filled with fas-

cinating facts" and personal impressions. Includes also central Asia,
the Steppes, Moscow and Leningrad.
Farrar, Straus, 1971.

St. George, G.   SIBERIA; THE NEW FRONTIER
Description and history of the industrial cities, the "science" cities,
Lake Baikal, a diamond mine; also helpful tourist information for
those planning a trip to Siberia.
McKay, 1969.

Ukraine and the Baltic States

Allen, W.E.D.   THE UKRAINE, A HISTORY
Russell & Russell, 1963.

Berzins, A.   UNPUNISHED CRIME
Story of the takeover and elimination of Latvia as a nation.
Speller.

Blodnieks, A.   UNDEFEATED NATION
Another book about Latvia.
Speller, 1959.

Gerutis, A., et al   LITHUANIA: SEVEN HUNDRED YEARS
Manyland, 1969.

Von Rauch, G.   THE BALTIC STATES
"The years of independence, 1917-1940," of the three Baltic states,
Estonia, Latvia and Lithuania.
Univ. of California Press, 1974.

"Russia Under Western Eyes"

Beloff, N.   INSIDE THE SOVIET EMPIRE
British journalist describes a car trip and many places closed to visi-
tors.
Times Books, 1980.

Cartier-Bresson, H.   ABOUT RUSSIA
Picture book with text ". . . conveys this vast country today."
Viking, 1974.

Chase, I.   WORLD'S APART
One of Ms. Chase's typically amusing, deft, perceptive guides.
Doubleday, 1972.

Cross, A.   RUSSIA UNDER WESTERN EYES, 1517-1825
An anthology of visitors' descriptions of Russia over three centuries;
interesting to compare with contemporary observers' descriptions.
St. Martin's, 1971.

Feifer, G.   OUR MOTHERLAND AND OTHER
                                       VENTURES IN RUSSIAN REPORTAGE
"Slice of life stories . . . into the real U.S.S.R."
Viking, 1973.

Gambino, T.   NYET: AN AMERICAN ROCK MUSICIAN
                               ENCOUNTERS THE SOVIET UNION
Collective memoir of a jazz/rock ensemble; responses of the people
to their performances and the willingness of Soviet citizens to risk
meeting with the Americans.
Prentice-Hall, 1976.
Kaiser, R.G.   RUSSIA: THE PEOPLE AND THE POWER
"Soviet life and society . . .for a curious amateur" by a Washington
Post correspondent.
Atheneum, 1976.
Kaiser, R.G. and H.J.   RUSSIA FROM THE INSIDE
Photographs accompanied by expert comments as a way of outwit-
ting Russia's determination to present a carefully contrived impres-
sion for tourists.
Dutton, 1980.
Kampen, I.   ARE YOU CARRYING ANY GOLD
                               OR LIVING RELATIVES?
A very "light" narrative of traveling in Russia accompanied by
a Russian-born friend; problems with Intourist (the Soviet travel
agency), small disasters, etc.
Doubleday, 1970.
Kuhn, D. and F.   RUSSIA ON OUR MINDS
Another of the memoirs of travels by Americans in Russia.
Doubleday, 1970.
McDowell, B.   JOURNEY ACROSS RUSSIA:
                               THE SOVIET UNION TODAY
Prepared by the Special Publications Division of the National Geo-
graphic Society.
The Society, 1977.
Martin, J.   WINTER DREAMS; AN AMERICAN IN MOSCOW
Enjoyable reading and good reporting; personal account of a five-
month stay as a visiting professor.
Houghton, 1979.
Salisbury, C.Y.   RUSSIAN DIARY
Mrs. Salisbury writes of her experiences as a "month-long tourist in
Moscow and Leningrad" accompanying her reporter husband; a per-
ceptive account of experiencing Russia as a tourist, and of the con-
fined lives of Russian friends under the political system.
Walker, 1974.
Schecter, L. and J.   AN AMERICAN FAMILY IN MOSCOW
Written jointly by husband, wife, and children.
Little, Brown, 1975.
Schulthess, E. and Salisbury, H.   SOVIET UNION
Photographs with commentary by the noted reporter Harrison Salis-

bury. One reviewer commented: "Probably the most graphic presentation of the Soviet Union . . . done in this country since 1918."
Harper, 1973.

Smith, H.   THE RUSSIANS
A "compendium of his finest reporting . . . polished and amplified . . . (and including) some of the more reflective pieces he never had a chance to write while he was there."
Quadrangle, 1976.

Van Der Post, L.   A VIEW OF ALL THE RUSSIAS
Chronicle of a three-month trip, alone, by plane, train, and ship, from north to south and from west to east. The trip and the writing were commissioned by a travel magazine. The scope and the level of writing make this a unique book.
Morrow, 1964.

Wilson, E.   A WINDOW ON RUSSIA
                        FOR USE OF FOREIGN READERS
Papers written by this noted critic on major Russian writers: Gogol, Pushkin, Chekov, etc., as well as pieces on Alliluyeva (Stalin's daughter), Solzhenitzyn and other aspects of the Soviet Union.
Farrar, Straus, 1972.

Russia Under Russian Eyes

Alliluyeva, S.   TWENTY LETTERS TO A FRIEND
The letters of Stalin's daughter giving her observations of the Soviet system from a unique perspective.
Harper, 1967.

Kuznetsov, E.   PRISON DIARIES
"The latest stunning addition to the most significant genre of contemporary Soviet letters."
Stein & Day, 1975.

Panin, D.   NOTEBOOKS OF SOLOGDIN
An account of thirteen years in Russian prisons and labor camps.
Harcourt, 1976.

Sakharov, A.D.   MY COUNTRY AND THE WORLD
A dissident who believes that detente has only strengthened the Sovient Union and will eventually undermine American democracy and the West.
Knopf, 1975.

Shostakovich, D.   TESTIMONY
Anecdotal and witty memoirs dictated during the four years preceding the death of this prominent Soviet composer. The memoirs were smuggled abroad, and clearly reflect his hatred of the regime under which he lived while pretending to be "a faithful Party member."
Harper, 1979.

Solzhenitsyn, A.   THE GULAG ARCHIPELAGO
His personal experience in Russian labor camps, and those of 227
other survivors of that system.
Harper, 1974.
Vladimir, L.   THE RUSSIANS
The book is written by a defector to the West who had been editor
of a Russian science magazine. "Highly readable and informative."
Praeger, 1968.
Wayne, K.P.   SHURIK; A STORY OF THE
                                      SIEGE OF LENINGRAD
A Russian actress and nurse tells of her experience caring for an or-
phan boy during part of the three-year siege of Leningrad.
Grosset, 1970.

History

Billington, J.H.   THE ICON AND THE AXE
"An interpretive history of Russian culture . . . a most readable sur-
vey of Russian cultural history" through the post-Kruschev era and
the important role of organized religion in Russia's past.
Knopf, 1966.
Daniels, R.V.   RUSSIA
A "remarkably comprehensive survey" for a slim volume.
Prentice-Hall, 1964.
Dmytryshyn, B.   A HISTORY OF RUSSIA
A formal, college-level history.
Prentice-Hall, 1977.
Dukes, P.   A HISTORY OF RUSSIA; MEDIEVAL, MODERN
                                      AND CONTEMPORARY
McGraw-Hill, 1974.
Grey, I.   THE HORIZON HISTORY OF RUSSIA
American Heritage, 1970.
Pipes, R.   RUSSIA UNDER THE OLD REGIME
It is the author's premise that the police state and totalitarian govern-
ment in Russia have their roots "in the very nature of the Russian
state since its inception" rather than in communism alone.
Scribner, 1974.
Riasanovsky, N.V.   A HISTORY OF RUSSIA
Oxford Univ. Press, 1977.
Salisbury, H.E.   THE 900 DAYS: THE SIEGE OF LENINGRAD
Harper, 1969.
Seton-Watson, H.   THE RUSSIAN EMPIRE 1801-1917
The period as it was rather than in terms of what happened after the
abdication of Nicholas II.
Oxford, 1967.

The Czars and the Revolution

Bergamini, J.   THE TRAGIC DYNASTY; A HISTORY
OF THE ROMANOVS
Putnam, 1969.

Carmichael, J.   A SHORT HISTORY
OF THE RUSSIAN REVOLUTION
Basic Books, 1964.

Cowles, V.S.   THE ROMANOVS
Popular history, more concerned with personalities, daily routine, and love affairs of the royal dynasty than straight history—"reads with the compelling excitement of a novel."
Harper, 1971.

Crankshaw, E.   SHADOW OF THE WINTER PALACE
"Russia's drift to revolution, 1825-1917" seen through the lives of its last four czars, and portraits of many other key people.
Viking, 1976.

Dumas, A.   ADVENTURES IN CZARIST RUSSIA
Contemporary memoir of the famous French writer; ". . . pungent and vivid glimpse of a bygone era."
Chilton, 1961.

Hingley, R.   THE TSARS
A visually beautiful book with many illustrations, drawings, and a "collective biography of Russian rulers"—from Ivan IV to Nicholas II. Written for the popular market.
Macmillan, 1968.

Massie, R.K. and S.   NICHOLAS & ALEXANDRA
The last czar and czarina and their dependence upon Rasputin because of their son's tragic illness, which in turn led to disastrous appointments and decisions that helped lead to their own abdication. This is ". . . intimate history at its magnificent best."
Atheneum, 1968.

Palmer, A.   RUSSIA IN WAR AND PEACE
"Places the events of (Tolstoy's) *War and Peace* in their historical context."
Macmillan, 1972.

Pearlstein, E.W., ed.   REVOLUTION IN RUSSIA!
"As reported (at the time) by the New York Tribune and the New York Herald, 1894-1921."
Viking, 1967.

Pearson, M.   SEALED TRAIN
Lenin's return to Russia in 1917—"readers will be fascinated by this well-written unfolding of one of this century's most remarkable historical dramas."
Putnam, 1975.

Troyat, H.   DAILY LIFE IN RUSSIA UNDER THE LAST TSAR
Reprint of the 1962 edition.
Stanford Univ. Press, 1979.

Architecture, Theatre and the Arts

Bank, A.   ·   BYZANTINE ART IN THE
                                        COLLECTION OF SOVIET MUSEUMS
Puts the influence of Byzantine art on Russia in perspective.
Abrams, 1978.

Berton, K.   MOSCOW: AN ARCHITECTURAL HISTORY
"A breezy history of building in Moscow . . ."—one of the few books,
in English, on Russian architecture.
St. Martin's, 1978.

Carmichael, J.   A CULTURAL HISTORY OF RUSSIA
Painting, sculpture, architecture, literature, philosophy, film, ballet,
—an overview with many photographs.
Weybright and Talley, 1968.

Descargues, P.   THE HERMITAGE MUSEUM
Abrams, 1961.

Duncan, D.D.   GREAT TREASURES OF THE KREMLIN
Abrams, 1968.

Jacobson, S.and E., eds.   THE DANCE HORIZONS TRAVEL GUIDE
See entry under France, page 80.
Dance Horizon, 1978.

Kennett, A. and V.   THE PALACES OF LENINGRAD
Putnam, 1973.

Massie, S.   LAND OF THE FIREBIRD:
                                        THE BEAUTY OF OLD RUSSIA
A new book that is excellent pre-travel reading; "a dazzling history
of the now-vanished culture of pre-revolutionary Russia . . . ." See
also this author's (with husband) book *Nicholas and Alexandra,*
listed on page 227.
Simon & Schuster, 1980.

Onassis, J.K., ed.   IN THE RUSSIAN STYLE
A book on Russian art prepared with the assistance of the Metropoli-
tan Museum of Art.
Viking, 1976.

Pokrovskii, B.A.   THE BOLSHOI
"Opera and ballet in the greatest theatre in Russia."
Morrow, 1979.

Voronin, N.N., ed.   PALACES AND CHURCHES
                                        OF THE KREMLIN
Hamlyn, 1965.

Novels

Adler, W.   TRANS-SIBERIAN EXPRESS
  KGB mystery on board a train.
  Putnam, 1977. fc/s77
Aksenov, V.   THE STEEL BIRD, AND OTHER STORIES
  "Contemporary voice from the Soviet Union."
  Ardis, 1979. fc/s79
Bulgakov, M.   BLACK SNOW, A THEATRICAL NOVEL
  Autobiographical novel giving an "inside view of the Soviet theatre."
  Simon & Schuster, 1968. brd/68
Clark, E.   BLACK GAMBIT
  Suspense novel of unofficial steps taken by Washington to reunite a
  Soviet dissident with his wife.
  Morrow, 1978. fc/s78
Garve, A.   THE ASHES OF LODA
  Foreign correspondent gets involved in local intrigue.
  Harper, 1965. fc
Gavin, C.   THE SNOW MOUNTAIN
  Romance and death of the Romanov's eldest daughter.
  Pantheon, 1973. fc
Koestler, A.   DARKNESS AT NOON
  Autobiographical novel of imprisonment of the early Bolsheviks.
  Macmillan, 1941. fc
Krotkov, Y.   THE NOBEL PRIZE
  A novel based on Pasternak's winning of the Nobel prize for his writ-
  ing of *Doctor Zhivago.*
  Simon & Schuster, 1980. brd/80
Maximov, V.   FAREWELL FROM NOWHERE
  Chronicle of a twelve-year old's wandering throughout the Soviet
  Union.
  Doubleday, 1979. brd/80
Maximov, V.   THE SEVEN DAYS OF CREATION
  Three generations of a Russian family from the revolution until today.
  Knopf, 1975. fc
Pasternak, B.   DOCTOR ZHIVAGO
  Chronicle of a doctor-poet during the period of the Russian revolu-
  tion and communist takeover.
  Pantheon, 1958. fc
Romains, J.   THE WORLD IS YOUR ADVENTURE
                                        IN THE NEW DAY
  An Englishman's involvement and experiences in the revolution.
  Knopf, 1942. fc

Salisbury, H.   THE GATES OF HELL
Fictionalized account of Solzhenitsyn's experiences.
Random House, 1975. fc/s76
Solzhenitsyn, A.   THE CANCER WARD
Bantam, 1969. fc
Solzhenitsyn, A.   AUGUST 1914
Russia at the outbreak of WWI.
Farrar, Straus, 1972. fc
Sulzberger, C.   THE TOOTH MERCHANT
A parody of espionage—Stalin, Nasser, Ben-Gurion, Eisenhower are
among the cast of characters.
Quadrangle, 1973. fc
Suslov, I.   HERE'S TO YOUR HEALTH, COMRADE SHIFKIN
A satire on present-day Russia and the efforts of a Jew to climb the
publishing ladder—"... satiric episodes ... the small lies and hy-
pocrisies of every day Moscow life."
Indiana Univ. Press, 1977. brd/77
Thomas, C.   FIREFOX
England, U.S.S.R. and the United States involved in a novel of sus-
pense and intrigue.
Holt, 1977. fc/s77
Trifonov, Y.   THE LONG GOODBYE
Contemporary Russian stories.
Harper, 1978. brd/78
Troyat, H.   BROTHERHOOD OF THE
                                              RED POPPY
1814 love affair of a czar's officer and a French widow which involves
the politics of the period.
Simon & Schuster, 1961.fc
Troyat, H.   THE BARONESS
A sequel to above novel; 1819-1825 in feudal Russia as the Baroness
attempts to improve the life of the serfs.
Simon & Schuster, 1961. fc
Troyat, H.   MY FATHER'S HOUSE
A second family epic; this one begins with the period 1888-1914.
Duell, 1951. fc
Troyat, H.   THE RED AND THE WHITE
A sequel to *My Father's House*; chronicles the effect of the revolu-
tion on the middle class. The trilogy continues with *Strangers on
Earth*, set in Paris (see entry on page 89).
Crowell, 1956. fc
Voinovich, V.   IN PLAIN RUSSIAN
"Ordinary Soviet citizens going about the ordinary business of life."
Farrar, Strauss, 1979.

Voinovich, V.   THE LIFE AND EXTRAORDINARY
                    ADVENTURES OF PRIVATE IVAN CHONKIN
    Life in the Russian military.
    Bantam, 1979.
Waring, M.W.   THE WITNESSES
    Panorama of Russian life from the end of the czarist period through
    the beginnings of revolution in 1917.
    Houghton, 1967. fc
Wingate, J.   RED MUTINY
    Navy story.
    St. Martin's, 1978. fc/s78
Zinoviev, A.   THE YAWNING HEIGHTS
    A satire of socialist achievement in the tradition of Swift and Voltaire.
    The author creates the imaginary country of Ibansk to deliver his
    " . . . tirade in the wilderness."
    Random House, 1979. brd/79

Caucasus

Heaven, C.   HEIR TO KURAGIN
    Romance of an English girl in the U.S.S.R.
    Coward, McCann, 1978. fc/s79

Kiev

Anatoli, A.   BABI YAR
    The killing of Jews and Russians by the Nazis in 1941-43.
    Farrar, Straus, 1970. fc
Malamud, B.   THE FIXER
    This novel won a Pulitzer prize.
    Farrar, Straus, 1966. fc

Leningrad

Bely, A.   PETERSBURG
    Novel of the revolution. Originally published in 1913.
    Indiana Univ. Press, 1978. fc/s78
Butler, G.   THE RED STAIR CASE
    1912, czarist Russia; fact and fiction.
    Coward, McCann, 1979. fc/s79
Dostoevsky, F.   CRIME AND PUNISHMENT
    Dodd. fc
Dostoevsky, F.   THE IDIOT
    Dutton. fc
Elliott, J.   BLOOD ON THE SNOW
    1899-1906; Bloody Sunday.
    St. Martin's, 1977. fc/s77

Goncharov, I.   OBLOMOV
  Novel of a wealthy, fat, lazy Russian in the nineteenth century.
  Macmillan, 1915. fc
Koning, H.   THE PETERSBURG-CANNES EXPRESS
  Turn-of-the-century mystery of two idealistic revolutionaries.
  Harcourt, 1975. fc/s76

Moscow

Francis, D.   TRIAL RUN
  An Englishman sent to Moscow in search of a man; takes place dur-
  ing fictional Olympic games.
  Harper, 1979. brd/79
Gallico, P.   MRS. 'ARRIS GOES TO MOSCOW
  Charwoman's adventure in Moscow.
  Delacorte, 1975. fc
Littell, R.   MOTHER RUSSIA
  "Modern day Russian Don Quixote."
  Harcourt, 1978. fc/s78
Ossorgin, M.   QUIET STREET
  Moscow during WWI and the revolution.
  Dial, 1930.
Pliévier, T.   MOSCOW
  Invasion by Germany in 1941.
  Doubleday, 1954. fc
Rothberg, A.   THE STALKING HORSE
  A story of espionage.
  Sat. Review Press, 1972. fc
Solzhenitsyn, A.   THE FIRST CIRCLE
  A technical institute staffed by political prisoners who are working
  for favored treatment.
  Harper, 1968. fc
Tolstoy, L.   CHILDHOOD, BOYHOOD & YOUTH
  Oxford, 1957.

Rural Settings

Ehrenburg, I.   A CHANGE OF SEASON
  Rural love story.
  Knopf, 1962. fc
Markish, D.   A NEW WORLD FOR SIMON ASHKENAZY
  An incarcerated Jewish family at the end of Stalin's regime.
  Dutton, 1976. fc/s76
Sholokhov, M.   AND QUIET FLOWS THE DON
  Revolution as experienced by the Cossacks; first of several on this

group of Russians, and this area of Russia. Also: *The Don Flows Home to the Sea* (Knopf, 1941), and *Tales of the Don* (Knopf, 1962). Knopf, 1934. fc

Siberia

Dostoevsky, M.   MEMOIRS FROM THE HOUSE
OF THE DEAD
  Oxford, 1965. fc

Rasputin, V.   LIVE AND REMEMBER
  Siberia in 1945.
  Macmillan, 1978. fc/s78

Shalamov, V.   KOLYMA TALES
  Survival of seventeen years as a prisoner in Siberia.
  Norton, 1980. brd/80

Solzhenitsyn, A.   ONE DAY IN THE LIFE
OF IVAN DENISOVICH
  A modern classic by the Soviet dissident on prison life.
  Dutton, 1963. fc

Verne, J.   MICHAEL STROGOFF
  First published in 1876.
  Scribner, 1927.

Vladimov, G.   FAITHFUL RUSLAN
THE STORY OF A GUARD DOG
"A compelling anthropomorphic tale" of the guard dog's bewilderment when turned loose from his concentration camp duties.
Simon & Schuster, 1979. brd/79

Stalingrad (Volgograd)

Pliévier, T.   STALINGRAD
  The Nazi invasion of the city.
  Appleton, 1948. fc

Simonov, K.   DAYS & NIGHTS
  The Nazi invasion of the city.
  Simon & Schuster, 1945. fc

Travel Articles

CAR & DRIVER
  1979   Sep   To Russia with Saab (a tale of proles, pepsis and paranoia, mostly paranoia), M. Knepper - p. 121

234

GEO

1980   Jun   Mullah and the commissar (Soviet Muslims),
             N. Lubin - p. 10

MOTHER EARTH NEWS

1980 Jan-Feb   Travels with Mother (travel tours sponsored by the
               magazine) - p. 98
1979 Mar-Apr   Easter's most elegant eggs (Ukrainian Easter
               eggs) - p. 96

NATIONAL REVIEW

1980   Jan 25   Welcome to Russia, W. Buckley - p. 117
1979   Nov 9   But leave me out (visit to Moscow),
                N. Jernakoff - p. 1422

NEW YORKER

1980   Jun 30   Summer and fall (Part 1), Journal of an American liv-
                ing in Moscow, L. Andrea - p. 72
       Jul 7   Winter and spring (Part 2), Journal of an American
                living in Moscow, L. Andrea - p. 70

N.Y. SUNDAY TIMES TRAVEL SECTION (10)

1979   Mar 18   Pskov: a journey into Russia's past, F. Maclean - p. 1
       May 20   The Black Sea resort of Yalta, a place in the Crimean
                Sea, J. Rippetau - p. 9

READER'S DIGEST

1980   Oct   Russian scenes, Russian voices, G. Feifer - p. 207

ROAD & TRACK

1979   Jul   Driving in Russia (we didn't see any joggers),
             D. Clendenin - p. 70
       Nov   On the road in Latvia, W. Hoyt - p. 134

SATURDAY REVIEW

1979   Jun 23   R & R (rock music) in the U.S.S.R., B. Cohen - p. 28

SMITHSONIAN

1979   Oct   Get the message: U.S.S.R. is a happy medium,
             R. Thurston - p. 150

SOVIET LIFE

Articles for this publication are not listed individually because it is dif-
ficult to determine from the Magazine Index listings, whether the article is aimed at travelers or not. Nevertheless, if your library stocks

the magazine, it is well worth your time to look over current and back issues for articles that may help you plan an itinerary for Russia.

TRAVEL/HOLIDAY
1979   May   Leningrad, C.E. Adelsen and H. Angelo-
                Castrillon - p. 108

VOGUE
1979   Sep   A great Russian poet's guide to a city of mystery,
                Leningrad, J. Brodsky - p. 494

WORKING WOMAN
1980   Jan   Women of Russia, R. Plutzik - p. 6

WORLD PRESS REVIEW (formerly Atlas)
1980   Jul   Surviving in the Soviet Klondike: Russia's "wild east,"
                C. O'Clery - p. 58
1979   Oct   Longest train ride: Trans-Siberian Railroad,
                A. Serra - p. 69

Notes - Spain

1. Abbreviations of reference sources for novels:
   fc - Fiction Catalog, 9th Edition
   fc/s76 (77, etc.) - Supplement to 9th Edition
   fc/8ed - Fiction Catalog, 8th Edition
   brd/78 (79, etc.) - Book Review Digest for the year

2. Standard Series Guidebooks for Spain:
   Blue Guide (Southern Spain)
   Fodor
   Frommer (Lisbon-Madrid-Costa del Sol)
   Frommer $ (Spain-Morocco-Canary Islands)
   Michelin Green Guide
   Michelin Red Guide (Spain and Portugal)
   Nagel (Spain plus Balearics)
   Foreign Area Study

3. See Appendix 1 for more complete data on the above.

4. See Europe, at end of country sections, for additional possible sources of reading and information for Spain.

Spain

INCLUDING: ANDORRA
GIBRALTAR

Background Reading

Ballard, S. and J.   TRAVEL GUIDE TO
                                          THE PARADORS OF SPAIN
   The atmospheric alternative to hotels.
   Ballard's Travel Guides, 1978.
Brenan, G.   THE FACE OF SPAIN
   "A day-to-day account of the author's return to his Andalusian house
   and village after an absence of thirteen years . . ." as well as travels in
   other parts of Spain. Descriptive, and beautifully written.
   Pellegrini, 1951.
Chase, I.   THE VARIED AIRS OF SPRING
   One of several books by Ms. Chase—"anecdotal and informative."
   Spain is part of the itinerary.
   Doubleday, 1969.
Chetwode, P.   TWO MIDDLE-AGED LADIES IN ANDALUSIA
   The "two ladies" are the wife of English poet John Betjemann and
   a Spanish mare. This is a diary of their month-long trip to remote
   areas of Andalusia with details of where they stayed, people they
   met, and the spectacular landscape.
   Transatlantic, 1966.
Clissold, S.   SPAIN
   A profile of Spain—regions, history, political and economic situation,
   everyday life.
   Walker, 1969.

Croft-Cooke, R.   THROUGH SPAIN WITH DON QUIXOTE
A British novelist and poet retraces the route of the Don as a basis
for this travelogue—"vivid and instructive."
Knopf, 1960.

Crow, J.A.   SPAIN: THE ROOT AND THE FLOWER
A history of the civilization of Spain and of the Spanish people.
Harper, 1963.

Deardorff, R.H.   A DAY OUTSIDE THE CITY
Pleasant and interesting day trips using Madrid and Barcelona as base
cities.
Holt, 1968.

Feldkamp, F.   NOT EVERYBODY'S EUROPE
A grand tour of nine unique cities including Granada.
Harper's Magazine Press, 1976.

Hemingway, E.   DEATH IN THE AFTERNOON
The classic book on bullfighting—see also Hemingway novels listed
below.
Scribner, 1933.

MacKendrick, P.L.   THE IBERIAN STONES SPEAK
Archaeology in Spain and Portugal. An introduction to archaeology
and cultural history based on archaeological findings.
Funk & Wagnall, 1969.

Maugham, S.   DON FERNANDO
The noted author intended to write a novel on sixteenth century life
in Spain. Instead, he incorporated his notes and the "results of his
reading and observations (into this) series of informal chapters on a
variety of topics, from Spanish food and wines to El Greco and Cervantes." Intelligence and good writing by one of the best.
Doubleday, 1935.

Michener, J.S.   IBERIA
A travelogue and interpretation of Spanish life, history, politics, mys-
tique, with chapters on bullfighting and on the wildlife preserve, Las
Marismas.
Random House, 1968.

Morris, J.   SPAIN
The "writing of a country's character" by a leading travel genre author. Originally written in 1965; the author revisited the country
and retraced some of the journeys. One reviewer says: "One of the
best descriptive essays on that country every written."
Oxford Univ. Press, 1979.

Morton, H.V.   A STRANGER IN SPAIN
"Cities and their treasures of art and buildings . . . festivals, the wild
remote hills and the warm plains."
Dodd, 1955.

Pritchett, V.S.   THE SPANISH TEMPER
The author "has written what is virtually a pocket analysis of the
Spanish character" with insight and perception.
Greenwood, 1954.

Streeter, E.   ALONG THE RIDGE
See full entry under France on page 79
Harper, 1964.

Tracy, H.   WINTER IN CASTILLE
Travels in Spain—cathedrals, monasteries, other places—by an acerbic
"compassionate satirist . . . (with a) knack for conveying a sense of
place."
Random House, 1974.

Andorra

Deane, S.   THE ROAD TO ANDORRA
An account of a family living in Andorra (with a brief stint in Ibiza).
Vividly written description of the adventures and daily life with
some history of Andorra and Ibiza.
Morrow, 1960.

Balearic Islands

Colas, J.L.   THE BALEARICS: ISLANDS OF ENCHANTMENT
Rand McNally, 1967.

Cox, R., ed.   TRAVELLERS GUIDE TO MAJORCA,
                                MINORCA, IBIZA, AND FORMENTERA
Thornton Cox, 1979.

Basque Country

Moore, C.   FREE SPIRITS OF THE PYRENEES
"A guide to the Basque country."
IPS, 1972.

Morris, J.   PLACES
Literate essays by a leading travel writer—includes an essay on the
Basque country of Spain.
Harcourt, 1972.

Canary Islands

Brander, B.   CANARY ISLANDS
Description, travel and views.
Doubleday, 1967.

Eldridge, P.   TALES OF THE FORTUNATE ISLES
Social life and customs..
T. Yoseloff, 1959.

Walter, R.   CANARY ISLAND ADVENTURE
"A young family's quest for the simple life." Vignettes of a year spent
in the Angostura Valley of the Canaries, with wife and four children.
Dutton, 1956.

Gibraltar

Dennis, P.   GIBRALTAR
David & Charles, 1977.
Stewart, J.D.   GIBRALTAR: THE KEYSTONE
Houghton, 1967.

History

Kamen, H.   A CONCISE HISTORY OF SPAIN
First settlements to Franco.
Scribner, 1974.
McKendrick, M.   HORIZON CONCISE HISTORY OF SPAIN
American Heritage, 1972.
Miller, T.   THE CASTLES AND THE CROWN
"A biography of the monarchs who shaped Spain's destiny."
Coward, McCann, 1963.
O'Callaghan, J.F.   HISTORY OF MEDIEVAL SPAIN
See entry under Portugal, page 200.
Cornell Univ. Press, 1975.
Read, J.   MOORS IN SPAIN AND PORTUGAL
See entry under Portugal, page 200.
Rowman & Littlefield, 1975.
Smith, R.M.   SPAIN; A MODERN HISTORY
From ancient times to present, with major emphasis on period since
·1800.
Univ. of Michigan Press, 1965.

The Spanish Civil War

Brenan, G.   THE SPANISH LABYRINTH
"An account of the social and political background" of the war.
Macmillan, 1943.
Kozantzakis, N.   SPAIN
A journal of two trips to Spain by the author, before and during the
civil war, by one who admired Franco's Spain.
Simon & Schuster, 1963.
Kurzman, D.   MADRID; MIRACLE OF NOVEMBER
"Madrid's epic stand"—reconstruction of events from interviews with
participants.
Putnam, 1980.

Landis, A.H.   THE ABRAHAM LINCOLN BRIGADE
History of Americans in the international brigade that fought during the Spanish Civil War on the side of the Republican Army.
Citadel, 1967.

Orwell, G.   HOMAGE TO CATALONIA
An account of the war by a writer who participated in the fighting.
Harcout, 1952.

Thomas, H.   THE SPANISH CIVIL WAR
A history, from the origins (20's and 30's) to Barcelona's fall in 1939.
Harper, 1961.

Yglesias, J.   THE FRANCO YEARS
Bobbs, 1977.

Novels

Braider, D.   RAGE IN SILENCE
Fictional account of Goya's life.
Putnam, 1969. fc

Cervantes, M. de   DON QUIXOTE DE LA MANCHA
The universal classic, set in sixteenth-century Spain.
Dodd. fc

Condon, R.   THE OLDEST CONFESSION
Art heist by American businessman.
Random House, 1969. fc

Gironella, J.M.   THE CYPRESSES BELIEVE IN GOD
First of a trilogy, by one of Spain's leading writers. This novel takes place in the years before the Civil War, told through the experiences of a middle class family. The second book, *One Million Dead*, is an account of the family during the Spanish Civil War; third (following the Civil War) is *Peace After War*.
Knopf, 1955. fc

Godden, J.   IN THE SUN
A retired English spinster, living on the Spanish coast, is terrorized by her nephew.
Knopf, 1965. fc

Goytisolo, J.   MARKS OF IDENTITY
The narrator, living in France, recalls his life in Spain.
Grove, 1969. fc

Hemingway, H.   FOR WHOM THE BELL TOLLS
The international brigade and the Spanish Civil War.
Scribner, 1940. fc

Hemingway, E.   THE SUN ALSO RISES
Novel of the "lost" generation of the 1920's and a group of Ameri-
cans and Britons who drift between Paris and Spain.
Scribner, 1926.
Herrick, W.   HERMANOS!
An American communist in the Spanish Civil War.
Simon & Schuster, 1969. fc
Murphy, J.   PAY ON THE WAY OUT
Complicated, intricate plot—set mostly in Spain. Concerns double
and triple-crossing and three apparently unconnected murders in
Spain, London and Washington.
Scribner, 1975. fc/s76

Rathbone, J.   ¡CARNIVAL!
BBC film crew working on a documentary in Spain and Portugal be-
come involved in murder and the CIA.
St. Martin's 1976. fc/s77
Wahlöö, P.   A NECESSARY ACTION
Norwegian couple in a grim story of the secret police in Franco's
Spain.
Pantheon, 1969. fc

Andalusia

Alarcón, P.A. de   THE THREE-CORNERED HAT
Folk tale of a miller and his perfect wife; a Spanish classic first pub-
lished in 1874.
Penguin, 1975. fc
Bates, R.   THE OLIVE FIELD
A picture of village life and politics of the 1930's.
Dutton, 1936, 1975. fc
Feibleman, P.S.   THE COLUMBUS TREE
Americans in Spain and a tragic encounter.
Atheneum, 1973. fc
Jiménez, J.R.   PLATERO AND I
Life in a small community, 1907-1910. First published in 1914.
Univ. of Texas Press.
Sprigge, E.   CASTLE IN ANDALUSIA
An English girl married to a Spanish nobleman and the revolution.
Macmillan, 1935.

Balearic Islands

Godwin, G.   THE PERFECTIONISTS
Set on Majorca; a British psychiatrist, his new American wife, and
his illegitimate young son.
Harper, 1970. fc

Basque Country

Herron, S.   THE BIRD IN LAST YEAR'S NEST
The Basque separatist movement.
Evas, 1974. fc

Canary Islands

Cadell, E.   CANARY YELLOW
Young woman's adventures in the CIA.
Morrow, 1965. fc

Carr, P.   THE LION TRIUMPHANT
Historical romance during reign of Elizabeth I; set in England and on
the Islands.
Putnam, 1974. fc

Gibraltar

Masters, J.   THE ROCK
Story of Gibraltar's historic past and present.
Putnam, 1970. fc

Madrid

Del Castillo, M.   THE DISINHERITED
The Spanish Civil War and its effect on a young man from Madrid.
Knopf, 1960. fc

Peréz Galdós, B.   FORTUNATA AND JACINTA
Bourgeois life, 1869-1875; originally published 1886.
Penguin, 1973.

Peréz Galdos, B.   THE SPENDTHRIFTS
Comic novel of a wife who cannot resist spending more money than
she has. First published 1868.
Farrar, Straus, 1952. fc

Sender, R.J.   SEVEN RED SUNDAYS
Madrid and the revolution.
Liveright, 1931.

Malaga

MacInnes, H.   MESSAGE FROM MALAGA
Plot involves a Spanish dancer, the CIA and a Soviet defector.
Harcourt, 1971. fc

Perera, V.   THE CONVERSION
A trip to Spain has profound effect on an American Sephardic Jew
whose family want him to be a rabbi.
Little, Brown, 1970. fc

Seville

Cervantes, M. de   RINCONETE AND CORTADILLO
In *The Portable Cervantes*. Seventeenth-century Seville.
Viking, 1951. fc
Conrad, B.   MATADOR
Seville and bullfighting. Originally published in 1952.
Houghton, 1975. fc

Travel Articles

COSMOPOLITAN
  1980   Sep   The Costa del Sol, K. Olson - p. 160

ESSENCE
  1979   Sep   Si! Spain, J. Harris - p. 36

GLAMOUR
  1980   Oct   The Europe where summer lasts longer - p. 170

GOURMET
  1980   Dec   Gourmet holidays: Extremadura,
                          P.T. Mitchell - p. 36
  1979   Dec   Gourmet holidays: Valencia, P.T. Mitchell - p. 40

HOUSE BEAUTIFUL
  1980   Aug   Six continents in search of a traveler, M. Gough - p. 24
  1979   Aug   Classical Spain, M. Gough - p. 18

N.Y. TIMES SUNDAY TRAVEL SECTION (10)
  1980   Feb 10   A quiet holiday on Minorca, S.H. Anderson - p. 1
            Sep 13   The Moorish flavor of Malaga, M. Carpenter - p. 1
            Sep 28   What's doing in Madrid, J.M. Markham - p. 5
  1979   May 6   The tour bus way of seeing castles in Spain,
                          J. Egan - p. 1
            Jun 17   Galatia, the magnet for pilgrims in Spain,
                          D.M. Alpen - p. 1
            Jul 15   Inns where Spaniards stay in Spain, J. Man and
                          S.R. Markham - p. 1
            Aug 12   The Barcelona of Antonio Gaudí, S. Ferrell - p. 1
            Nov 4   Partaking of a rich past in old Spanish city of Ronda,
                          W. Plummer - p. 1

SAIL
1979   Jun   Looking both ways (Balearic Islands),
                      M.D. Hoyt - p. 78

SATURDAY REVIEW
1980   Feb 2   Fruits of the sea in Barcelona, G. Feifer - p. 42
        Feb 16   A Spanish treasure chest (Santiago), P. Brooks - p. 22

SOUTHERN LIVING
1980   Sep   Looking for Flamenco? (Spanish guided tour) - p. 56

SPORTS ILLUSTRATED
1979   May 14 Olé (bullfighting resurgence in Spain),
                      R.H. Boyle - p. 18

SUNSET
1979   Sep   Sleeping in Spain (central reservation office for
                      paradores) - p. 42

TOWN & COUNTRY
1980   Apr   Golfing in Spain, D. Miller - p. 85
1979   Apr   The Ritz, L. Gwinn - p. 134
1979   Jul   Sybaritic Ibiza, L. Ashland - p. 56

TRAVEL & LEISURE
1980   Jan   A taste of Spain, J. Morgan - p. 56
        Mar   The princely paradors of Spain, H.B. Livesey - p. 121
        Apr   Zaragoza, Spain - B.F. Carruthers - p. 161
        May   Diminutive domains (Andorra), H. Koenig - p. 90
        Dec   Small museums of Madrid, D. Cochrane - p. 20
1979   Feb   Worth a detour—Salamanca, J. Egan - p. 27
        Apr   Resorting to the high life in France and Spain,
                      W.A. Krauss - p. 86
        Aug   The restaurants of Seville, G. Lang - p. 18

TRAVEL/HOLIDAY
1980   Jun   Two faces of Tenerife, T. Bross - p. 39
        Sep   Castles in Spain, B. Matthiessen - p. 66
1979   Nov   Cordoba, I.C. Kuhn - p. 70

VOGUE
1979   Mar   Celebrating sherry in Spain's Jerez de la Frontera,
                      D. Messinesi - p. 26

WORLD PRESS REVIEW (formerly Atlas)
1980   Oct   Living like a gypsy (Spanish gypsies), R. Herren - p. 62

Notes - Sweden

1. Abbreviations of reference sources for novels:
   fc - Fiction Catalog, 9th Edition
   fc/s76 (77, etc.) - Supplement to 9th Edition
   fc/8ed - Fiction Catalog, 8th Edition
   brd/78 (79, etc.) - Book Review Digest for the year

2. Standard Series Guidebooks for Sweden:
   Fodor (Scandinavia)
   Frommer $ (Scandinavia)
   Nagel

3. See Appendix 1 for more complete data on the above.

4. See Europe, at end of country sections, and items with an asterisk under Denmark, for additional possible sources of reading and information for Sweden.

Sweden

Background Reading

Deardorff, R.A.   A DAY OUTSIDE THE CITY
Interesting and pleasant day trips with Stockholm as a base city.
Holt, 1968.

Foote, P.G. and Wilson, D.M.   THE VIKING ACHIEVEMENT
"A comprehensive survey of the society and culture of early medieval Scandinavia."
Praeger, 1970.

Huntford, R.   THE NEW TOTALITARIANS
This book is in the "de-bunking" tradition and presents a picture of Sweden that contradicts the usual praise it receives for its social achievements; it presents the country as "totally controlled by a bureaucracy which . . . discourages all signs of individuality."
Stein & Day, 1972.

Källberg, S.   OFF THE MIDDLE WAY
"Report from a Swedish village"—the lives of twelve ordinary Swedes. ("Middle Way" refers to Marquis Childs' book of the 30's which extolled the Swedish economic system.)
Pantheon, 1972.

Lorénzen, L.   OF SWEDISH WAYS
Written by a teacher of Swedish at the University of Minnesota. The book is a "charming account of Swedish customs and traditions"—handicrafts, myths and legends, drinking and eating.
Dillon, 1964.

Lottman, H.   DETOURS FROM THE GRAND TOUR
"Off-beat, overlooked, and unexpected Europe"—travel writing that
includes material on the city of Stockholm.
Prentice-Hall, 1970.

Magnusson, M.   VIKINGS!
Based on ten-part public television series; Viking culture, religion,
mythology, literature, and a reconstruction of origins.
Dutton, 1980.

Moberg, V.   A HISTORY OF THE SWEDISH PEOPLE
                      FROM RENAISSANCE TO REVOLUTION
A popular history that reconstructs daily life of the people. See also
two novels by the same author, listed below, the first of which deals
with the great emigration of Swedes in the nineteenth century.
Pantheon, 1973.

Roberts, M.   THE EARLY VASAS
A history of Sweden during the period 1523-1611 with the first
Vasa king installed, who was founder of the modern Swedish state.
Cambridge Univ. Press, 1968.

Sansom, W.   THE ICICLE AND THE SUN
Four essays on Scandinavia by a gifted travel writer. First published
in 1959.
Greenwood, 1976.

Scott, F.D.   SWEDEN: THE NATION'S HISTORY
"A most readable . . . thorough account of the strangely shifting destiny" of Sweden—primarily concerns eighteenth and nineteenth century Sweden.
Univ. of Minnesota Press, 1977.

Simpson, C.   THE VIKING WORLD
". . . an authentic and vivid picture of life in Viking times."
St. Martin's, 1980.

Streeter, E.   SKOAL SCANDINAVIA
Perceptive and pleasant account of the author's trip by car through
Scandinavia with his wife and another couple.
Harper, 1952.

Novels

Barroll, C.   SEASON OF THE HEART
A love story set in fifteenth century Sweden and an accurate picture
of the life of that period.
Scribner, 1976. fc/s77

Bjorn, T.F. PAPA'S WIFE
An autobiographical novel that begins in Swedish Lapland and ends
in New England. The author's father marries their housemaid and
the family emigrates to America in the early 1900's; a story of family life. (The sequel, *Papa's Daughter*, goes on with their life in America, and the daughter's yearnings to be a writer.)
Rinehart, 1955. fc

Budd, L. APRIL SNOW
A peasant woman's life in the nineteenth century.
Lippincott, 1951. fc/8ed

Eden, D. WAITING FOR WILLA
A spy mystery involving an English author in Stockholm.
Coward, McCann, 1970. fc

Gardner, J. FREDDY'S BOOK
Two stories. An American is invited to visit a renowned Swedish re-
cluse and a novel turns into the re-telling of King Gustav-Vasa and
the liberation of Sweden from the Hanseatic League.
Knopf, 1980. brd/80

Lagerkvist, P. THE ETERNAL SMILE
A collection of stories that won a Nobel prize in 1951.
Random House, 1954. fc

Lagerlöf, S. GÖSTA BERLING'S SAGA
Rural setting; adventures of a young man who eventually marries
and settles down.
American-Scandinavian Foundation, 1918. fc

Lagerlöf, S. THE GENERAL'S RING
Charles XII's ring brings disaster to three generations of a family; a
good eighteenth century story.
Doubleday, 1928. fc

Moberg, V. THE EMIGRANTS
Emigration of Swedish farmers and peasants to America in the 1850's.
Simon & Schuster, 1951. fc

Moberg, V. A TIME ON EARTH
A transplanted Swede in California (for over forty years) reflects on
his life and his early days in Sweden.
Simon & Schuster, 1965. fc

Sjöwall, M. and Wahlöö, P. ROSEANNA
A murder mystery set in Lake Vatern, and leading to Nebraska. This
and following several books listed are all basically murder mysteries
written by a husband and wife team. Their books have been very fa-
vorably reviewed as being much more than simply stories of murder
and police investigations; they are well written, perceptive, probing
social commentary. Since there is a dearth of novels set in contemporary Sweden, I have listed the entire series of Sjöwall-Wahlöö myster-

ies and perhaps at least one or two of them will be in your library.
Pantheon, 1967. fc

Sjöwall, M. and Wahlöö, P.   THE MAN ON THE BALCONY
Murder of a child in Stockholm.
Pantheon, 1968. fc

Sjöwall, M. and Wahlöö, P.   THE FIRE ENGINE THAT DISAPPEARED
Suicide and a fire leads to a trail all over Europe.
Pantheon, 1970. fc

Sjöwall, M. and Wahlöö, P.   THE LAUGHING POLICEMAN
Mass murder on a bus.
. Pantheon, 1970. fc

Sjöwall, M. and Wahlöö, P.   MURDER AT THE SAVOY
Murder in a hotel in Malmo (the route to the ferry to Denmark).
Pantheon, 1971. fc

Sjöwall, M. and Wahlöö, P.   THE ABOMINABLE MAN
Murder of a policeman in a hospital room in Stockholm.
Pantheon, 1972. fc

Sjöwall, M. and Wahlöö, P.   THE LOCKED ROOM
Suicide in a locked room, with no weapon.
Pantheon, 1973. fc

Sjöwall, M. and Wahlöö, P.   THE COP KILLER
Murder of a divorced woman.
Pantheon, 1975. fc/s76

Sjöwall, M. and Wahlöö, P.   THE TERRORISTS
Involves the visit of a reactionary American senator and terrorist ac-
tivities. This is also the last of the writing team's mysteries.
Pantheon, 1976. fc/s76

Strindberg, A.   THE SCAPEGOAT
Lawyer in a small village. Originally published in 1906.
Eriksson, 1967. fc

Strindberg, A.   THE NATIVES OF HEMSÖ
Nineteenth century rural life; a serious work by one of Sweden's
classic writers published originally in 1887.
Eriksson, 1965. fc

Sundman, P.O.   THE FLIGHT OF THE EAGLE
Fictitious account of a true story. Three men leave Spitsbergen in 1897
in a balloon, to reach the Arctic. The balloon falls onto White Island
after sixty-five hours, and the story is reconstructed through records
recovered in 1930.
Pantheon, 1970. fc

Wallace, I.   THE PRIZE
Behind the scenes in Stockholm during the Nobel prize preliminaries
and ceremonies.
Simon & Schuster, 1962. fc

Travel Articles

BACKPACKER
1979 Jun-Jul   Sweden's royal route, W.E. Reifsnyder - p. 52

BLAIR & KETCHUM'S COUNTRY JOURNAL
1979 Jul   Scurrying through the Skerries, D. Rath - p. 30

CRUISING WORLD
1980 Oct   Exploring Scandinavia's heartland,
              J.E. McKelvey, Jr. - p. 134

CUISINE
1980 Nov   Scandinavia: Sweden's specialties (cheese),
              B.J. Ojakaugas - p. 14

ESSENCE
1980 Nov   Keeping the faith in Sweden (a black writer living in
              Sweden), N. Grimes - p. 92

GOURMET
1979 Sep   To and through Sweden's Varmland,
              L. Langseth-Christensen - p. 36

N.Y. SUNDAY TIMES TRAVEL SECTION (10)
1980 Apr 13   What's doing in Stockholm, J. Norquist - p. 17
      Jul 20   Sweden's unsullied Vaxholm, J. Vinocur - p. 1

TOWN & COUNTRY
1979 Apr   Grand Hotel, L. Gwinn - p. 132

TRAVEL & LEISURE
1979 Mar   A warm time in the Old Town tonight (Stockholm's
              historic area), D. Butwin - p. 102

YACHTING
1979 Oct   Sweden: a land for cruising, M. Lostrom - p. 62

Notes - Switzerland and Liechtenstein

1. Abbreviations of reference sources for novels:
   fc - Fiction Catalog, 9th Edition
   fc/s76 (77, etc.) - Supplement to 9th Edition
   fc/8ed - Fiction Catalog, 8th Edition
   brd/78 (79, etc.) - Book Review Digest for the year

2. Standard Series Guidebooks for Switzerland:
     Blue Guides (Lucerne, Bernese Oberland)
     Fodor
     Michelin Green Guide

3. See Appendix 1 for more complete data on the above.

4. See Europe, at end of country sections, for additional possible sources of reading and information for Switzerland and Liechtenstein.

Switzerland

INCLUDING: LIECHTENSTEIN

Background Reading

Bonjour, E.   A SHORT HISTORY OF SWITZERLAND
  Oxford, 1952.
Brody, E.   THE MUSIC GUIDE TO BELGIUM, LUXEMBOURG,
                    HOLLAND AND SWITZERLAND
  See entry under Belgium on page 11.
  Dodd, 1977.
Bunting, J.   SWITZERLAND INCLUDING LIECHTENSTEIN
  Hastings House, 1973.
Clark, R.W.   THE ALPS
  Knopf, 1973.
Cole, R. and James, T.   EUROPE: A SECOND TIME AROUND
  "An informal guide to selected places you may have missed on your
  first trip"—off-the-beaten track places to visit in Switzerland.
  Funk & Wagnall, 1971.
Deardorff, R.H.   A DAY OUTSIDE THE CITY
  Interesting and pleasant day trips with Geneva or Zurich as a base.
  Holt, 1968.
Hillaby, J.   A WALK THROUGH EUROPE
  See full entry under Belgium on page 11.
  Houghton, 1972.
Hughes, C.   SWITZERLAND
  Comprehensive and definitive—" . . . a window onto Swiss life."
  Praeger, 1975.

253

Kranz, W.   LIECHTENSTEIN
   Photographs and text.
   Hubert Gassner, 1977.

Lunn, Sr. A.H.M.   THE SWISS AND THEIR MOUNTAINS
   "A study of the influence of mountains on man."
   Rand McNally, 1963.

Maeder, H., ed.   THE MOUNTAINS OF SWITZERLAND:
                    THE ADVENTURE OF THE HIGH ALPS
   A book about "the mountain experience, what it is and what its satis-
   factions are" and of mountain climbing, with photographs.
   Allen & Unwin, 1968.

Martin, L.   SWITZERLAND; AN UNCOMMON GUIDE
   "Uncommon in its pleasant discursiveness"—it describes principal
   cities, towns and areas worth seeing by travelers, and it also includes
   practical travel information.
   McGraw-Hill, 1965.

Raton, P.   LIECHTENSTEIN
   "History and institutions of the principality."
   Liechtenstein-Verlag, 1970.

Sauter, M.R.   SWITZERLAND FROM EARLIEST TIMES
                          TO THE ROMAN CONQUEST
   Written by the archaeologist for the canton and city of Geneva; for
   travelers with an interest in archaeology and antiquities.
   Westview Press, 1976.

Sorrell, W.   THE SWISS: A CULTURAL PANORAMA
                              OF SWITZERLAND
   Cultural history, ". . . well written and easy to read." Achievements
   in intellectual and cultural areas from theologians to painters.
   Bobbs, 1972.

Steinberg, J.   WHY SWITZERLAND?
   The author is a lecturer in history at Cambridge University, and is
   married to a member of a Swiss-German family. It is his premise that
   Switzerland is unique, much can be learned from its institutions, and
   that "democracy rests ultimately on the community level." An enthusiastic and knowledgeable account of the Swiss success story.
   Cambridge Univ. Press, 1976.

Sutton, H.   FOOTLOOSE IN SWITZERLAND
   An informal guidebook by a leading travel reporter. "The author is a
   pleasant, witty . . . and knowledgeable traveling companion."
   Rinehart, 1952.

Thürer, G.   FREE AND SWISS; THE STORY OF SWITZERLAND
   Univ. of Miami Press, 1971.

Zellers, M.   THE INN WAY . . . SWITZERLAND
   Swiss inns, with line drawings and enticing descriptions; guidelines

for choosing those that will fit in with your tour plans, and local information on festivals, etc.
Berkshire Traveller Press, 1977.

Ziegler, J.   SWITZERLAND, THE AWFUL TRUTH
In this polemic, Switzerland is the "fence" of world imperialism; highly critical view of what seems to most of us, a contemporary utopia.
Harper, 1979.

Novels

Ambler, E.   THE INTERCOM CONSPIRACY
Ingenious novel of espionage, set in Geneva.
Atheneum, 1969. fc

Bryher, W.   ROMAN WALL
Story of third century Roman city Orba, now part of Switzerland.
Pantheon, 1954. fc

Cronin, A.J.   A POCKETFUL OF RYE
A British doctor in Switzerland is reunited with his lover and their son.
Little, Brown, 1969. fc

Daudet, A.   TARTARIN ON THE ALPS
In *Tartarin of Tarascon;* a nineteenth-century novel of climbing the Alps. First published in 1885.
Dutton, 1954. fc

Davies, R.   THE MANTICORE
Set in Zurich; a Canadian lawyer in the Jung Institute for analysis.
Viking, 1972. fc

Duerrenmatt, F.   THE PLEDGE
A murder mystery that highlights the role mere chance plays in helping or hindering police work.
Knopf, 1959. fc

Edwards, A.   THE SURVIVORS
A woman in a small town in Switzerland trying to forget her past.
Holt, 1968. fc

Fleming, I.   ON HER MAJESTY'S SECRET SERVICE
James Bond on the ski trails.
New American Library, 1963. fc

Frisch, M.   MAN IN THE HOLOCENE
Profound novel of a man living alone in a mountain valley in the canton of Ticino, and under threat from rockslides and avalanches.
Harcourt, 1980. brd/80

Gallico, P.   LUDMILA
In *Three Legends: The Snow Goose, The Small Miracle, Ludmila.* Set
in Liechtenstein; story of a cow who wants to be beautiful.
Doubleday, 1966. fc

Gilman, D.   A PALM FOR MRS. POLLIFAX
Espionage, with the ubiquitous Mrs. Pollifax as amateur sleuth.
Doubleday, 1973. fc

Greene, G.   DOCTOR FISCHER OF GENEVA
A translator in a chocolate factory; serious.
Simon & Schuster, 1980. brd/80

James, H.   DAISY MILLER
An American girl in Vevey; first published in 1878.
Harper, 1975. fc

Kirst, H.   THE NIGHTS OF THE LONG KNIVES
Story of a murder investigation set in Lugano.
Coward, McCann, 1976. fc/s77.

Koestler, A.   THE CALL GIRLS
Intellectual prostitutes at a symposium in Switzerland.
Random House, 1973. fc

MacInnes, H.   PRAY FOR A BRAVE HEART
Story of American counter-intelligence.
Harcourt, 1955. fc/8ed

Mackenzie, D.   SLEEP IS FOR THE RICH
Jewel robbery caper—"...a most interesting tale of a foolproof
plan that is beset at every turn by unpredictables."
Houghton, 1971. brd/71

Silone, I.   THE FOX AND THE CAMELLIAS
Set on a Swiss farm near Brissago; story of anti-fascist underground.
Harper, 1961. fc

Solzhenitsyn, A.   LENIN IN ZURICH
Fictional account of Lenin, and his exile in Switzerland during WWI
until his departure in 1917 for Russia.
Farrar, Straus, 1976. fc/s76

Spark, M.   NOT TO DISTURB
Set in Geneva; witty comedy about the aristocracy seen through the
eyes of the servants.
Viking, 1972. fc

Stead, C.   THE LITTLE HOTEL
Story set in a Montreux pension hotel in the late 1940's.
Holt, 1973. fc/s76

Stewart, F.M.   THE METHUSELAH ENZYME
Novel of suspense; three couples at a gerontology clinic and seeking
regained youth through the Methuselah enzyme.
Arbor House, 1970. fc

Troyat, H.   THE MOUNTAIN
   Rescue in the Alps that reveals the character of two brothers.
   Simon & Schuster, 1953. fc
Ullman, J.R.   THE WHITE TOWER
   Adventure story set in the Alps; this was a best seller in its day.
   Lippincott, 1945. fc
Waller, L.   THE SWISS ACCOUNT
   Set in Basel; story of power struggle in the Swiss banks.
   Doubleday, 1976. fc/s76

Travel Articles

APARTMENT LIFE
   1980 Jun   Switzerland: feast on the Alps and taste five more
                    countries, J. Newman - p. 24

BACKPACKER
   1979 Feb-Mar   Skiing the haute route, D. Ford - p. 48

BETTER HOMES & GARDENS
   1980 Nov   Family skiing in Switzerland - p. 22

COUNTRY GENTLEMAN
   1980 Winter   Alpenfest, A. Parker - p. 42

CUISINE
   1980 Nov   The day of the onion (Bern onion festival),
                    E. Sheldon - p. 52

DANCE MAGAZINE
   1980 May   Fribourg, Switzerland: folk dance to try, educate and
                    entertain, D. Sanders - p. 124

ESQUIRE
   1980 Feb   Lunch in the Alps, T. Theodoracopulus - p. 95

GOURMET
   1979 Mar   Regensberg—a Swiss surprise, J. Wechsberg - p. 30

HOUSE & GARDEN
   1980 Dec   Tennis and ski escapes - p. 46

LADIES' HOME JOURNAL
 1980   Dec   The non-skiing ski vacation: high season at St. Moritz,
                 D. de Dubovay - p. S1

MADEMOISELLE
 1980   Oct   Grab your bags and

NEW YORKER
 1980   Dec 15   A reporter in Europe, Zurich, J. Kramer - p. 118
        Dec 29   Rapido (travel by train from Switzerland to Italy),
                 B. Roueche - p. 45

N.Y. TIMES SUNDAY TRAVEL SECTION (10)
 1980   Mar 9   What's doing in Bern, P. Hofmann - p. 13
        Aug 31 New Swiss tunnel cuts driving time - p. 8
        Dec 14 What's doing in St. Moritz, P. Hofmann - p. 7
 1979   Apr 8   Into the Alps on the new Heidi trail, A. Levy - p. 1
        May 13 What's doing in Geneva, P. Lewis - p. 11

READER'S DIGEST
 1980   Apr   Switzerland: safest, smoothest-running country on
                 earth, C. Lucas - p. 185

SATURDAY EVENING POST
 1979   Mar   Swiss cheesemaking: the eyes have it, F. Geiser - p. 122

SATURDAY REVIEW
 1979   Feb   Getting high on an Alp; the Trotte, near Lucerne,
                 M. and F. Morton - p. 45

SKIING
 1980   Spring   Think sommer-ski, J.W. Bradshaw - p. 96
 1979   Sep   Ski the Alps (Switzerland and Liechtenstein),
                 M. and T. Grimm - p. 14
        Dec   Small, special Andermatt, T. Veun - p. 154

SUNSET
 1979   Nov   Out-of-the-way Swiss skiing (Andermatt, Notschen),
                 p. 30

TOWN & COUNTRY
 1979   Apr   The prince and princess of Liechtenstein, P. Dragadze
                 and S. Aarvas - p. 98
        Apr   Switzerland: land for all seasons, A. Rand - p. 73

TRAVEL & LEISURE

TRAVEL/HOLIDAY

VOGUE

Notes - Wales

1. Abbreviations of reference sources for novels:
   fc - Fiction Catalog, 9th Edition
   fc/s76 (77, etc.) - Supplement to 9th Edition
   fc/8ed - Fiction Catalog, 8th Edition
   brd/78 (79, etc.) - Book Review Digest for the year

2. Standard Series Guidebooks for Wales:
   Blue Guide
   Guides to Great Britain (under England)

3. See Appendix 1 for more complete data on the above.

4. See Europe, at end of country sections, and items with an asterisk under England, for additional possible sources of reading and information for Wales.

Wales

Background Reading

Brody, E.   MUSIC GUIDE TO GREAT BRITAIN;
ENGLAND, SCOTLAND, WALES, IRELAND
   See full annotation for this series under Austria (Brody), page 1.
   Dodd, 1975.

Fellows, A.   ENGLAND AND WALES,
A TRAVELLER'S COMPANION
   See full entry under England, page 33.
   Oxford, Clarendon, 1964.

Fishlock, T.   WALES AND THE WELSH
   Cassell, 1972.

Hilling, J.B.   HISTORIC ARCHITECTURE OF WALES
   Personal survey by an architect, of the architecture of Wales from
early times to the present—". . . from fortresses to religious buildings
to country houses . . . an excellently designed book for anyone touring Wales and interested" in architecture.
   Verry, 1976.

Jones, F.   THE PRINCES AND PRINCIPALITY OF WALES
   Univ. of Wales Press, 1969.

Jones, R., ed.   ANATOMY OF WALES
   Geography, history, society, religion, politics, language, literature,
music, economy and industry—each written by a specialist in his
field and in Wales.
   Gwerin, 1972.

Lockley, R.M.   WALES
A Batsford guide—"takes the form of seventeen tours, the reader
may be imagined to be making . . . to places the author feels are
worth seeing." There is also an introductory essay that "places Wales
in context of time and race."
Hastings House, 1966.

Lofthouse, J.   NORTH WALES FOR THE COUNTRYGOER
Hale, 1970.

Morris, J.   PLACES
Literary essays by a leading travel genre writer that includes material
on Wales.
Harcourt, 1972.

Morris, R.   CATHEDRALS AND ABBEYS OF
                                                 ENGLAND AND WALES
See full entry under England, on page 44.
Norton, 1979.

Reid, A.   THE CASTLES OF WALES: CASTELLU CYMRU
IPS, 1974.

Rhys, Sir. J.   THE WELSH PEOPLE
"Origin, history and laws, language, literature and characteristics."
Haskell, 1969.

Styles, S.   WELSH WALKS AND LEGENDS
J. Jones, 1972.

Williams, G.   THE LAND REMEMBERS; A VIEW OF WALES
Faber, 1977.

Williams, G.   RELIGION, LANGUAGE AND
                                        AND NATIONALITY IN WALES
Historical essays by an outstanding authority—" . . . provides the es-
sential background to understanding modern Welsh nationalism."
Univ. of Wales Press, 1979.

Novels

Aldridge, J.   THE MARVELOUS MONGOLIAN
A "child's book for adults"—a Mongolian stallion captured and sent
to Wales for breeding meets a Shetland mare and they try escape.
Little, Brown, 1974. fc

Bainbridge, B.   ANOTHER PART OF THE WOOD
"Focuses on the relationships between people who are vacationing at
a camp . . . in Wales"; revised version of novel published in 1968.
Braziller, 1980. brd/80

Cordell, A.   THE RAPE OF THE FAIR COUNTRY
"Family chronicle set in Wales of the 1830's" and a brutal story of
ironworkers' attempts to unionize. Originally published in 1959.
Doubleday, 1975. fc

Cordell, A.   ROBE OF HONOUR
A sequel to *The Rape of the Fair Country.*
Doubleday, 1960. fc

Cronin, A.J.   THE CITADEL
Career of a young doctor in a Welsh mining town who becomes dis-
illusioned and moves on to London, with unhappy consequences.
Little, Brown, 1937. fc

Delderfield, R.F.   CHARLIE, COME HOME
Suspense tale in Welsh town, 1929.
Simon & Schuster, 1976. fc/s76

Delving, M.   DIE LIKE A MAN
Suspense story; American antiques dealer in Wales.
Scribner, 1920. fc

Graham, W.   WOMAN IN THE MIRROR
Twentieth-century mystery based on earlier book (1938) by author.
Doubleday, 1975. fc/s76

Hanley, J.   A KINGDOM
Two sisters: one leaves to marry, one stays with father on farm—are
reunited at father's death.
Horizon, 1978. brd/79

Hanley, J.   THE WELSH SONATA
Small town tramp disappears; medley of reactions. (First published
in England twenty years ago.)
Horizon, 1978. brd/79

Howatch, S.   THE DEVIL ON LAMMAS NIGHT
Satanic mystery in modern day South Wales.
Stein & Day, 1972. fc

Hubbard, P.M.   THE DANCING MAN
Mystery involving archaeologist victim.
Atheneum, 1971. fc

Hughes, J.L.   BEFORE THE CRYING ENDS
Welsh mining town, Pontypridd.
Braziller, 1977. brd/78

Llewellyn, R.   GREEN, GREEN, MY VALLEY NOW
Wealthy man returns to Wales and gets involved with IRA plot.
Doubleday, 1975. fc/s76

Llewellyn, R.   HOW GREEN WAS MY VALLEY
Coal mining lays waste the "green valley"—story of a memorable
family.
Macmillan, 1940. fc

Martin, G.   PASSAGE OF TIME
   A marriage disintegrates.
   Scribner, 1978. fc/s79
Melville, J.   NUN'S CASTLE
   Twentieth-century gothic mystery and romance.
   Fawcett, 1975. fc
Norris, L.   SLIDING
   Short stories of the Welsh countryside, pre-WWII days.
   Scribner, 1976. brd/78
Peters, E.   CITY OF GOLD AND SHADOWS
   Suspense—Welsh border setting, and archaeological digs.
   Morrow, 1974. fc
Powell, A.   THE VALLEY OF BONES
   In *A Dance to the Music of Time: Third Movement;* Welsh infrantry-
   man in Wales, military life away from the war front.
   Little, Brown, 1971. fc
Rees, B.   PROPHET OF THE WIND
   Rural mystery, 1937.
   Harcourt, 1973. fc
Roberts, D.J.   KINSMEN OF THE GRAIL
   Twelfth century; quest for the Holy Grail.
   Little, Brown, 1963. fc
Rofheart, M.   GLENDOWER COUNTRY
   Fourteenth-century reigns of Richard II and Henry IV, Chaucer,
   his wife, etc.
   Putnam, 1973. fc
Rubens, B.   I SENT A LETTER TO MY LOVE
   Rural coastal setting "tour de force."
   St. Martin's, 1978. fc/s78
Smollett, T.   THE EXPEDITION OF HUMPHREY CLINKER
   Dickenesque plot; first published in 1771.
   Dutton. fc
Stafford, C.   THE TEVILLE OBSESSION
   Nineteenth-century gothic.
   Simon & Schuster, 1978. fc/s78
Stewart, M.   THE CRYSTAL CAVE
   Merlin, fifth century.
   Morrow, 1970. fc
Stubbs, J.   AN UNKNOWN WELSHMAN
   Live of Henry VII, fifteenth century.
   Stein & Day, 1972. fc
Thomas, D.   REBECCA'S DAUGHTERS
   1840's; rural revolt.
   Little, Brown, 1966. fc

Wain, J.A.   A WINTER IN THE HILLS
University professor visiting in Wales (with hopes of going to Sweden
to study blonds!) but suspense and surprises change his plans.
Viking, 1970. fc

Travel Articles

BACKPACKER
1979 Aug-Sep Walking in Wales (trails to take), D. Wickers - p. 28

BETTER HOMES & GARDENS
1979 Aug   Touring Wales: a fascinating London side trip - p. 24

N.Y. SUNDAY TIMES TRAVEL SECTION (10)
1980 Apr 20 A country home for Monarchs, S. Carr - p. 1
      Apr 20 Descent to history at a mine in Wales, J.E. Mann - p. 6
1979 May 13 Seeing Wales by pony, R.J. Walton - p. 3
      Sep 9   A village built just to amuse, S. and M. Sawyer - p. 1

SOUTHERN LIVING
1980 Aug   Across Wales by bus (south to north service) - p. 22

TRAVEL & LEISURE
1980 May   Portmeiron, E. Morris - p. 73

TRAVEL/HOLIDAY
1980 Apr   In July, Wales goes for a song (Eisteddfod "Olympics"
                  for choral and folk music and dance),
                  E. Antrobus - p. 110
      May   Portmeiron, Wales, F.E. Heard - p. 4
1979 Apr   Exploring the back roads: North Wales,
                  B. Dunne - p. 79

Notes - *Yugoslavia and Albania*

1. Abbreviations of reference sources for novels:
   fc - Fiction Catalog, 9th Edition
   fc/s76 (77, etc.) - Supplement to 9th Edition
   fc/8ed - Fiction Catalog, 8th Edition
   brd/78 (79, etc.) - Book Review Digest for the year

2. Standard Series Guidebooks for Yugoslavia
   and Albania:
     Blue Guide
     Fodor
     Nagel
     Country Study (Yugoslavia)
     Foreign Area Study (Albania)

3. See Appendix 1 for more complete data on the
   above.

4. See Europe, at end of country sections, for additional possible sources of reading and information
   for Yugoslavia and Albania.

Yugoslavia

INCLUDING: ALBANIA

Background Reading

Adamic, L.   **MY NATIVE LAND**
    Portraits and sketches of Serbs, Slovenes and Croats and the under-
    ground struggle in 1943 of the Partisans.
    Harper, 1943.

Ardagh, J.   **A TALE OF FIVE CITIES; LIFE IN EUROPE TODAY**
    See entry under France on page 77.
    Harper, 1980.

Chase, I.   **FRESH FROM THE LAUNDRY**
    See entry under Bulgaria on page 17.
    Doubleday, 1967.

Clissold, S., ed.   **A SHORT HISTORY OF YUGOSLAVIA**
                               FROM EARLY TIMES TO 1966
    Cambridge Univ. Press, 1966.

Cuddon, J.A.   **THE COMPANION GUIDE TO JUGOSLAVIA**
    Anecdotal, narrative travel guide—"... covers almost all subjects
    that the ordinary traveler to this beautiful country needs to know
    about." A first-rate guide that fills a gap, since there are very few
    guides for this varied country.
    Harper, 1968.

Dedijer, V. and others   **HISTORY OF YUGOSLAVIA**
    This is a "chronological outline of the social, economic, political and
    intellectual development of the various Yugoslav nationalities."
    McGraw-Hill, 1974.

Dedijer, V.   THE BELOVED LAND
Written by an associate of Tito and other revolutionists who set up
the communist state in Yugoslavia. A very personal book—". . . life
in a backward and intolerant country" traced through the career of
the author's great-grandfather, to the end of WWII.
Simon & Schuster, 1961.

Doder, D.   THE YUGOSLAVS
An emigrant from Yugoslavia returns twenty years later as bureau
chief for the Washington Post. Description of the history, culture
and ideology, with profiles of Tito and Djilas. A personal, panoramic
survey by a sympathetic and skilled observer.
Random House, 1978.

Durrell, L.   SPIRIT OF PLACE
See entry under France on page 77—includes material on Yugoslavia.
Dutton, 1969.

Edwards, L.F.   THE YUGOSLAV COAST
Hastings House, 1974.

Feldkamp, F.   NOT EVERYBODY'S EUROPE
A grand tour of nine unique cities including Dubrovnik.
Harper's Magazine Press, 1976.

Heppell, M. and Singleton, F.   YUGOSLAVIA
"An outline history of the six Balkan countries which comprise to-
day's Federal People's Republic of Yugoslavia."
Praeger, 1961.

Kimbrough, E.   WATER, WATER EVERYWHERE
Details ". . . a six weeks' tour of Greece with homeward bound stop-
overs in Yugoslavia and England."
Harper, 1956.

Kindersley, A.   THE MOUNTAINS OF SERBIA
"Travels through Yugoslavia."A very personal, sympathetic and perceptive account of a series of journeys taken in 1964 and 1967, written by the wife of a British diplomat. "Art and architecture of religious buildings along with an account of succeeding waves of conquer-
ors who tried to destroy them."
John Murray, 1976.

Lasic-Vasojevic, M.M.   ENEMIES ON ALL SIDES:
                                               THE FALL OF YUGOSLAVIA
The author fought with the nationalist forces of the Serbian people
in WWII, and feels the Partisans, under Tito, are as evil as the Nazis
or Croatians. Written from an anti-communist viewpoint.
North American Int., 1976.

Logoreci, A.   THE ALBANIANS: EUROPE'S
                                               FORGOTTEN SURVIVORS
Westview, 1978.

Marmullaku, R.   ALBANIA AND THE ALBANIANS: A HISTORY
    C. Hurst, 1975.
Myrdal, J.   ALBANIA DEFIANT
    Description and background.
    Monthly Review, 1976.
Perl, L.   FOODS AND FESTIVALS OF THE DANUBE LANDS
    World, 1969.
Perl, L.   YUGOSLAVIA, ROMANIA, BULGARIA
                                        NEW ERA IN THE BALKANS
    History, government, culture and people.
    Nelson, 1970.
Robinson, G.J.   TITO'S MAVERICK MEDIA
    "The politics of mass communications." Written for media people,
    but interesting also to all. It is a study of "how the press, radio and
    television operate in multi-national Yugoslavia."
Stillman, E.   THE BALKANS
    Time, Inc., 1964.
Tornquist, D.   LOOK EAST, LOOK WEST
    "The socialist adventure in Yugoslavia." The author, in preparation
    for this book, learned Serbo-Croatian, and worked for publishing
    companies to support himself so that he could live in conditions ap-
    proximately those of a native. "Conveys the flavor of everyday life."
    Macmillan, 1966.
West, R.   BLACK LAMB AND GREY FALCON;
                                A JOURNEY THROUGH YUGOSLAVIA
    This is a classic and important book. "It is a travel diary of an Easter
    trip through Yugoslavia in 1937," along with much history and anal-
    sis of European culture and ideas.
    Viking, 1943.
Wilson, D.   TITO'S YUGOSLAVIA
    A "good account of the events of WWII, of the Yugoslav revolu-
    tion . . . ." The author served as British ambassador to Yugoslavia.
    Cambridge Univ. Press, 1979.

Novels

Andric, I.   BOSNIAN CHRONICLE
    Nineteenth-century Bosnia, before the fall of Napoleon, by a leading
    author of Yugoslavia who won a Nobel prize in 1961.
    Knopf, 1963. fc

Andric, I.   THE BRIDGE ON THE DRINA
History of a bridge in the Bosnian town of Visegrad through three and
a half centuries of Turkish overlords.
Macmillan, 1959. fc

Andric, I.   THE WOMAN FROM SARAJEVO
Twentieth-century Belgrade and Sarajevo. Originally published in 1945.

Arnold, E.   PROVING GROUND
A World War II ferry pilot is shot down over Albania, while taking
wounded Yugoslavian partisans to Italy.
Scribner, 1973. fc

Ball, B.   MONTENEGRIN GOLD
Search for World War II gold in Montenegro.
Walker, 1978. fc/s78

Bridge, A.   ILLYRIAN SPRING
An English woman on respite in Dalmatia; beautiful portrait of the
country.
Little, Brown, 1935. fc

Cosic, D.   REACH TO ETERNITY
Serbia at war with Austro-Hungary, in 1915.
Harcourt, 1980. brd/80

Cosic, D.   A TIME OF DEATH
Story of a World War I battle after the country has been abandoned
by the Allies.
Harcourt, 1978. fc/s78

Djilas, M.   UNDER THE COLORS
Story of a family fighting against the Turks; Montenegro in 1870.
Harcourt, 1971. fc

Durrell, L.   WHITE EAGLES OVER SERBIA
Espionage; man infiltrates the country as a peasant to solve the mur-
der of a British agent.
Criterion, 1957. fc/8ed

Fagyas, M.   DANCE OF THE ASSASSINS
Serbia at the beginning of the twentieth century; the assassination of
King Alexander and his wife, which led to the start of World War I.
Putnam, 1973. fc

Gilman, D.   THE UNEXPECTED MRS. POLLIFAX
Espionage involving amateur sleuth Mrs. Pollifax and a chase from
Mexico to Albania.
Doubleday, 1966.

Keneally, T.   SEASON IN PURGATORY
The "experiences of a young English surgeon in WWII" who ends up
serving the partisans; he runs a ramshackle hospital on the Island of
Mus and falls in love with a Yugoslav nurse.
Harcourt, 1977. brd/77

MacLean, A.   FORCE 10 FROM NAVARONE
A World War II suspense and adventure story.
Doubleday, 1968. fc
Pekic, B.   THE HOUSES OF BELGRADE
A wealthy landlord's obsession with his buildings.
Harcourt, 1978. brd/80

Travel Articles

GEO
1980   Feb   Ruritania revisited, J. Morris - p. 64

HOUSE & GARDEN
1980   Jun   A walk-on island in the Adriatic, P. Brooks - p. 126

LADIES' HOME JOURNAL
1979   Jul   Rites of summer (festivals), P. Funke - p. 56

NATIONAL GEOGRAPHIC
1980   Oct   Albania alone against the world, M. Biber - p. 57

N.Y. TIMES SUNDAY TRAVEL SECTION (10)
1979   May 6   Yugoslav resorts after the quake,
                    D.A. Andelman - p. 21
          Nov 18 What's doing in Zagreb, D.A. Andelman - p. 9

SKIING
1979   Sep   Ski the Alps, P. Gordon - p. 163

SMITHSONIAN
1979   Dec   Yugoslavia's old images become bright and shiny,
                    J. Phillips - p. 93

TOWN & COUNTRY
1979   Jul   Yugoslavia: at the center of the cosmos,
                    L. Gwinn - p. 80

TRAVEL/HOLIDAY
1979   Dec   Ski Yugoslavia, H. and G. Koenig - p. 8

YACHTING
1979   Apr   Island summer (off the Yugoslavian coast),
                    G. Beiser - p. 80

Notes - Europe

1. Standard Series Guidebooks for Europe as a whole:
   Fielding (Europe; Hotels and Inns, Europe;
      Low-Cost Europe; Sightseeing Guide)
   Fodor's Europe
   Frommer (Dollarwise and $ a day)

2. See Appendix 1 for more complete data on
   the above.

Europe

Background Reading

The books listed here are applicable to Europe as a whole, or may just offer an idea for an over-all "theme" for a planned trip to Europe.

Baylis, R.H.   EUROPE ON PURPOSE
THE CHRISTIAN TRAVELER'S GUIDE
     Pilgrimage, 1977.

Benarde, A.   BEACH HOLIDAYS,
FROM PORTUGAL TO ISRAEL
     For sun and sea worshippers; Mediterranean beaches in Cyprus, Elba, France, Malta, Portugal, Sardinia, Spain, Yugoslavia.
     Dodd, 1974.

Braider, D. PUTNAM'S GUIDE TO THE ART CENTERS OF EUROPE
     Putnam, 1965.

Brandel, F.   THE MEDITERRANEAN
     A two-volume "total history"—geography, history, inventions, biography, environment, war and peace, kings and peasants, language and literature.
     Harper, 1976.

Bridgeman, H. and Drury, E. VISITING THE GARDENS OF EUROPE
     Lists practical information (hours, fees, etc.) for 1200 gardens open to the public—botanical, formal, romantic, cottages, great country houses, cloisters , tour parks, etc.
     Dutton, 1979.

Calvert, P.   INLAND WATERWAYS OF EUROPE
  IPS, 1975.
Chandler, D., ed.   TRAVELLER'S GUIDE TO THE
                                           BATTLEFIELDS OF EUROPE
  British Book Centre, 1974.
Cleare, J.   THE WORLD GUIDE TO MOUNTAINS AND
                                              MOUNTAINEERING
  Mayflower Books, 1979.
Crosland, M., ed.   A GUIDE TO LITERARY EUROPE
  For the literary-minded traveler, linking stories and plays and their
  authors with towns, villages, views, cafes, theatres. Each country is
  handled by a contributor who is a specialist in the country's litera-
  ture. Three volumes in one: northern Europe, Great Britain and Ire-
  land, southern Europe—includes all of Europe except the commun-
  ist countries. See also several other literary guides listed under coun-
  try sections for Great Britain and Ireland.
  Chilton, 1966.
Davidson, M.B.   THE HORIZON BOOK OF
                              GREAT HISTORIC PLACES OF EUROPE
  McGraw-Hill, 1974.
Dulles, F.R.   AMERICANS ABROAD;
                            TWO CENTURIES OF EUROPEAN TRAVEL
  Univ. of Michigan Press, 1964.
Hilowitz, B., ed.   A HORIZON GUIDE:
                              GREAT HISTORIC PLACES OF EUROPE
  American Heritage, 1974.
Jackson, N.   SEXY EUROPE
  Pinnacle Books, 1976.
Kane, R.S.   GRAND TOUR A TO Z
                                      THE CAPITALS OF EUROPE
  Doubleday, 1973
Klein, J.S. and Reader, N.   GREAT SHOPS OF EUROPE
  National Retail Merchants.
Lancaster, O.   A CARTOON HISTORY OF ARCHITECTURE
  A lovely idea for introducing the novice to the basics of identifying
  architecture, which is so much a part of tours and travel in every
  country in Europe.
  Gambit, 1975.
McNaspy, C.J.   A GUIDE TO CHRISTIAN EUROPE
  Loyola, 1971.
Madden, D.M.   A RELIGIOUS GUIDE TO EUROPE
  "A unique guide, opening up whole new vistas of travel pleasure—
  the religious pilgrimage."
  Collier, 1975.

Massee, W.E.   MASSEE'S GUIDE TO EATING
                                      AND DRINKING IN EUROPE
A bit out of date, but much general information on food and drink-
ing styles and customs.
McGraw-Hill, 1963.
Norman, J. and T.   TRAVELER'S GUIDE TO EUROPE'S ART
Galleries, cathedrals, museums.
Appleton, 1965.
Pepper, E.   MAGICAL AND MYSTICAL SITES;
                                  EUROPE AND THE BRITISH ISLES
Delphi, Malta, Stonehenge, Granada, and other sites reputed to have
magical qualities.
Harper, 1977.
Postal, B.   THE TRAVELER'S GUIDE TO JEWISH
                            LANDMARKS OF EUROPE
Fleet, 1971.
Rubinstein, H., ed.   EUROPE'S WONDERFUL
                        LITTLE HOTELS AND INNS: 1979-80
Dutton, 1979.
Rudner, R.   WANDERING: A WALKER'S GUIDE TO
                            THE MOUNTAIN TRAILS OF EUROPE
In two parts: 1) the pleasures of wandering and advice for walkers;
2) a trail guide based on the author's past "wanderings."
Dial, 1972.
Simpson, N.T.   COUNTRY INNS AND BACKROADS
                            EUROPEAN EDITION
Berkshire Traveller, 1978.
Skurdenis, J.V. and Smirich, L.J.   WALK STRAIGHT THROUGH
                                     THE SQUARE
"Walking tours of Europe's most picturesque cities."
McKay, 1976.
Sutton, H.   TRAVELERS: THE AMERICAN TOURIST
                        FROM STAGECOACH TO SPACE SHUTTLE
"Honest, witty, social history of American behavior as tourists and
travelers and of how they affect those they visit." Concerns travel as
a whole, including much about Europe.
Morrow, 1980.
Von Kuenhelt-Leddihn, E.   THE INTELLIGENT AMERICAN'S
                                GUIDE TO EUROPE
"To acquaint (American readers) . . . with the more or less permanent
characteristics of Europe, its nations and religions, historic back-
grounds, social structures, political institutions and economic trends."
An ideal general introduction to the continent.
Arlington House, 1979.

APPENDIX 1

Reference Sources:

Books in Print, R.R. Bowker Co., New York, NY
Book Review Digest, H.W. Wilson Co., New York, NY
Fiction Catalog, H.W. Wilson Co., New York, NY
   (Ninth Edition, and supplements 1976-79; also Eighth Edition)
The Magazine Index, Information Access Corporation, Menlo Park, CA*
The Travel Book Guide to the Travel Guides, R.R. Bowker, Co., New
   York, NY
Travel Guidebooks in Review (University of Michigan International Cen-
   ter), Gaylord Professional Publications, Syracuse, NY

Guidebooks listed in the Notes for each country:
   (A full review of these guidebooks can be found in either *The Travel
   Book* **or** *Travel Guidebooks in Review,* **listed above.)**

Blue Guide Series, Ernest Benn, London, England (distributed by Rand
   McNally & Co., Chicago, IL)
Fielding Guides, Fielding Publications, New York, NY
Fodor Guides and Budget Guides, David McKay Co., New York, NY
Frommer Guides, Arthur Frommer/Pasmantier (Distributed by Simon
   & Schuster, New York, NY)
Michelin Green Guides, Michelin Co., Paris, France (distributed by Mi-
   chilen Guides and Maps, Roslyn Heights, NY)
Michelin Red Guides, same as above.
Nagel Encyclopaedia-Guides, Nagel Pub, Geneva, Switzerland (distrib-
   uted by Hippocrene Books, New York, NY)

Foreign Area and Country Studies

These are published by the U.S. Government and available from the
Superintendent of Documents, Washington DC 20402.

   "Studies of a country's social, economic, political and military organization designed for the nonspecialist."

APPENDIX 2
Supplementary Information — England

1. **Literary Guides**: The following reference books (in addition to the literary guides listed on page 45) are useful especially for classic and standard British authors—Dickens, Trollope, the Brontes, Hardy, Jane Austen, D.H. Lawrence, etc. etc.—and the various places connected to them and to their literary works:

   Eagle, D. and Carnell, H., *The Oxford Guide to the British Isles*, Oxford University Press, 1977.

   Hardwick, M., *A Literary Atlas and Gazetteer of the British Isles*, Gale, 1973.

2. **Author List**: As explained in the introduction to Volume 1, there were far too many books for England to list them all, or even most of them in this reading list. Following, therefore, is a list of authors of books included in *Fiction Catalog* and *Book Review Digest* which you can use as a convenient, alphabetical, checklist against the card files or bookshelves in your library in order to locate additional titles which may be of interest. Authors marked with an asterisk (*) were listed by the *Fiction Catalog* under "Mystery and Detective Stories" therefore the author's books may be partially, or entirely, housed in the mysteries section of your library.

Adams, Richard
*Aiken, Joan
*Aird, Catherine
*Allingham, Margery
*Amis, Kingsley
*Anderson, J.
*Armstrong, C.
Ashe, Rosalind
Atwater, James D.
Bagley, Desmond
Bagnold, Enid
Bainbridge, Beryl
Ballard, J.G.
Banks, Lynne Reid
Barker, A.L.
*Barnard, Robert
Bates, H.E.
Bawden, Nina
Beckett, Samuel

Bedford, Syville
*Bell, Josephine
Benedictus, David
Benson, E.F.
Berckman, Evelyn
Bermant, Chaim
Billington, Rachel
Blackstock, Charity
Blackwood, Caroline
*Blake Nicholas
Bowen, Elizabeth
Bradbury, M.
Braddon, Russell
Bradford, Barbara T.
Bragg, Melvyn
Braine, John
Brent, Madeleine
*Brett, Simon
Bryher

Buchan, John
*Burley, W.J.
Burnley, Judith
Burroway, Janet
Butler, Gwendoline
Butterworth, Michael
Byatt, A.S.
*Cadell, Elizabeth
Caine, Jeffrey
*Canning, Victor
*Carr, John Dickson
*Carter, Youngman
*Carvic, Heron
*Charteris, Leslie
Christopher, J.
*Christie, Agatha
*Clarke, Anna
*Cleary, Jon
Clifford, Francis

*Collins, Wilkie
Connolly, Roy
Cook, Lennox
Cooke, Judy
Cookson, Catherine
*Creasey, John
Christopher, J.
Chrichton, Michael
*Crispin, Edmund
Crofts, Freeman W.
Cronin, A.J.
Danby, Mary
Dane, Clemence
*Davidson, Lionel
Davies, L.P.
Deighton, Len
Delderfield, R.F.
*Delving, Michael
*Derleth, August
*Dexter, Colin
*Dibdin, M.
Dick, R.A.
*Dickinson, Peter
Donleavy, J.P.
Drabble, Margaret
DuMaurier, Daphne
Duffy, Maureen
Durrell, Gerald
Eden, Dorothy
Emecheta, Buchi
Estleman, Loren D.
Ewing, Barbara
Eyre, Katherine W.
*Ferrars, E.X.
Fletcher, Inglis
*Fleming, Joan
Ford, Hilary
Fowles, John
*Francis, Dick
Frankau, Pamela
Freeman, Cynthia
*Fremlin, Celia
French, Marilyn

Gadney, Reg
*Gallico, Paul
Gardam, Jane
*Gardner, John
*Garve, Andrew
*Gash, Jonathan
Gaskin, Catherine
Gibbons, Stella
*Gilbert, Anthony
Gilbert, Harriett
*Gilbert, Michael
Glanville, B.
Godden, Rumer
Golding, William
Goudge, Elizabeth
Graham, W.
Greene, Graham
Haldeman, Linda
Hardwick, Mollie
Harris, Marilyn
*Heald, Tim
Heath, Catherine
*Heyer, Georgette
*Hill, Reginald
Hilton, James
*Hilton, John B.
Hoban, Russell
Hodge, Jane A.
Holland, Isabelle
Holt, Victoria
Household, Geoffrey
Howatch, Susan
*Hubbard, P.M.
Hughes, Richard
*Hunter, Alan
*Innes, Michael
*James, P.D.
Jameson, Storm
*Jeffreys, J.G.
Johnson, Pamela H.
Jones, Merwyn
*Keating, H.R.F.
Kennedy, Lena

*Kenyon, Michael
King, F.
Larkin, P.
*Lemarchand, E.
Lessing, Doris
*Lindop, Audrey E.
Llewellyn, Richard
Lofts, Norah
Lovell, Marc
*Lovesey, Peter
Macardle, Dorothy
McCrum, Robert
*MacDonald, Philip
MacDonald, Malcolm
MacInnes, Colin
MacKenzie, Donald
McNeish, J.
Mankowitz, Wolf
Marchant, Catherine
Maric, J.J.
*Marsh, Ngaio
Martin, Gillian
Masters, John
Maybury, Anne
Mayhew, Margaret
*Melville, Jennie
*Meyer, Nicholas
Meynell, Laurence
Michaels, Barbara
*Milne, A.A.
Mitchell, A.
Moggach, Deborah
*Morice, Anne
Mortimer, Penelope
*Moyes, Patricia
Murdoch, Iris
*Parrish, Frank
Patterson, Sarah
Pearce, Mary E.
Pearson, John
*Perowne, Barry
*Perry, Anne
*Peters, Ellis

Pilcher, R.
*Porter, Joyce
Powell, Anthony
*Priestley, J.B.
Pritchett, V.S.
*Procter, Maurice
Pym, Barbara
Pynchon, Thomas
*Radley, Sheila
Raphael, Frederic
Raymond, Ernest
Rayner, Claire
Read, Miss
Read, Piers Paul
Redmon, A.
*Rendell, Ruth
Rhys, Jean
Richler, Mordecai
Roberts, Dorothy J.
Robinson, Derek
Rock, M.
Sackville-West, V.
Salisbory, Carola
*Sayers, Dorothy L.
Scholefield, Alan

*Selwyn, Francis
Seymour, G.
Sharp, Margery
Sharpe, Tom
Shelby, Graham
Shute, Nevil
Sillitoe, Alan
Smith, Dodie
Smith, Godfrey
Snow, C.P.
Spark, Muriel
Spring, Howard
Stevenson, D.E.
Stewart, J.I.M.
Stewart, Mary
Storey, David
Stow, Randolph
Straub, P.
Struthers, Jan
*Stubbs, Jean
*Symons, Julian
Tattersall, Jill
Taylor, Elizabeth
Tey, Josephine
Thane, Elswyth

Theroux, Paul
Thirkell, Angela
Tracy, Honor
Tremain, R.
*Underwood, M.
Unsworth, Barry
Vaughan, M.
Wade, Jennifer
Wain, John
*Warner, Mignon
Warner, Sylvia T.
*Watson, Colin
Webb, E.
Webb, Mary
Weldon, Fay
Wells, Dee
Wells, H.G.
West, Rebecca
White, Patrick
Whitney, Phyllis A.
*Williams, David
Wilson, Angus
*Winslow, P.G.
Wodehouse, P.G.
Woodhouse, Martin
*Woods, Sara

3. **Errata**: These books should have been cross-indexed or listed under England. The Ardagh, Cole, Deardorff and Durell books all described on page 77; the Gunther book described on page 2; the Jacobson book listed on page 80; the Lottman book listed on page 78; the Morris book listed on page 161.

IN APPRECIATION

Thanks must certainly be expressed to many people.

First, to those who helped in editing and publishing this first volume of the series—

to Maria and Christine for becoming involved in the project at a time when their participation was crucial;

to Rhoda Van der Clute, and her mother, Rhoda Sawkins, for their professional expertise in book design, production and printing as well as for their friendship and generous assistance;

to Gini Nicoll for suggesting a way out of the dilemma that England presented, and for generally being a good listener and sounding board;

to Andrea Wandelt and Ariel Graphics for never turning down a request to meet rush deadlines—no matter how inconvenient;

to Helen Ports for her expertise in English and willingness to share it when asked;

to the public libraries in Bayport, Patchogue and Sayville (New York), Coronado (California), Bremerton (Washington), Cheshire and Waterbury (Connecticut) for providing the research tools needed in compiling the *Reading Guides;*

the charming illustrations are from *Victorian Fashions and Costumes, 1867-1898,* edited by Stella Blum and published by Dover Publications, New York.

Then to those who provided the personal support and friendship so necessary in a lengthy project of this kind—

to the members of my various families—Batchelders, Donovans, Heuthes, Meszaros's, Simonys—for never uttering a "discouraging word" even though I know they may have wondered at times what on earth I was doing working on what is a rather odd kind of book;

to the Fallers, Nicolls and Barbara and Pete Meszaros, where I could always stop by for a meal, or a drink, or some conversation when a break from work was desperately needed—their friendship and support was invaluable at times;

finally to Alice Van Horn who literally rescued me from potential disaster by providing the wherewithal to meet that final printer's deadline.

INDEX

TRAVEL ARTICLE SUPPLEMENTS

Supplements, listing newly published travel articles, will be printed semi-annually. The Supplement that covers articles for the period January through June 1981 will be available in September 1981 at the time the first volume is available.

Thereafter, Supplements will be printed for July through December 1981, by February 1, 1982; for January through June 1982, by August 1, 1982 and so on.

It is advisable for libraries to clip the order forms at the time a volume of the series is acquired, and return them to the publisher so that supplements will be received automatically.

Supplements may also be ordered *without* an accompanying form by sending a check or money order for $1.50 for each 6-month supplement desired. Be sure to specify the Volume number, and calendar period of the Supplement being ordered. Address these orders to:

Freelance Publications Ltd
Attn: TA Supplements
Box 8
Bayport, N.Y. 11705

TO: Freelance Publications, Box 8, Bayport, NY 11705

Please send the Travel Article Supplement to TRAVELER'S READING
GUIDES, Volume 1 - Europe, for the period:

January - June 1981

Enclosed is $1.00 to cover shipping & handling.

(Signature)_____

(Library/Firm)_____

(Address)_____

_____

This offer is valid through December 1982

- -

TO: Freelance Publications, Box 8, Bayport, NY 11705

Please send the Travel Article Supplement to TRAVELER'S READING
GUIDES, Volume 1 - Europe, for the period:

July - December 1981

Enclosed is $1.00 to cover shipping & handling.

(Signature)_____

(Library/Firm)_____

(Address)_____

_____

This offer is valid through December 1982

TO: Freelance Publications, Box 8, Bayport, NY 11705

Please send the Travel Article Supplement to TRAVELER'S READING
GUIDES, Volume 1 - Europe, for the period:

January - June 1982

Enclosed is $1.00 to cover shipping & handling.

(Signature)_____

(Library/Firm)_____

(Address)_____

_____

This offer is valid through December 1982

- -

TO: Freelance Publications, Box 8, Bayport, NY 11705

Please send the Travel Article Supplement to TRAVELER'S READING
GUIDES, Volume 1 - Europe, for the period:

July - December 1982

Enclosed is $1.00 to cover shipping & handling.

(Signature)_____

(Library/Firm)_____

(Address)_____

_____

This offer is valid through December 1982